P9-DES-996

Latin America
and the Transformation
of U.S. Strategic Thought,
1936–1940

Latin America
and the Transformation
of U.S. Strategic Thought,
1936–1940

David G. Haglund

University of New Mexico Press
Albuquerque

UNIVERSITY
OF NEW BRUNSWICK

WITHDRAWN

LIBRARIES

For Susan

Library of Congress Cataloging in Publication Data

Haglund, David G.
  Latin America and the transformation of U.S. strategic
thought, 1936–1940.

  Bibliography: p.
  Includes index.
  1. World War, 1939–1945—Causes. 2. World War, 1939–
1945—United States. 3. World War, 1939–1945—Latin
America. 4. World War, 1939–1945—Diplomatic history.
5. United States—Foreign relations—Latin America.
6. Latin American—Foreign relations—United States.
7. United States—History—1933–1945. 8. Latin America—
History—20th century. I. Title.
D742.U5H3 1984   940.53'22   83-27442
ISBN 0-8263-0747-7

©1984 by the University of New Mexico Press.
All rights reserved.
Manufactured in the United States of America.
Library of Congress Catalog Card Number 83-27442
International Standard Book Number 0-8263-0747-7.
First edition.

Contents

Acknowledgments

This book is based on my doctoral dissertation at the Johns Hopkins University School of Advanced International Studies, Washington, D.C. I was fortunate enough to have been able to work at SAIS with Robert W. Tucker, my thesis supervisor, and Piero Gleijeses, and to both of whom I am deeply indebted. I also wish to thank Riordan Roett, Frederick Holborn, and Simon Serfaty for reading and commenting upon the earlier version of this book.

Research grants were provided by SAIS and by the Eleanor Roosevelt Institute, Hyde Park, New York. My sincere thanks go to both these institutes. William Emerson and the staff of the Franklin D. Roosevelt Library, Hyde Park, provided invaluable research guidance, as did the staff of the National Archives, Washington.

To Robert A. Divine, of the University of Texas, I am very grateful for having contributed helpful suggestions for revision of the original manuscript. I wish also to thank David V. Holtby, of the University of New Mexico Press, for the deft editorial touch he applied to the pages that follow.

Betty Greig, of the Institute of International Relations, University of British Columbia, performed yeoman duty in her dual capacity of typist and solecism-hunter, and Mark Zacher, director of the Institute and benefactor of numerous young scholars, provided with his customary good cheer and generosity the encouragement and support necessary to turn this project into a book. Warmly I thank them both.

Finally, my wife Susan Murphy, to whom I dedicate this book, contributed more than she can know to make it all possible.

1

The Relationship
of Latin America
to U.S. Isolation

It is impossible to understand why the United States abandoned its policy of noninvolvement in European political and military affairs and entered into a de facto alliance with Great Britain during the late summer of 1940 without taking account of the important role that Latin America occupied in the international strategic calculations of policymakers in Washington. Much has been written about both the specific question of American entry into the Second World War and the broader issue of U.S.–Latin American relations in this century, but little attention has been paid—at least in the past twenty-five years—to the nexus between the specific question and the broader issue. It is with that nexus that this book is concerned; for in what follows I shall argue that real or perceived developments in Latin America were of utmost significance in shaping the course of American policy toward the war that broke out in Europe in September 1939.

It is perhaps not too great an overstatement to claim that students of American foreign policy have assimilated, explicitly or not, what would today be termed a *dependencista* perspective in assessing the relative importance of Latin America in the wider context of international politics as well as in the narrower one of American foreign policy. By this I mean that writers on U.S. foreign policy have adopted a mode of analysis with respect to Latin America that is posited upon the assumption of Latin marginality; not only is Latin America held to be a geographic, economic, and political periphery, but it is likewise deemed a conceptual one.[1] In the world of the dependencistas, systemic variables seem to be the only ones that matter; Latin America, in this view, has for centuries been a "dependent variable," a region perpetually forced to respond to events over which it has little, if any, control.[2] Similarly, in the world inhabited by students of U.S. Latin Amer-

1

ican policy, the important questions all too often involve either what the United States can do for Latin America, or (to those critical of the country's Latin policies) what the United States has done *to* Latin America.

One can, to be sure, err in the opposite direction and consistently conjure up seminal roles for Latin America, at the present time or at any other juncture in American foreign policy. Indeed, the analytical distortions introduced by a dependencista perspective would pale in comparison with those occasioned by a *Latino-centric* one. (Nor would the *policy* implications of a Latino-centric perspective necessarily be benign, either for the United States or for its Latin neighbors.) The point is not that, as a general rule, one analytical school is preferable to another; it is rather that given the major changes in the international political system that have occurred in just the past four decades, no *general* model can inform the analysis of Latin America's relationship either to world politics or to the foreign policy of the United States.

For the years 1936 to 1940 in particular, one would be hard-pressed to sustain an argument for Latin marginality to U.S. foreign policy. Far from being marginal, Latin American issues were of greater relevance to overall foreign policy goals of the United States in the half decade preceding American entry into World War II than they had ever been before. It is unlikely, given the obvious effect that developments in military technology have had on America's ability (or inability) to guarantee its physical security, that Latin America will ever again loom as large in American strategic thought as it did in those prewar years, when the U.S. policy of isolation was premised upon an expectation that the defense of the United States also entailed the defense of much of Latin America (and, some held, *all* of Latin America). Because of its bearing on the U.S. policy of isolation, Latin America was enmeshed, in strategic conceptions, with the nation's utmost foreign policy goals and interests. This was so, to repeat, because the most vital national interest, the physical security of the United States, was deemed to be contingent upon the maintenance of a Western Hemisphere immune to the contagion of "European" war.

The hemisphere represented the legitimate extent of American security interests to the country's strategic planners and most of its political leaders—as it did, for that matter, to most Americans who bothered to think about their nation's place in world affairs. But since hardly anyone in the United States imagined that any European power or collection of powers would either dare or be able to violate the territorial and political integrity of Canada, for all practical purposes "hemisphere security" was synonymous with Latin American security in U.S. strategic thinking. Those who thought primarily about the defense of the New World were most concerned with the least defensible regions of the hemisphere; and though a febrile mind could work up scenarios about attacks on North American military or civilian targets, it was infinitely easier for strategic planners to envision an armed Axis presence in the streets of Montevideo or Santiago de Chile than in the streets of New York or Montreal.

For several reasons, which will become evident in subsequent chapters, Americans during the late 1930s and early 1940s were growing extremely worried about the possibility of European power politics spilling over into what all but a very few considered to be the sphere of vital national interest. To most Americans in the year and a half before Pearl Harbor, the idea that the United States might soon be confronting a formidable challenge from German power in the Western Hemisphere seemed frighteningly obvious. In August 1941, *Fortune* reported that only a tiny fraction, fewer than 7 percent, of the American public believed that Hitler had no political designs on either North or South America; more than 72 percent, on the other hand, were convinced that "Hitler won't be satisfied until he has tried to conquer everything including the Americas."[3]

It was a time when international political forces were, perhaps ironically, thrusting Latin America to the forefront of America's collective consciousness. Insofar as people *above* the Rio Grande were concerned, Latin America had become what F. S. Northedge calls an "epicenter" of world politics.[4] This development had not taken place overnight; America's "great fear" for its southern neighbors had been increasing for some years before the United States finally entered World War II in December 1941. But despite its lengthy gestation period, the idea that the security of the United States was intimately bound up with the immediate political and economic future of Latin America really only took root in the fearsome aftermath of the German western offensive during the spring of 1940.

With the twin citadels of democracy in Europe, France and

England, either collapsed or collapsing, the American public turned its attention in a dramatic way to the part of the world that the Roosevelt administration had been insisting for some years was of fundamental importance to the safety of the United States. "Cultural rapprochement" between the United States and its southern neighbors became both a catchword and an imperative for the Roosevelt Good Neighbor Policy. Hubert Herring captured the American mood when he wrote in 1941 that a nervous affection for Latin America had recently broken out "like a speckled rash on the skin of the North American body politic. Clubwomen read papers on the Humboldt Current, dress up as Aymaras, listen to guitarists strum tunes reputed to come from the Amazon. College presidents substitute courses on the Incas for those on the Age of Pericles."[5] And a leading public opinion journal reported that the "wooing of Latin America had developed . . . into what is substantially a shotgun wedding," as the United States scrambled to gain the affection of lands below the Rio Grande.[6]

Skeptics like Nicholas John Spykman, who taught international politics at Yale, scoffed that a marriage of such obvious geopolitical convenience was bound to fail, primarily because it was based on nothing other than an unexamined notion that if the peoples of the hemisphere could only get to know each other they would come to like each other, and that if they liked each other a thousand German divisions could not threaten them. "If the cooperation of our Latin neighbors is dependent on the popular appreciation of the rhumba in the United States," wrote Spykman, "the future is indeed bright." But of course the future wasn't, and he explained why: However noble such administration policies as "cultural rapprochement" might be in inspiration, in practice they were going to fail, for "sympathy does not determine policy; policy tends to determine sympathy." Spykman thought that American policy was in flagrant violation of the canons of common sense. Rather than attempt to hold off Hitler from a Western Hemisphere redoubt, he wanted the United States to follow the dictates of realism and declare war immediately on the Axis.[7]

Spykman's analysis of the implications of the administration's policy of isolation—only *one* of whose features was the pursuit of cultural rapprochement—was in some ways unfair; for no one in the White House imagined that cultural rapprochement by itself would do very much to ensure the isolation of the hemisphere from the European war. The administration, in reacting to the breakdown of world order from 1936 on, had placed great emphasis upon constructing political, economic, and military links between the United States and the other republics in the hemisphere—links that would serve as the substance of a powerful Pan-Americanism which, it was hoped, would keep the Axis at bay on the far side of the Atlantic. But if Spykman was guilty of oversimplification, he was, by dint of simplification, placing America's strategic situation in proper perspective. As Spykman noted, the great debate over American foreign policy, which raged from the late 1930s until the Pearl Harbor attack, was essentially a question of alternative security schemes: alliance with Great Britain versus a renewed commitment to the "Fortress America," by which was usually (though not always) meant the ideal of an impregnable Western Hemisphere.

To Spykman and other internationalists like Percy Bidwell and Arthur Upgren, there could be no question that the British alliance was the only choice the country could make. "Hemisphere self-sufficiency," wrote these two critics of isolationism early in 1941, "is an impracticable dream. . . . There is no way of defending adequately either our interests in the Western Hemisphere, or the other member states, except in close association with the British Empire."[8] It was not simply a matter, argued the internationalists, of political and military unity on this side of the Atlantic; the economic existence of many of the states in the hemisphere depended on European markets, specifically on markets that were either under Hitler's control or in danger of becoming so. "Let Britain's economic life be destroyed," warned Eugene Staley in April 1941, "or let it come under the domination of Hitler's New Order, and the effect on the economic defense of the Americas is analogous to the effect the sinking or capture of the British fleet would be on the naval defense of the Americas."[9]

To the isolationists such arguments were guaranteed prescriptions for disaster. Rather than see the United States once again involve itself in the moils of Europe, the isolationists wanted the country to adhere to what they considered the bedrock principle of American foreign policy: nonentanglement in the affairs of Europe. The best way to do this, while at the same time maintaining peace at home, would be for the administration to concentrate on making the Western Hemisphere invulnerable. Once American security was taken care of, there would be no call for the nation to again get mixed up in a European fight. For all but a few isolationists, the hemisphere was tantamount to the nation; the security of the latter could not be preserved without guaranteeing that of the former. Indeed, many who shared this outlook vehemently denied that they were "isolationist" at all, precisely for the reason that their concern for the security of the entire New World was as great as their concern for the security of the United States itself. Indicative of this perspective, and a prominent figure in the America First Committee, was Gen. Hugh S. Johnson, who addressed an angry letter to the interventionist Douglas Fairbanks, Jr., following a pro-British speech that the actor delivered in September 1940. "You are being a propagandist's little agent—and the direction of that propaganda is disaster," stated the former head of Roosevelt's National Recovery Administration. "When you call me an isolationist, you are calling names. It isn't isolation to prepare to defend—and get ready to defend—half a world."[10]

For those Americans who wanted the nation to spring to England's defense, efforts by Johnson and others to show that they were not isolationists only offered further proof that the "myth" of the continents was a dangerous one, in that it encouraged the belief that the United States could remain aloof from the European war. To the interventionists, this attitude was not only craven but stupid; for if the nation refused to help England stop Hitler, it would soon have to stop him alone. As they saw it, the "myth" of the continents rested on a central fallacy: that territoriality (in the sense that both the North and South American continents share a hemisphere) implied a kind of political unity. The anti-isolationists had minimal faith in Pan-Americanism, holding that history and ethnographic diversity did far more to divide the hemisphere than "territoriality" did to unite it.[11]

As the interventionists correctly perceived, the ideal (if not the reality) of an impregnable hemisphere—a Fortress America—had been a fundamental pillar of American isolationism since the birth of the United States. Two related theses dominated historical American thinking about the New World: first, it was considered a geographical unit clearly distinct from Europe; second, it was also regarded as politically and ideologically distinct from, and purer than, Europe. Of these two themes, the former was greater importance in the formulation of American policy towa. the great powers of Europe, because so long as Americans felt themselves and their neighbors to be safe from the wars of the Old World, then so long would they be able to advocate a policy of isolation.

The concept of the geographical distinctness of the Western Hemisphere is not the tautology it might appear to be at first glance, for how one assimilates geographic data is conditioned by many non-geographic factors.[12] For example, although Canada has been as much a Western Hemisphere land in a physical sense as the United States, it has never experienced the same attraction toward the Latin American nations as its southern neighbor. "Canadians," John Holmes has written, "never having shared the Washington-Bolívar mystique and the revolutionary republican tradition, have not taken very seriously the idea that they have special links with peoples of vastly different political traditions merely because they happen to be linked by an almost intraversable neck of land. History has bound Canada across traversable oceans to the northern hemisphere."[13]

The political traditions linking the United States with Latin America perhaps were not as strong as Holmes seems to be implying. Actually, the notion that the New World (Canada excepted) was *politically* unique was a relatively late addition to America's repertory of geopolitical conceptualizations. In 1820, John Quincy Adams brusquely dismissed the idea that the United States and the nascent Latin republics were evolving in a similiar manner: "As to an American System, we have it; we constitute the whole of it; there is no community of interests or principles between North and South America."[14] The secretary of state's viewpoint, if not his bluntness, tended to dominate thinking in policy circles (with some important exceptions) until the twentieth century. It was not until their widespread disillusionment with Europe during the interwar years that Americans and their leaders really began to talk as if they actually believed in the political solidarity and superiority of the Pan-American system.

In the first two administrations of Franklin Roosevelt the "idea" of a politically superior Western Hemisphere reached its apex. The demise of democracy nearly everywhere in Europe seemed to corroborate in a political sense what had long been perceived in a geographical sense—that the hemispheres were truly separate. No one has better traced the rise and decline of the Western Hemisphere as a politically significant concept than Arthur Whitaker, in his seminal work, *The Western Hemisphere Idea.*[15] Whitaker's chief concern in this book, written in the early 1950s, was to demonstrate that the conception of a distinct and superior Western Hemisphere was inseparable from the tradition of American isolationism; once the latter became extinct, so too did the former. He employed the metaphor of a glacier to demonstrate that the "idea" of the hemisphere was valid only so long as Latin America was of paramount strategic importance to the United States. Glaciers are formed from snow falling and accumulating over a lengthy period of time; when the snow stops falling, the glacier does not immediately alter in any perceptible way. To Whitaker, the "snow" that gave birth to the "glacier" of the Western Hemisphere idea consisted in the events of the international political system. When this system was fundamentally altered as a result of World War I and the rise of America to world-power status, Americans did not initially understand that the Western Hemisphere no longer mattered in the sense that it once had—that it no longer possessed the same strategic significance, for technology and changed political conditions had altered the meaning of distance and spatial configuration. Although the snow had ceased to fall, the glacier had not ceased to exist. Only after the onset of World War II did it become obvious in Washington (and even then not until July 1940) that international political realities had been fundamentally and irrevocably altered.[16]

In Whitaker's analysis, the vectors of influence run from isolationism (the independent variable) to the hemisphere "idea" (the dependent variable). In this perspective, the United States is seen to have outgrown isolationism as a policy, and in so doing, to have adjusted accordingly its position on the issue of Pan-Americanism. What I propose to do in this book is to argue—mindful of the dangers inherent in imputing causation—that the vectors in Whitaker's model can profitably be reversed, and that if they are, an interesting relationship emerges. It may be more meaningful to regard the demise of isolationism as a function of the decline of the hemisphere "idea" than to construe the latter as solely a consequence of the former. What I am suggesting is that it may be that the ending of isolation was, in a way heretofore only dimly recognized, part and parcel of the eroding American belief in a Western Hemisphere that was at once distinct from and impregnable to Old World political systems. In sum, I maintain that the decision of the Roosevelt administration to abandon isolationism and to construct a de facto alliance with Great Britain (which occurred in the summer of 1940) simply cannot be understood without analyzing the effect that events below the Rio Grande had on perceptions and actions of American policymakers.

In the following chapters, I propose to show how the president and his advisers perceived the hemisphere's economic, military, and political developments, and what the influence of those perceptions was on their decision to align the United States with Great Britain. Causal explanations are probably impossible in history and political science, so I am not suggesting here a causal model in the sense that my analysis supplies the necessary *and* sufficient conditions that led the United States into World War II. But I do argue that *one* of the necessary conditions for the abandonment of isolation—the belief that the security of much of Latin America (and by extension, of the United States) was imperiled by the Axis—has never been given the attention that it deserves by historians or political scientists. I will return to this argument later; at this juncture, however, it is necessary to digress slightly and to address three highly important and related topics: the historiography of American interventionism in World War II; the meaning of isolationism; and the question of whether Franklin D. Roosevelt was following isolationist policies from late 1936 until the middle of 1940.

The great historiographical debate over American intervention in World War II turns on one fundamental question: Was the security of the United States endangered by the prospect of a Nazi conquest of Europe in 1940? Not surprisingly, students of the problem have, ever since the immediate postwar years, been in disagreement about the answer to this question. Although disagreement over an issue of such historical importance is to be expected, what *is* surprising is the tremendous lack of attention that students on either side of the issue have paid to a part of the world that was arguably of critical significance in the Roosevelt administration's decision to enter an undeclared, but nonetheless real, war with Germany after July 1940. Latin America figures little, if at all, in most accounts of United States involvement

in the war. Indeed, even scholars whose main concern is not World
War II but Latin America have misconstrued some basic facts
about the part of the world they study.

Howard J. Wiarda, for example, has written that "prior to Fi-
del Castro's coming to power . . . Latin America had been largely
ignored, both in the literature on social change and political development and in the councils of the world's nations."[17] Wiarda's
statement is partly correct, for the literature on change and development has indeed achieved more Latin American content
since January 1959; but it is a large oversight to fail to mention that for the government of the United States between 1936
and 1940, Latin America was of far greater importance than it
has ever been to any subsequent administration, including that
of John F. Kennedy in the immediate aftermath of the Castro
triumph—and, perhaps more to the point, of Ronald Reagan,
who gives the impression lately of being profoundly convinced
that the national security of not only the United States, but
"of all the Americas is at stake in Central America."[18] Mexican author Carlos Fuentes has committed the fallacy of writing, apropos recent revelations of Mexico's oil wealth, that "for
the first time since the 1830s, Mexico has become strategically
important to the United States."[19] Fuentes was a century off
the mark; for in the 1930s it would have been hard to find a nation of greater imagined strategic importance to the United States
than Mexico.

Writers who have concentrated on American intervention have
likewise overlooked the strategic significance of Latin America
during the half decade leading up to Pearl Harbor. Even those political scientists and historians who argue that a genuine threat
to American security did exist in the late 1930s and early 1940s,
and that the Roosevelt administration acted wisely in getting the
nation into the war, have given minimal attention to the lands
below the Rio Grande. For example, Robert Osgood's *Ideals and
Self-Interest in America's Foreign Relations* has surprisingly little to say about hemisphere events, although it was arguably these
events which made it apparent to the White House that what Walter Lippmann called America's era of "effortless security" was
coming to an end.[20] Osgood's slighting of the Latin American
"contribution" to American security worries is curious, in that
he gives a detailed account of security concerns in the hemisphere

during the First World War, while also arguing (correctly, I think) that American intervention in *that* war was not attributable to any recognition on the part of Woodrow Wilson that the nation's physical security was seriously at issue.[21]

Other students of American involvement in World War II have similarly discounted the Latin American factor. Basil Rauch maintained that it was the German invasion of Denmark that "brought the danger of aggression geographically and strategically closer to the United States than any other Axis move to date."[22] Robert Sobel attempted to explain the origins of interventionism in terms of the Finnish-Soviet war of 1939–40.[23] And, more recently, Arnold Offner managed to concentrate an entire book on United States foreign policy and the coming of the Second World War without so much as mentioning Latin America.[24] I have chosen to highlight these works not because they are poor specimens of scholarship, for they are anything but that. It is my intention to establish the claim of neglect insofar as it concerns the Latin American factor in American intervention—and how better to demonstrate that neglect than by citing not the irrelevant but the salient analyses of the general problem of intervention? And if I do cite these writers for neglecting Latin America, I nevertheless hold that they are correct in appreciating that the White House was acting because it came to believe (albeit not as quickly as some Americans wanted it to) that the growth of German power posed a threat to the physical security of the United States. Not everyone thinks that Germany actually did constitute a menace to America's safety—a point to which I shall return presently—and many scholars would even argue that Roosevelt did not *perceive* such a challenge to exist, irrespective of whether it really did.

Among those who make the case that Roosevelt was not motivated by any great sense of concern for America's physical security are the radical revisionists. I use the modifier *radical* to distinguish between two important schools of revisionist historiography of the postwar years. The earlier of the two revisionist schools tended to be composed (but not entirely) of right-wing critics who concentrated their efforts on showing that Roosevelt led, lied, or otherwise duped the nation into a war that did not involve any vital interests of the United States. In the main, these earlier critics—let us call them the "conservative" revis-

ionists—were continuing to fight the good fight for the prewar
isolationism they had espoused. The later wave of revisionists,
the radicals, have interpreted American foreign policy in the context of the nation's domestic, capitalist economic system; they
have tried to demonstrate, as Robert W. Tucker has argued, "not
simply that America is aggressive and imperialistic, but that it is
so out of an institutional necessity. It is the central assumption
that American imperialism must ultimately be traced to the institutional structure of American capitalism that is the common
denominator of radical criticisms."[25]

The radical revisionists, in placing primary emphasis on economics as the cutting edge of American foreign policy, have contributed to our understanding of that policy, but at the same time
they have presented us with a tool for policy analysis that ultimately is too inflexible for sustained and effective use. It is one
thing to argue, as they do, that economic interests predominated
in the formulation of United States policy toward Latin America
during the 1920s and the first half of the 1930s; for, in that period,
America seemed so secure that even its army and navy war planners had to display much dexterity in conjuring up a plausible enemy to plot against, in the end settling upon the British Empire
or Japan (or an alliance of the two).[26] It is quite another matter,
however, to maintain that the same order of interests informed
the policymaking process of the latter part of the 1930s—a time
when, I would argue, the perceived threat to American security,
via the Axis penetration of Latin America, was so awesome that
economic *qua* economic interests were necessarily relegated to
an inferior position on the scale of concern.[27] It is the radicals'
contention, on the other hand, that American entry into World
War II was ultimately a function of the belief not that the nation's
physical security was menaced, but that its economic frontiers—in
Latin America and elsewhere—were threatened by the expansion
of German and Japanese power.[28]

The conservative revisionists also contend that America's physical security was not at issue in the late 1930s and early 1940s,
but they do not maintain that economics explains the nation's
entry into World War II. The core of their more eclectic position
is contained in the following four propositions: 1) that Germany
did not pose a threat to the security of the Western Hemisphere;
2) that Roosevelt adopted policies that he knew (or should have

known) would lead to war; 3) that he took the nation into war while insisting that he wanted it to remain at peace; and 4) that by getting mixed up in the fight against Hitler, the United States made possible the rise of a menace at least as great, Stalinist Russia.[29] The first three of these propositions need some elaboration; the fourth, whether Nazi Germany and Stalinist Russia were equally abhorrent, requires no further comment here.

The first proposition is probably the most difficult to address, not because the revisionists are correct, but because serious epistemological obstacles preclude anything but a hypothetical response to what is an immanently hypothetical question; namely, Did Germany pose a serious threat to the security of the Western Hemisphere? To answer this, one must consider German intentions as well as German capabilities. Let us assume, as those who specialize in strategic studies nearly always do, that it is both wiser and safer to concentrate upon the enemy's capabilities and not his intentions.[30] On this assumption, one would be tempted to conclude that since Germany could not even conquer Europe, it would have been no threat to lands on other continents. Of course, without the American intervention that the conservative revisionists denounced, Hitler *might* have attained victory in Europe, and he might then have gone on to subjugate the Soviet Union. It is easy to speculate upon whether Germany might have developed into a world power on the scale of the United States. But because it is just speculation, such activity really does us little good from an empirical standpoint. All that one can conclude is that Germany *might* have been in a position eventually to challenge the physical security of the United States.

A more pertinent consideration, perhaps, is the question of German intentions. If Berlin's numerous public disavowals are to be credited, one might be justified in concluding that the Reich had no designs on any nations in the New World. Time and again in the late 1930s and early 1940s, top German officials (including Hitler) emphasized that all they wanted was a Monroe Doctrine of their own in the Old World. It is well known that no plans for the invasion of a single Latin American state were discovered when German archives were ransacked after the war, nor were any plans discovered that related to the United States.[31] Therefore, it has been asserted by many writers since the end of the war, most suggestively by Bruce Russett, that the United States faced "no clear and present military danger" from the actions of Germany and its allies.[32]

This proposition, of course, is as impossible to prove or disprove as the related one concerning German power. One cannot say what Hitler, assuming an initial triumph in Europe, might have had in store for Latin America. In private, on the rare occasions during the 1930s when he discussed Latin America, he apparently made statements that would support the conclusion that Germany intended to play a dominant role in the affairs of certain Latin republics.[33] Nor is the absence of plans for the violation of the Western Hemisphere any indication that such violation would not have been attempted *(pace* the revisionists). One need only recall that until December 1940 no plans existed for the German invasion of the Soviet Union.

There is no agreement among scholars on the question of German intentions. Those who, like A. J. P. Taylor, minimize German aspirations, argue that when he began Hitler had no clear conception of exactly what he wanted, other than to make of Germany a European power.[34] But others maintain that Hitler wanted nothing less than world dominion, and because of this, in the words of Meir Michaelis, he "would have posed a very grave challenge indeed, not only to U.S. hegemony in the Western Hemisphere, but to the 'American way of life' as well."[35] It is not my purpose here to take sides in this dispute; the point is simply that the question of German intentions remains open.

Even if it cannot be determined whether Germany constituted an objective potential menace to the security of the United States, one can nevertheless speak with more certainty to the second and third of the theses advanced by the conservative revisionists; namely, that Roosevelt was following a course which he knew would involve the United States in war, and that he did this while lying to the public that he wanted peace. That the president recognized the likelihood of American participation in the war after the destroyers-for-bases exchange of September 1940 would seem to be a just conclusion: he did not know for certain that this act would lead to others that, in turn, would lead to an undeclared naval war against Germany; but he was prepared to accept such consequences as part of his decision to abandon isolationism. Likewise, it must be acknowledged that much of what he said during 1940—especially in the heat of that year's election campaign against Wendell Willkie—tended to leave the impression that he would never take the country into war, and in this sense it can be charged that he lied America into the Second World War.

Having said this, one has nevertheless to take into consideration this most relevant aspect of American intervention: that Roosevelt and the men around him *perceived* the security of the United States to be imperiled by the growth and spread of German power, whether or not it was or would have been so imperiled. "Security in international politics," Hedley Bull has written, "means no more than safety: either objective safety, safety which actually exists, or subjective safety, that which is felt or experienced."[36] The small but growing body of writing on threat perception in international politics suggests that subjective safety is by far the more significant of the two kinds of safety. Indeed, because the inference of a threat is much more common an occurrence than the direct issuance of one, the problem of identifying security threats becomes practically coextensive with that of identifying *perceptions* of security threats.[37] Thus, in assessing the conservative revisionist charge that Roosevelt, for whatever reason, involved the United States in a war that did not threaten the country's security, it is germane to ask not whether Germany intended to menace American security but whether and why Franklin D. Roosevelt inferred such a threat.

Of course, Roosevelt's anti-interventionist critics, having livelier topics to explore, did not seem to be too concerned with the dynamics of threat perception in the White House. But if they had somehow been more aware of the element of subjective safety, they would likely not have advanced the kinds of answers they did to the question, Why should Roosevelt have taken the United States into war? It is simply not adequate to argue, as Charles Beard and others have done, that defects in the president's character were responsible for what they considered to be his disastrous policy of interventionism.[38] And it is even less fruitful to attempt, as Charles Callan Tansill did, to prove that Roosevelt conspired to get Americans into combat so that he could secure "the preservation of the British Empire."[39]

Nor does Bruce Russett's provocative restatement of the Beardian position have any greater persuasive power than the earlier version. Russett belittles the fear widely felt in Washington after the collapse of France in June 1940—the fear that Hitler would soon be moving against the Western Hemisphere. "All of this of course," Russett says, "seems more than a little absurd in light of known—then as well as now—German capabilities."[40] Frederic Maitland, the famous English jurist and historian, observed some years ago that "it is very hard to remember that events long in the past were once in the future." Perhaps now we know (though, given Hitler's quixotic planning style, we can never be sure) that Germany had no designs on the Western Hemisphere; but Russett is misleading when he states that in the middle of 1940 Americans considered Germany incapable of threatening their hemisphere and therefore themselves as well.

It is my argument that Roosevelt and his circle of advisers did indeed perceive a strong actual and potential threat to American physical security—a threat stemming principally from their assessment of Axis (mainly German) activities and intentions in Latin America, the most vulnerable part of the Western Hemisphere. Given the information reaching him from advisers in Washington and official and unofficial representatives in Latin America—and taking into account that Nazi and Fascist political activities were on the upswing in many lands south of the border; that millions of persons with German, Italian, and even Japanese blood lived in those lands; that several Latin countries had strong economic links with Germany (and German-occupied Europe after 1939); and that Axis airlines were operating throughout South America and would continue to operate until 1941—there were indeed understandable grounds for Roosevelt to have become alarmed over what represented, at the time, the most conceivable manner in which the security of the United States could be challenged.

The president's awareness of an Axis threat to Latin America had two important dimensions. The first dimension consisted in the flow of information reaching him in respect of German, Italian, and even Japanese activities or alleged activities in Latin America. In the matter of information (or intelligence) alone, Roosevelt and his anti-interventionist opponents were separated by one enormous barrier: he had access to confidential information from and concerning Latin America—information, we shall shortly discover, that was often of an alarmist nature—and they did not. As two correspondents covering the White House at the time put it: "Neither the President, nor Hull, nor the Senate really *makes*

American foreign policy. The cables make it. Senators, who do not read the cables, may be isolationists. But men who see the cables coming in, week by week and month by month, are either enlightened or afflicted with a professional deformation."[41]

In a literal sense, the cables did not, of course, "make" U.S. policy; they never do, neither between 1936 and 1940 nor today. To be sure, they (or, more precisely, the information flow that is represented by the expression "the cables") are an indispensable element in the making of foreign policy; but they do not process themselves. Rather they get read by, and are acted upon (or are not acted upon, as the case may be) by policymakers whose minds are far from being tabulae rasae. It may be a truism, but it still bears noting that the mind operates by imposing an ordering structure—call it an "image"—upon the disparate and confusing facts that make up reality.[42] Thus the second important dimension of Roosevelt's cognition of an Axis threat appears to be the image he possessed of Latin America's role in the strategic framework of the United States. Like nearly all Americans— and certainly like his closest advisers—the president conceived of American security during the latter 1930s, to use the metaphor of Isaiah Bowman, "in terms of the mollusk. The hemisphere was our shell."[43]

Robert Jervis has argued that policymakers, to enable themselves to make more effective decisions, should encourage the formulation and application of "alternative images" of reality; they should strive to build structural conflicts into the cognitive apparatus of the state—in a word, they should promote the use of devil's advocates to filter out, to the maximum extent, possible misperceptions.[44] The striking aspect with regard to Roosevelt's circle of advisers is that, insofar as the perception of a threat to the hemisphere was concerned, there were no devil's advocates to take the position that the United States and its Latin neighbors were safe from the contamination of European politics. It could be argued that this lack of "alternative images" was primarily a function of the essentially internationalist world views of the president and most of his closest advisers. I do not accept such an interpretation, for I contend that by the middle of the 1930s, Franklin Roosevelt and other top policymakers were more inclined to support isolationist than internationalist policies. As supporters of isolation, they naturally thought of American

security in terms of both the United States and its New World
neighbors. If my argument is correct, it was the administration's
predilection for isolationism, not internationalism, that largely
explains the absence of alternative images of strategic reality. But
these isolationist predilections, paradoxically, contained the seeds
of the destruction of the Roosevelt policy of isolation, for the good
reason that men who equated American security with the security of the hemisphere would prove to be extremely sensitive to
any potential dangers below the Rio Grande—and, beginning in
late 1936, the more evidence of danger in Latin America that
Washington searched for, the more evidence of danger "the cables" revealed.

If one is to claim that Roosevelt, during the latter part of the
1930s, was following "isolationist" policies, then one must seek
to make it clear what he means by the word *isolation*. Like all political concepts, isolation is an abstraction, and as such, permits
of no "true" definition. And, like quite a few political concepts,
isolation has given birth to a welter of conflicting definitions,
so much so that one scholar, only half in jest, threw up his hands
and concluded that isolationism was "not a theory but a predicament."[45] The most important distinction to be made in
thinking about isolationism is that between policy and ideology.
Governments follow policies; individuals (including those in
government) think in terms of ideology.

Let me make this distinction clearer. Isolationism as ideology
essentially implies the myths, symbols, or distinguishing personal
traits (such as ethnicity) that influence individuals to desire that
their own nation have as little political contact as possible with
particular regions of the world, or even with particular nations.[46]
Of the two kinds of isolationism, it is the ideological variant that
has been subject to most attention from scholars and others. Perhaps as a result of this attention, it is the more confusing of the
two types of isolationism. A wide variety of theories has emerged
in recent decades attempting to prove that American isolationism was a function of (to cite only the most frequently mentioned
variables) region, ethnicity, progressivism, conservatism, history,
personality—even I.Q.[47] Most of these studies are irrelevant to
the argument I make in this book, namely that Franklin Roosevelt was following isolationist policies until his concern for the
security of Latin America led him to enter into a de facto alli-

ance with Great Britain in the late summer of 1940. But there is one theory from the ideological studies that bears directly on my thesis: the theory that American isolationism of the interwar years is in large part explained by the widespread image of a Europe that was beyond redemption—an image stemming from the historical perception (one could even say the accepted wisdom) that the United States had blundered terribly by getting involved in World War I.

I will have more to say about this last point shortly, but before I do, it would be opportune to turn to the question of isolationism as *policy*. Perphaps the best way to begin is to state what isolationism as a policy of the United States has *not* meant. It has not meant economic isolationism. This is worth a brief comment, for it is sometimes argued that because the United States has never practiced economic isolation, it has never been isolationist. The most forceful and articulate exponent of this view has been revisionist historian William Appleman Williams, who doubts that the United States has ever followed isolationist policies (at least in this century), because the leaders of the country's political and business communities have faithfully adhered to an expansionary strategy aimed at "keeping the world safe for the Open Door."[48] Williams has made a careful study of the Republican administrations of Harding, Coolidge, and Hoover—administrations often seen as epitomizing twentieth-century isolationism—and has concluded that under these presidents the United States was a consummately interventionist power, if not politically then certainly economically.[49] Lloyd C. Gardner has grafted this approach to his examination of the Roosevelt foreign policy, thereby reaching an identical conclusion: the United States "never contemplated self-containment and moved towards greater participation in the world economy. . . ."[50] Yet another scholar, Bernard Fensterwald, has protracted the Williams-Gardner perspective backward in time and has discovered that since the United States has never attempted isolationism in its "pure form"—the kind experienced, say, by Tibet or Yemen—"our policies have never amounted to anything more than pseudo-isolationism."[51]

Two things must be claimed in respect of the above statements. First, they are correct; with the exception of one year in the presidency of Thomas Jefferson, the United States never tried to adopt economic isolationism.[52] Second, they are beside the point: for isolationism has traditionally and justifiably been construed as a political orientation and not as an economic one. In one of the earliest arguments for isolation ever penned in North America, *Common Sense*, Thomas Paine called for a policy of noninvolvement in European political controversies, while simultaneously urging that the new nation seek to broaden its trade ties to the fullest extent, and to do so on a basis of commercial equality with all countries.[53] Even George Washington's Farewell Address, cited ad nauseam as an unerring Baedeker of foreign policy, explicitly separated economic from political entanglements: "The great rule of conduct for us, in regard to foreign nations, is in extending our commercial relations to have with them as little *political* connection as possible."[54]

An additional confirmation of the view that isolationism has usually carried only political connotations comes, as it were, directly from the horse's mouth, in a work by Charles Beard, the dean of isolationist academicians during the interwar years. In a 1946 study of Roosevelt's foreign policy, Beard established the following criteria as being necessary and sufficient conditions of an isolationist policy: rejection of membership in the League of Nations; noninvolvement in the political affairs of Europe and Asia; and the pursuit of friendly relations with all nations willing to reciprocate. No mention is made, in Beard's index, of economic isolation.[55]

If isolationism as a policy of the United States has not meant economic self-containment, it has also not meant a renunciation of political entanglements in every region of the globe. An examination of the historical record reveals that proscriptions on political (including military) connections with other lands have traditionally been applied most often to only one continent, Europe. Towards Latin America, particularly towards her nearby neighbors in the Caribbean area, the United States has been nothing if not interventionist. In the Far East, more self-restraint has characterized American activity, but by comparison with its behavior towards Europe, the United States has followed policies that can only with difficulty be called isolationist.[56]

Indeed, it is well known that, during the isolationist interwar years, demands for a more active policy toward Japan frequently came from public figures who were among the most ardent foes of "internationalism." Livingston Hartley correctly observed in 1937 that "our active role in Far Eastern affairs forms a strong contrast to our flight from the affairs of Europe. . . ."[57] When President Roosevelt announced in July 1939 that he intended to "get tough" with Japan by abrogating the Japanese-American commercial treaty of 1911, no less an isolationist than Sen. Arthur Vandenberg applauded—and well he should have, because the Michigan Republican had sponsored a resolution in the Foreign Relations Committee calling for just that action. Even Sen. William Borah, no shrinking violet when it came to steering clear of European affairs, gave his assent.[58] All of this prompted Assistant Secretary of State Adolf Berle to note in his diary that "it is a curious fact that the United States, which bolts like a frightened rabbit even from remote contact with Europe, will enthusiastically take a step which might very well be a material day's march on the road to a Far Eastern war." Berle could only conclude that the American public felt that "getting into trouble is quite all right if the trouble is in the Western Pacific; but very, very bad if in Europe."[59]

Charles A. Lindbergh could serve as an example of what Berle meant. Lindbergh, who became a star attraction for the isolationist America First Committee in the fall of 1940, was an anti-interventionist who could bring himself to endorse stern measures against Japan. Although he claimed to be against war with Japan or with anyone else, he did tell a Yale University rally in late October that the time had come for the United States to adopt decisive policies in the Pacific. "If we intend to fight a war in in the Orient," he said, "it is long past time for us to begin the construction of bases in the Pacific, and to stop our wavering policy in the Philippines—we should either fortify these islands adequately, or get out of them entirely." Like some other nonpacifist isolationists, Lindbergh felt that the United States could easily defeat Japan, and could do so without the encumbrance of allies.[60]

Lindbergh's preference was for acting without allies, and it was precisely this that constituted the defining characteristic of isolationism as policy. Manfred Jonas's excellent study of isolationism during the interwar years has concluded that the essential feature of this policy was the belief in unilateralism as the modus operandi of American diplomacy.[61] If there is a wide variety of theories about isolationism as ideology, there is a surprising

consensus among scholars on the meaning of isolationism as
policy. Echoing Jonas, Warren Kimball has observed that a more
accurate name for isolationism as policy would be "unilateral
internationalism."[62] To Kalman Silvert, "the functional distinction which should interest us is between acting alone and acting
in concert with others, and not the misleading words 'isolationism'
and 'internationalism.' The former involves working abroad with
no entangling alliances."[63] And for Robert W. Tucker, isolationism as policy has meant, above all, a "refusal to enter into alliances and to undertake military interventions."[64]

Keeping in mind this *consensus auctorum* on unilateralism as
a hallmark of American foreign policy, one can now state what
isolationism, as a policy followed by the Roosevelt administration until the late summer of 1940, implied: In the words of
Tucker, "what isolationism as a policy signified . . . was nothing
more nor less than the refusal to guarantee the post-World War I
status quo in Europe and Asia against change by force of arms."[65]
Although it is true that America had not adhered strictly to an
isolationist policy in the Far East before the 1930s, it is nevertheless true that Franklin Roosevelt was not, until 1941, prepared
to use military power to enforce the post-World War I status quo
in that part of the world. To many Americans, European developments of the late 1930s were spilling over into Asia, making it
appear that unilateral solutions to problems there were no longer
as feasible as they once were. Thus, when a reluctant Adolf Berle
was asked to enter the State Department in late 1937, he remarked
that, while not eager to accept the appointment he nonetheless
believed that the "foreign affairs of the United States . . . have to
go on and somebody has to do the work and I would rather do it
myself than leave it to some second-rate intriguer picked from
the political basket who will get us into a British alliance and a
European Asiatic war."[66]

It might be argued that to define isolationist policy in the above
manner is to put too fine a point on the matter, to refine the concept nearly out of existence. I would prefer to think that the failure to delimit sufficiently the meaning of "isolationist policy"
would render footless any discussion of the isolationist phase of
the Roosevelt presidency, for Roosevelt and most of the men
around him cannot be considered to have been isolationists in
the classic ideological sense. Failure to understand this point has

led countless writers to insist, almost to their last drop of ink, that Franklin Roosevelt was born, lived, and died as a confirmed "internationalist." Plainly, Roosevelt did not fit the usual categories of isolationist ideology discussed above.[67] He did not hail from the Midwest. He was not, despite an exaggerated claim to more Dutch ancestry than he in fact possessed, a member of a non-English ethnic group. His liberalism (or was it his conservatism?) did not make him chary of foreign entanglements. And he was not generally considered, except by his most uncharitable critics, either to be deficient in basic intelligence or to possess more than his portion of psychological difficulties.

By all the normal criteria of isolationist idelogy, then, Roosevelt appears to be a misfit. However, one very important qualification must be made: like most Americans of the interwar period, Franklin Roosevelt believed that there was a profound historical "lesson" to be derived from the experience of 1917, when the United States abandoned its policy of isolationism for the bloody trenches of the western front. It was this belief, an immanently ideological characteristic, that reinforced and to a large measure explained Roosevelt's determination to stay with an isolationist policy during the late 1930s and the first half of 1940. Only when it became evident that the United States risked losing more by remaining aloof from Europe's war than it did by getting involved in it would Roosevelt abandon isolationism.

What was this great perception of the two interwar decades? It was that America had been duped into entering war in 1917 by an unholy alliance of bankers, munitions makers, and Allied propagandists. This perception was so widespread that it nearly became a national credo. One political scientist estimated that it was an article of faith for 99 percent of the American public. "It is, of course, utter nonsense," Robert Strausz-Hupé reflected many years later, "to assert that the internationally minded were restrained by the isolationist few: except for an exceedingly small but influential minority, *all* Americans were isolationist."[68] Ernest Hemingway drew a somber picture for his fellow Americans in his 1936 essay, "Notes on the Next War," in which he wrote that "of the hell broth that is brewing in Europe we have no need to drink. Europe has always fought; the intervals of peace are only armistices. We were fools to be sucked in once in a European war, and we should never be sucked in again."[69] And in a similar vein, Hubert Herring bitterly observed that America was being betrayed by the very people it had gone to war to save. "Contrary to some commentators," he wrote in 1938, "the Americans fought in the World War for noble purposes, without self-interest. . . . We gave the kind of teamwork which can't be bought, but we were bought—and sold. One may be proud of being pure but not of being simple. We were both."[70]

In their excursuses on international politics, the Hemingways and the Herrings (and there were many of them) were cultivating a field that had been first made fertile the decade before, when revisionist writers examined the standard interpretation of the origins of the World War and discovered that it was not only Germany—some even held it was not Germany at all—that was responsible for the conflict. In 1922 Albert Jay Nock's *Myth of a Guilty Nation* advanced the thesis that ultimate responsibility for the carnage of 1914–18 lay not with the Central Powers, but with Russia and France. Over the course of the next several years there appeared a flood of literature reiterating this theme and stating a second one: that the United States had been drawn into the war through the malign efforts of Wall Street and British propagandists.[71]

By November 1933 hardly any American could find fault with the editorial that William Allen White wrote to commemorate the fifteenth anniversary of the signing of the Armistice. Had the killing and destruction of war made the world any better than it had been in 1914? wondered the editor of the *Emporia* (Kansas) *Gazette*. "Would it have been any worse if Germany had won? Ask yourself honestly. No one knows. . . . War is the devil's joke on humanity. So let's celebrate Armistice Day by laughing our heads off."[72] It should be noted that White was no inveterate isolationist, no celebrant of the supreme virtues of unilateralism, as was his fellow editor, Arthur Vandenberg of the *Grand Rapids* (Michigan) *Herald;* indeed, after the outbreak of World War II, White was a leading campaigner for providing all aid short of war to Great Britain.[73]

Practically on the heels of White's editorial there appeared an article in *Fortune* that was to have tremendous repercussions on the development of interwar isolationism. "Arms and the Men," published in March 1934, stimulated public demands for an investigation of the armaments industry, which was by then widely thought to have been a prime agent in the backstage maneuvering that had got the nation into war in 1917. From September 1934 until April 1936, a Senate committee chaired by Gerald Nye, a North Dakota Republican and a staunch unilateralist, delved into the files of the country's biggest munitions makers, hoping to uncover evidence that the "merchants of death" were in fact the warmongers that everyone took them to be. Although in the future the Nye Committee would be castigated for damaging American foreign policy almost beyond repair, at the time it was doing its work it received nearly universal acclaim from a fascinated nation, which closely followed its well-publicized hearings. Even Secretary of State Cordell Hull, author of more than one ex post facto condemnation of the committee, was an early supporter, declaring himself in 1934 to be "in entire sympathy with the purpose of the committee."[74]

While the Nye investigators were hard at their job, isolationist policy was given solid legislative substance when the Congress passed, and the president signed, the Neutrality Act of 1935. This legislation sought to obviate a recurrence of the kind of events that most Americans thought had ensnared their nation in 1917. By preventing the sale of arms and munitions to *any* belligerent, Congress hoped to avoid the maritime disasters that had resulted in the diplomatic rupture with, and subsequent declaration of war upon, Germany. By its provision that the arms embargo be non-discriminatory (that is, applicable to aggressor and victim alike), the 1935 legislation marked a clear break with traditional American neutrality policy. It was also a departure from international neutrality law; for, according to Convention 5 of the Hague Convention of 1907 ("Respecting the Rights and Duties of Neutral Powers and Persons in War on Land"), a neutral state was "not called upon to prevent the export or transport, on behalf of one or the other of the belligerents, of arms, munitions of war, or, in general, of anything which can be of use to an army or a fleet."[75]

It is true that a precedent of sorts had been set the year before, when the United States applied an arms embargo on both sides in the Chaco War, but the 1934 legislation had been drafted in respect of a specific conflict—and a hemispheric one at that—while the 1935 law was intended to serve as a guide for American policy in all future wars. It was, as Robert Sherwood caustically remarked some years later, "carefully designed to prevent us from getting into the war in 1917. It was purely retroactive, . . . born of the belief that we could legislate ourselves out of the war, as we had legislated ourselves out of the saloons (and into speakeasies). Like Prohibition, it was an experience 'noble in motive' but disastrous in result."[76]

How determined were Americans in the mid-1930s to avoid "getting into the war in 1917"? Judging from the opinion polls, they were very determined: in April 1937 Gallup found that fully 70 percent of the nation thought American intervention in the World War had been an error. Even after the Second World War broke out in 1939, 68 percent of the public still maintained this belief.[77] Roosevelt and his top advisers, with a few exceptions, were not immune to what at the time seemed a persuasive thesis, notwithstanding later demurrers by scholars and policymakers alike that the administration had really wanted to pursue a more internationalist course but was continually prevented from doing so by public opinion.

What must be considered the dominant view of the isolationism of the Roosevelt administration (prior to 1940) is that it was essentially a function of expediency, with the president saying and doing things he really did not believe in but could not afford to reject for fear of the domestic political consequences. An early expression of this view came in 1943, when the State Department published *Peace and War,* a collection of selected documents that the department contended would prove that the administration had been fighting isolationist tendencies in the country since 1933—despite appearances to the contrary.[78] Since the publication of *Peace and War,* scholarship of the Roosevelt era has been dominated by the image of the president as a man who "during the paralyzing isolationism of the thirties . . . remained privately an internationalist willing only to work or toy with the isolationists."[79]

Proponents of the Roosevelt-as-internationalist interpretation argue that Roosevelt was destined by virtue of his family connections, his travels, and his education to become an ardent internationalist. In the prologue to his impressive study *Franklin D. Roosevelt and American Foreign Policy,* Robert Dallek depicts Roosevelt as the quintessential "American Internationalist," a politician who, with the exception of Theodore Roosevelt, "was the most cosmopolitan American to enter the White House since

John Quincy Adams in 1825."[80] Roosevelt, it is argued, was not one of the ethnocentric majority—a majority whose attitude toward the world beyond America's borders was best expressed by Sen. Thomas D. Schall's 1935 imprecation: "To hell with Europe and the rest of those nations!" Therefore, the argument continues, because he was cosmopolitan and most Americans were not, and because it was well known that the public would not support any political commitments to Europe, Roosevelt was at best able to make only small gestures in the direction of internationalism until 1940. He wanted to do more but could not; for he was a captive of public opinion, or of isolationists, or of both.[81]

This argument is plausible, especially since it rests on the assumption that Roosevelt had an internationalist background, which he did possess. Cosmopolitan by the standards of his or of any other day, the young Franklin Roosevelt was keenly interested in Europe, and when war broke out there in 1914 he wanted the United States to support the Allies to the fullest extent, even (by 1916) urging President Woodrow Wilson to declare war on Germany. When the United States did enter the war in the following year, Roosevelt applied for but was refused permission to leave his post as assistant secretary of the navy for active duty at the front. However, he did get sent on an inspection trip to France toward the end of the war, where he witnessed combat, even briefly coming under German shellfire. Although in the 1930s he would claim that this trip showed him the folly and wastefulness of war, at the time he was rather thrilled by all the excitement.[82]

Where the view of Roosevelt-as-internationalist breaks down is in the failure to consider that the revisionist historiography of the 1920s and 1930s might have had as persuasive an effect on Franklin D. Roosevelt as it did on William Allen White and on countless other Americans—cosmopolitan or not. It is simply incorrect to ascribe Roosevelt's "seeming" isolationism of the 1930s to expediency and to nothing but that. Roosevelt's disenchantment with Europe by the early 1930s was real, although it was not immutable. Thus, when the presidential aspirant agreed in February 1932 to repudiate the League of Nations, so as to assure the benign neutrality of party potentate William Randolph Hearst in the race for the Democratic nomination, expediency was not the motive, even if it was a consequence. As Robert Divine has

written, when Roosevelt told members of the New York State
Grange on 2 February that the League did not comply with "fundamental American ideals," and that consequently he could not support American entry, he was saying nothing that was repugnant
to his own beliefs, for he had given up on the League several years
before. Moreover, Roosevelt was genuinely surprised and hurt that
the press was interpreting his speech as a craven gesture of political expediency. To a politician who had not championed the
League since,the 1920 presidential campaign, the Grange address
represented the "culmination of [his] gradual disenchantment
rather than . . . a cynical act of political expediency."[83]

Following his election and inauguration, American foreign policy became, in the words of A. J. P. Taylor, "markedly more
isolationist" than it had been under Herbert Hoover.[84] The incoming president not only shunned Europe politically; he even
explored ways in which to lessen the economic and financial in-
terdependence between that continent and the United States.
When the departing Hoover proposed to him, in November 1932,
that the two men work together on the re-creation of a debt commission to assist bankrupt European states in meeting their wartime obligations to American creditors, Roosevelt demurred.
Raymond Moley, an important adviser to the president-elect on
this matter, rejoiced in the rejection of the Hoover proposal, because it constituted a "warning that the foreign policy of the New
Deal would not ally us with Britain and France as policemen of
the world determined to maintain the status quo by enforcing
peace through the threat of joint action in case of war."[85]

Moley opposed the debt commission because he was afraid of
multilateralism as a solution to international problems. Roosevelt shared this concern and showed it during the London Economic Conference of 1933, when he pulled the United States out
of any and all international attempts to achieve currency stabili-
zation. *New York Times* columnist Arthur Krock interpreted this
as a most significant indication of the nation's "retreat into the
furthest corner of isolationism. . . ."[86] The British chargé d'affaires
in Washington, like Moley, saw unmistakable political import
in the president's decision to restrict financial interaction with
Europe. "It seems clear," D'Arcy Osborne cabled Sir Robert Van-
sittart, permanent under secretary for foreign affairs, "that, largely
in conjunction with advancement of this programme, adminis-

tration and state department have turned their eyes from Europe towards South America." In a column of the Osborne communiqué, an unidentified foreign officer penciled in the comment that "Mr. Roosevelt is giving up hope in the old world and is turning his attention to the new."[87]

The flirtation with economic nationalism did not last long. Within a year, the administration, thanks mainly to the efforts of Cordell Hull, was moving in the direction of freer—but not free—trade, as the passage of the Reciprocal Trade Agreements legislation gave the president the power to reduce tariffs by up to 50 percent on imports from reciprocating nations.[88] While Roosevelt did not exactly become a Manchester Liberal by this deed, it was clear that he was moving away from the pronounced economic nationalism of his first year in office. It was also clear that he had not the slightest intention of altering the policy of *political* isolationism that he had promised as a candidate and had begun to implement as fledgling chief executive.

The most striking illustration of the president's isolationist tendencies is found in his handling of the divers arms embargo suggestions that crossed his desk, beginning in April 1933 when the Senate Foreign Relations Committee, chaired by Key Pittman, investigated the possibility of cutting off American munitions flows to future European belligerents. Cordell Hull wanted the committee to draft legislation allowing the president to embargo arms shipments to aggressor states—in short, to align the United States with the collective security sanctions of the League of Nations. But doughty Hiram Johnson, the Senate's foremost nationalist, insisted that any embargo law must include a prohibition on arms exports to *all* warring nations. When it became clear that no measure would make it out of committee unless it embodied Johnson's objections, Pittman turned to the White House for help in breaking the logjam. What is noteworthy, in view of the myriad claims that Roosevelt was a prisoner of the isolationists but never one himself, is that he was prepared to accept without any qualms the Johnson amendment. Only the strenuous objections of Hull, who felt the amended bill was worse than no bill at all, convinced Roosevelt, who was beginning to tire of the issue, to give up on neutrality legislation for the time being.[89]

In the following year Congress enacted its first neutrality legislation, the above-mentioned impartial embargo on munitions exports to the Chaco belligerents, Bolivia and Paraguay. Roosevelt saw the occasion as an opportune moment to stimulate public opinion, already agitated by revelations of the World War machinations of the "merchants of death," on the question of arms embargoes in future European wars. On 18 May 1934, he told the Senate that America's compassion was not limited to the suffering masses of Bolivia and Paraguay; peoples the world over were under the heel of tyrannical governments bent on conquest. Using words that could have come straight from the lips of Gerald Nye, the president declared that "this grave menace to the peace of the world is due in no small measure to the uncontrolled activities of the manufacturers and merchants of engines of destruction, and it must be met by the concerted action of the people of all nations." By "concerted action" Roosevelt meant no more than that each nation, acting independently, should control its own arms manufacturers.[90]

Roosevelt pursued his goal of reining in the arms makers. In December 1934, he appointed a prestigious committee, cochaired by Bernard Baruch and Hugh S. Johnson, to explore ways to "take the profit out of war." Gerald Nye feared that the president was trying to circumvent his own committee's investigation of the same subject; but, after a visit to the White House later that month, the North Dakotan was reassured that Roosevelt was serious about going after the arms traders. So serious, in fact, was the president that a few months later, in a subsequent interview with Nye, he suggested that the senator's committee take on the job of framing legislation that would guarantee a strict neutrality in case of another European war. Nye, flabbergasted by this suggestion, later claimed that his committee had not the slightest intention of proposing neutrality legislation until the president "laid it on our doorstep."[91]

Roosevelt's attempt to get enacted some form of legal proscription on future American involvement in war hardly appears to be the action of a man "held captive by the isolationists." Instead, it is a sterling demonstration of the depth of his own isolationism by the mid-1930s. So influenced had the president become by the "lessons" of postwar revisionist historiography that he was even willing to acknowledge the error of his own thinking during the World War. When William Jennings Bryan, Wilson's pacifistic secretary of state, had tendered his resignation in response to what he considered a bellicose note sent by Wilson to protest the *Lusitania* sinking, Roosevelt had been one of the pack baying after Bryan's blood. He hailed the appointment of Robert Lansing as successor to Bryan with the gratuitous remark that at long last the country had a secretary of state "who is a gentleman." But twenty years later Roosevelt would lament to his ambassador to Mexico, Josephus Daniels: "Would that W. J. B. had stayed on as secretary of state—the country would have been better off."[92]

Further evidence that Roosevelt's signature on the neutrality legislation of 1935 was not simply, as has been claimed, an instance of "almost Machiavellian expediency,"[93] was supplied by the president himself in 1941, when he recanted in print his earlier support of isolationist measures. Referring to the 1935 act, Roosevelt stated that "although I approved this legislation when it was passed originally and when it was extended from time to time, I have regretted my action."[94] While to some of the more internationalist members of the administration in 1935, like Norman Davis, the Neutrality Act was a "blunder of the first magnitude,"[95] to the president the legislation was, if not perfect, certainly acceptable. In a letter to his ambassador to Germany, who was disgruntled by the congressional action and threatening to resign because of it, Roosevelt preached calm. "If you had been here," he told William E. Dodd, "I do not think that you would have felt the Senate Bill last August was an unmitigated evil." It was true, the president informed Dodd, that he would have preferred more freedom for executive decision in the legislation, "quite aside from any connection with the League." What was sought was more presidential discretion, not for the purpose of collective security, but in case a European power tried to wrest raw materials from a Latin American state; in this event, the United States could, "without going to war ourselves, assist the South American nation with supplies of one kind or another."[96]

Two other events of 1935 have at times been misconstrued to give the appearance that Roosevelt was less isolationist than he in fact was. The first, occurring early in the year, concerned the president's encouragement of United States membership in the World Court. One writer has insisted that by taking action in this matter, Roosevelt for the first time "revealed himself as a statesman less isolationist than Congress. . . ."[97] The Senate, reacting to a publicity barrage erected by the extreme xenophobe Father Charles Coughlin (who called the Court the "perverted brain" of a "Frankenstein" League of Nations), failed to give the resolution of adherence the necessary two-thirds majority, and the measure went down to defeat on 29 January, fifty-two for to thirty-six against.[98]

Actually, as a gauge of internationalism, a more insipid issue than the World Court would have been hard to find; for the Court threatened none of the constraints on American unilateralism that membership in the League was seen to entail. So innocuous a step was it, in fact, that every president since Wilson—including even Calvin Coolidge—had felt obliged to recommend joining. It is doubtful, moreover, that Roosevelt's support for the Court was ever more than lackadaisical. That he moved at all in the matter was probably due to pressure from certain anti-isolationists in the State Department, such as Under Secretary of State William Phillips, who visited the president on the afternoon of the Senate vote and found him "not in the least disturbed that [things] were not going well."[99]

Later in 1935, following the Italian invasion of Ethiopia, Roosevelt had occasion to become annoyed with the anti-isolationists in the State Department, when they importuned him to delay proclaiming neutrality until the League had had a chance to act against the aggressor. "F.D.R. would have none of it," recalled Harry Hopkins, who was with the president on a fishing cruise when they heard of Mussolini's attack. Although it was certainly the case that stanching the flow of munitions to both belligerents affected Italy more than Ethiopia, which had neither funds to purchase them nor ships to deliver them, Roosevelt was primarily motivated by a desire to stop American war profiteers— and not because he was concerned with European collective security.[100] To be sure, the president's sympathies were with Ethiopia. But to conclude that he was attempting to align American policy toward the war in Africa with that of the League is to commit the fallacy of *cum hoc, propter hoc*—confusing correlation with cause. Cooperating with the League, or even giving the appearance of doing so, was something that Roosevelt was strongly opposed to. Least of all was he trying, as William E. Kinsella claims in a recent book, "to restrain Italy and provide leadership to those European nations floundering in the mire of appeasement."[101]

In August 1936 Roosevelt made his celebrated testament of isolationist faith, in a speech at Chautauqua, New York. According
to Samuel Rosenman, a close friend from the days when Roosevelt was governor of New York, this was the most important
speech he had made up to that time. The president began by stressing something he would repeat again and again over the next few
years; that the Old World could profit mightily from the example of the New. He then proceeded to spell out very carefully the
principal tenets of his foreign policy: "We shun political commitments which might entangle us in foreign wars; we avoid connection with the political activities of the League of Nations. . . ."

The United States, Roosevelt promised, would not divorce itself from the social and economic problems of the world. "We
are not isolationists except in so far as we seek to isolate ourselves completely from war." He could not guarantee—no one
could—that the country would never go to war again, but he made
very clear his determination to do his utmost to avoid American
participation in the kind of carnage that had taken place twenty
years before. In words whose vividness indicated the intensity of
the feelings they were conveying, Roosevelt declared: "I have seen
war. . . . I have seen blood running from the wounded. I have seen
men coughing out their gassed lungs. I have seen the dead in the
mud. . . . I have seen children starving. I have seen the agony of
mothers. I hate war."

He concluded his somber address by suggesting ways the United
States could help prevent future bloodshed. Collective security
was not one of these ways. Instead, the president offered the hope
that lowering the barriers to world trade might alleviate the causes
of war. In addition, he declared himself prepared to go to Congress for additional legislation aimed at preventing Americans
from participating in the business of war; for it was mandatory
that the great mistake of World War I, of succumbing to the temptation of reaping the "immediate riches—fools' gold" of wartime
trade, not be repeated. "If we face the choice of profits or peace,
the nation will answer—must answer—'We choose peace!' "[102]

As he made clear by the Chautauqua address, Roosevelt ab-
horred war. In this sentiment, he was at one with the American
public. He shared with that same public a world view that rested
on the belief that Europe truly was distinct from—and less enlightened than—the nations of the Western Hemisphere. So long

as the antiwar aspiration was given support by the perception that the Americas were safe from European struggles, then so long would it be possible for the administration to maintain a policy of isolationism. But once the safety of the hemisphere was seen to be imperiled by an increasingly powerful Germany, it became less and less easy for Roosevelt and his advisers to resist the persuasive conclusion that the best—perhaps, the only—way to keep the Americas both out of war and out of Hitler's grasp was to help Great Britain stay alive, so that the fight against the Nazis could continue in the part of the world where it had the best chance of success.

It is my contention that a necessary condition for American intervention in World War II was the uncertainty that the Latin American republics could or would resist the combined political, economic, and military threats and blandishments of a Germany that, by the middle of 1940, looked to be the conqueror of all Europe. This uncertainty over Latin America began to be experienced, mildly at first, by American policymakers in late 1936; by 1938 the uncertainty had turned to dread; by May and June 1940 the dread had become paranoia. It was this uncertainty and its sequelae that ultimately became, to borrow and slightly alter the phrase made famous by Charles Callan Tansill, not a "back door" but a "trap door to war" for the United States.

2

Buenos Aires:
An Attempt to Isolate
The New World

The trip was intended for "holiday purposes," or so newly re-elected Franklin D. Roosevelt confided to the publisher of the *New York Daily News,* Joseph M. Patterson.[1] But a second letter written by the president on the same Thursday, 9 November 1936, revealed that the upcoming Buenos Aires Conference for the Maintenance of Peace was much more than a convenient excuse to take another Rooseveltian fishing cruise: Roosevelt, anxious about European instability, expressed to his ambassador in Germany his hope that the Old World might profit from the happy demonstration of peacemaking that the New World was about to stage in Argentina.[2] The administration was not merely aspiring to show Europeans that international amity was still possible (even though New World amity had recently been compromised by the bloody Paraguay-Bolivia war). Washington was concerned with more than just the carnage in the Chaco Boreal; it was beginning to fear that European developments were spilling over into a part of the globe that, although it was no longer politic to admit it, the United States considered its own preserve.

Just a week before the conference was to open, an Argentine congressman delivered a ringing encomium for fascism. "Fascism is respectful of our social organization," Matías Sánchez Sorondo told his fellow senators. "States of this kind, no matter what their methods may be, are seeking to invigorate their national spirit and to raise the standard of living of their citizens."[3] A second publicized incident during the last week of November added to Washington's uneasiness: Carefully made up to resemble his apparent idol, German Fuehrer Adolf Hitler, a local Demosthenes of the soapbox harangued a crowd jammed into a downtown Buenos Aires theater with shouts of "Death to the Jews! Death to the Protestants! Death to the Masons!"[4]

35

Secretary of State Cordell Hull, making his second trip to southern South America in three years, was impressed with the extent of Axis inroads there. Contrasting the relatively tranquil aura of the 1933 Montevideo inter-American conference with the worrisome climate of Buenos Aires, Hull reflected some years later that "Axis penetration had made rapid, alarming headway."[5]

It was this mood of nascent apprehension that, to a certain extent, led the administration to propose in early 1936 that a special Pan-American meeting be called to deal with two nettlesome issues: banishing from the Americas such intrahemispheric conflicts as the Chaco War[6] and insulating the hemisphere (Canada excepted) from the next European war. With a regularly scheduled inter-American conference still two years away, there seemed ample reason for the White House to suggest that a special assembly be convened; for not only were German, Italian, and even Japanese activities on the increase in Latin America, but also the very real danger of war breaking out in the Old World suggested, at least to Washington, the urgency of creating a common policy of isolation in the New World. Elliott Roosevelt would later attest his father's growing belief in the imminence of European strife, remarking that by the early months of 1936 the latter's personal correspondence with his ambassadors was showing "an increasingly fatalistic tone."[7]

That Argentina volunteered to host the special assembly was fortunate for the United States, which hoped that the imperatives of hospitality would temper Buenos Aires' penchant for playing the Pan-American enfant terrible. Argentina, the largest Spanish-speaking republic in South America and the continent's strongest state, had traditionally opposed attempts by the United States to get the hemisphere aligned into a pro-American bloc; as much as its Yankee rival, Argentina had adopted a foreign policy credo of "no entangling alliances."

But very unlike the United States, Argentina felt a strong political attraction toward Europe—an attraction that had resulted in its foreign policy being opposed fairly consistently, and over time, to the integration of the hemisphere. In 1825, Buenos Aires had declined an invitation from Colombia to attend an inter-American gathering at Panama, on the grounds that the conference would prove inimical to the interests of certain European powers. Although in the ensuing century there would be moments when

Argentina showed signs of drawing closer to its neighbors, the major thrust of its foreign policy continued to be directed across the Atlantic. From time to time an influential figure would call for greater hemispheric solidarity, causing even more influential figures, like President Bartolomé Mitre in 1865, to explain that insofar as inter-American cooperation was concerned, "It is time to abandon the childish lie that we are brothers."[8]

What to Americans seemed like traditional Argentine stubbornness was magnified by the fact that the delegation of the host country of the 1936 conference was led by none other than the foreign minister, Carlos Saavedra Lamas, freshly garlanded with a Nobel Peace Prize for having arranged a cease-fire in the Chaco. To say that Saavedra Lamas was a thorn in the side of the American delegation is to grossly understate the matter; he was a jagged, rusting sword thrust into its midsection. Never before had a representative of a nation with which the United States was not at war been on the receiving end of so much American diplomatic vituperation (all of it off the record, of course). Spruille Braden, chief American negotiator at the Chaco peace talks and an observer at Buenos Aires, considered Saavedra Lamas a "vain, pathologically ambitious, . . . stupid and wicked man" who, because of his fondness for wing collars, had earned for himself the derisive nickname "Juan Cuello" (John Collar).[9]

Another American with experience at peacemaking in the Chaco, Francis White, reported that "every diplomatic officer in Buenos Aires has complained that he [Saavedra Lamas] has double-crossed him, misled him, and even directly lied to him."[10] Cordell Hull, who had worked assiduously if not entirely altruistically to help Saavedra Lamas get his Peace Price, was one who felt particularly double-crossed. Hull's putative subordinate, Assistant Secretary of State (later Under Secretary) Sumner Welles, claimed that the secretary's "violent antipathy" to Argentina—an antipathy that Welles noted would shortly develop into an "obsession" —came as a direct result of the frustrations Hull had suffered in his dealings with his Argentine counterpart at Buenos Aires.[11]

It is important to note that at this time (late 1936) Argentina's opposition to United States initiatives in the hemisphere had nothing to do with German intrigue. Although future Argentine rulers would try to establish warmer relations with Hitler, both Agustín Justo and his successor in the presidential palace, Ro-

berto Ortiz, were politically sympathetic to their country's principal trading partner, Great Britain. Indeed, to the extent that any
foreign influences could be said to be undercutting the American position at Buenos Aires, they were British. A member of the
American delegation (and soon to be assistant secretary of state),
Adolf Berle, recalled a few years after the conference that "British
influence in the Argentine has persistently been directed against
the United States, going even to the length of an attempt to break
up the Buenos Aires Conference . . ."[12]

A similar opinion was offered in 1941 by American author Hubert Herring, who regretted that the Buenos Aires conference had
been turned into a diplomatic defeat for the United States by the
machinations of "Perfidious Albion," which had "stolen Saavedra
Lamas from under Hull's very eyes."[13] One writer, Argentine po-
lemicist Ernesto Giudici, even reached the remarkable conclusion that Britain was seeking to advance *German* interests in Latin
America, on the assumption that a Hitler steered toward New
World riches would be a Hitler content to leave the British Empire unmolested. Whether this "Anglo-German coalition" had in
fact been operating at Buenos Aires was, to Giudici, immaterial;
what *was* important was that it could be invoked at a moment's
notice, to the great detriment of the American republics.[14]

In truth, Saavedra Lamas was doing no one's bidding at Buenos
Aires but his own, although the net effect of his work was no
doubt satisfactory to London. Rather than hewing to an anti-American stance, the Argentine diplomat was pursuing his country's
long-established policy of keeping open its lines of cooperation
with Europe, which meant in particular the League of Nations.[15]
Specifically, he fought against the United States attempt to have
the conference adopt a common neutrality policy patterned on
the isolationist legislation Congress had passed, and Roosevelt
had signed, the year before. Had the conference accepted the
United States proposal, the Latin American nations would, in the
event of a war breaking out between them, have been legally bound
to apply to the belligerent states an arms embargo that did not
discriminate between aggressor and victim—a clear departure from
League neutrality policy, which insisted on punishing the guilty
belligerent and assisting the innocent one.

In addition to the neutrality proposal, the American delegation
sought (and obtained) the passage of resolutions obligating the

hemisphere republics to settle all their disputes peaceably and to consult among themselves in case an external threat appeared likely to menace the security of the New World.[16] These other two proposals—the Convention to Coordinate, Extend and Assure the Fulfillment of the Existing Treaties between the American States; and the Convention for the Maintenance, Preservation and Reestablishment of Peace (commonly known as the Consultative Pact)—did pass and were much commented upon in the months following the Buenos Aires conference. Hull, for instance, wrote on his return to the United States that the two conventions constituted an "important step in the direction of the reestablishment and revitalization of international law and international order."[17] And Samuel Guy Inman, an unofficial observer at Buenos Aires, saluted the Consultative Pact for having "multilateralized" the Monroe Doctrine, thereby making that dogma of United States foreign policy a "joint responsibility" of the American republics.[18]

In fact, it did no such thing; nor did the Buenos Aires conference, as one historian has written, mark a "turning point in the attitude of the United States toward the defense of the Western Hemisphere. . . ."[19] It is not even the case, as William Everett Kane has stated, that "the United States and its southern neighbors sought to multilateralize neutrality and nothing else."[20] What *is* significant about the Buenos Aires conference is that it represented a singular failure of the Roosevelt administration to get the Latin American nations to adopt as their own the isolationist neutrality policy of the United States.

The draft convention on neutrality that the American delegation brought to Argentina contained a variety of measures designed to insulate the hemisphere from the strife of Europe, of which the two most important measures were an embargo on the export of arms and materiel to warring states, and a prohibition on loans to them. It was stipulated that both measures should apply "equally to all belligerents."[21]

No Latin American government was prepared to endorse such a radical departure from the collective security undertakings (such as they were) of the League of Nations. Strongest in their opposition were two of the southernmost states of South America, Uruguay and Argentina—states whose ties were eastward across the Atlantic, not northward. Uruguayan delegate Manini Rios summed up his country's position when he argued the unwisdom of further widening the Atlantic "which separates us from Europe. The truth is that the countries around the Rio de la Plata are more intimately related, culturally and economically, to some of the European countries than we are to America."[22]

It was left to Saavedra Lamas, fresh from a term as president of the League Assembly at Geneva, to put the quietus to Washington's bid to isolate the hemisphere. With a flurry of metaphors, the Argentine diplomat promised that the New World would never turn its back on the problems of the Old World. Throwing Hull a sop, he declared that the "dense clouds" on the world horizon, the "lightning flashes" signaling the onset of a "great storm," would find the American republics disposed to "noble consultation and to interchange of ideas for the protection of our continent." This pledge to join in the Consultative Pact notwithstanding, Saavedra Lamas made it clear that once the inter-American states had initiated consultation they would then turn toward "all the horizons and . . . offer the collaboration and cooperation that we are disposed to extend to the great human ideals—ideals having no limits or continental restrictions."[23]

Judged in the light of subsequent events, Saavedra Lamas's resistance to United States initiatives seems almost to have been providential, if premature; within four years the White House itself would be scrambling to get the nations of the hemisphere lined up behind Great Britain and against the Axis. Indeed, after the fall of France in June 1940 Washington would find in Saavedra Lamas an ally in the fight to keep Argentina from sliding into a pro-German neutrality.[24] However, all this was in the future; for, as we shall soon discover, from late 1936 until the summer of 1940 the administration of Franklin Roosevelt was as firmly committed to quarantining the United States and its southern neighbors from the effects of European war as were any congressional spokesmen for isolationism.

It seems obvious that, despite later impassioned justifications of his prewar policy, which he dared to label "internationalist," Cordell Hull was advocating isolationist measures at Buenos Aires. In his *Memoirs*, the secretary of state boasted that almost from their first day in office both he and the president were "strongly inclined toward international cooperation, sharply opposed to extreme nationalism and to isolation."[25] Buenos Aires indicates that the opposite was closer to the truth. Even Sumner Welles, not normally given to agreeing with Hull, exercised a similar kind of selective recall in his memoirs, when he termed Buenos Aires "intrinsically the most important inter-American gathering that has ever taken place." Welles was proud enough of the conference's achievements, the creation of intrahemispheric peace machinery and the adoption of the Consultative Pact, but he conveniently forgot to mention the third item in the American package of proposals—the one asking Latin America to imitate the isolationist neutrality policy of the United States.[26]

Unquestionably, the American neutrality package presented at Buenos Aires was harmful to the cause of European collective security, which is precisely why Saavedra Lamas combated it. There is good reason to wonder why the American delegation proposed it at all, particularly if the Hull-Welles view is taken seriously; for, unless the administration was committed to an isolationist policy toward Europe, why bother to extend the impact of the Neutrality Acts of 1935 and 1936?[27] An attempt was made by Nicholas John Spykman in 1941 to clarify the confused behavior of the Roosevelt administration at Buenos Aires. According to the Yale professor of international relations, President Roosevelt was actually seeking to create a League of American Neutrals capable of imposing sanctions against aggressor states outside the hemisphere. Claiming that it was "well known in South America" that the White House opposed the mandatory features of the neutrality legislation of 1935 and 1936 (a dubious claim), Spykman argued that there were hidden motives underlying United States action.

Specifically, said Spykman, the president was using the neutrality proposal as a means to get the other American republics to unite behind the United States on a common policy—even if that policy was a neutrality that Roosevelt himself found repugnant.[28] In this view, then, it was more important that the hemisphere be united than that it be united behind a worthwhile program. One can, of course, suggest as Spykman does that Roosevelt was putting the fox into the henhouse not to feast but to be converted by the chickens, but this stretches the bounds of credulity. What logic alone does not do to destroy Spykman's argument, however, historical evidence does.

For example, it is known that some of the northernmost states

of South America, led by Colombia, were advocating that the
conference create exactly what Spykman maintained Roosevelt
wanted: an American "League" that would have required its members to renounce neutrality in all wars of aggression (in effect, a
reversion to the neutrality policy of Grotius's Europe, where neutrals were expected to support the side waging the "just war")
that would have had the power to institute diplomatic and economic sanctions and that would have collaborated with the League
of Nations.[29] This Colombian proposal elicited nothing but a luke-
warm reaction from the American delelgation, indicating that the
United States was not disposed to let itself get mixed up in any
system of collective security that involved European powers.

To be sure, Roosevelt and the American delegates were not
against the concept of collective security per se. They had, after
all, journeyed all the way to Buenos Aires to try to attain security collaboration within the hemisphere. The Americans simply wanted their system to be confined solely to themselves and
to the nations of Latin America. And the Latin Americans clearly
did not. Thus Saavedra Lamas, who had been playing the part of
diplomatic gadfly throughout the conference, took care to insert
into the text of the Consultative Pact, which called upon the
American states to get together for discussion in the event of a
threat to any of them, the rider—"if they so desire."[30]

Despite his keen disappointment with this eleventh-hour caveat (Spruille Braden recalled Hull becoming "violently angry"
when informed of Saavedra Lamas's action),[31] Hull still managed
to convey the public impression that the conference had been an
unqualified success. In his valedictory address to the Buenos Aires assemblage, which was delivered by Welles because Hull had
a bad cold, the secretary stressed that the decisions taken by the
American republics would have a great influence on the rest of
the world. "Whenever twenty-one nations can forgather in such
a spirit and for such purposes," said Welles, "whenever they can
act together harmoniously in the cause of peace, all other nations
should find profit in their example."[32]

Hull's emphasis on the power of example in international relations was a classic American theme, as old as the country itself,
a theme that was intended to instruct Europe in the finer art of
good neighborliness.[33] It was as fundamental a part of isolation-

ism as was the refusal of the United States to "meddle" in the affairs of the Old World; indeed, it was what kept that refusal from appearing, in American minds at least, to be simply self-serving cant. The Roosevelt administration was not striving to exert a moral influence *despite* its isolationism, but rather *because* of it.

Despite having written flippantly prior to his departure for Buenos Aires that he intended to "carry the message to the Garcias of South America," the president was in real earnest about his mission, which he construed as speaking out against the spread of anti-democratic ideologies, not only in Latin America (where indigenous dictatorships were starting to be crowded out by German and Italian ideological imports), but in Europe and Asia as well.[34] Notwithstanding the existence of authoritarian governments in the three countries he planned to visit—Brazil, Uruguay, and Argentina—Roosevelt could not have selected a more fitting part of the world in which to preach the gospel of democracy; the Garcias of South America seemed to have fallen as much in love with him as had his own countrymen. According to a noted Latin American columnist for a Washington newspaper, Roosevelt's recent thrashing of Alf Landon was a triumph "that gave hope to Latin Americans in an almost hopeless world."[35]

It did not take long for Roosevelt to find out what this reporter meant. During a short stopover in Rio de Janeiro on 27 November, the president was accorded an extremely cordial welcome as his motorcade passed through the rain-slick streets of the Brazilian capital. "Never," reported the American military attaché in Rio, "has a national guest been received with so much enthusiasm, pride, and hospitality as was President Roosevelt."[36] Even more impressive was the reception in Buenos Aires, where exuberant crowds burst through police barriers to get closer to their famous visitor, leaving one astonished onlooker with the indelible memory of an "unforgettable outpouring of enthusiasm by a people that had never been especially friendly to the United States."[37]

Roosevelt did his oratorical best not to disappoint these adoring masses when the conference convened on 1 December. Touting the democratic ideal as the most worthwhile aim of peoples everywhere, he cautioned the hundred or so delegates and countless radio listeners that only if the American republics strengthened the democratic tradition could they hope to insulate themselves from the ravages of a European war and to ensure the triumph of social justice in their corner of the globe. But when they succeeded in perfecting their democratic institutions, the nations of the hemisphere would proudly assume their destined role as show-cases of man's capabilities. Confident that his hopes were well on the way to becoming political realities, Roosevelt declared that "our hemisphere has at last come of age. We are here assembled to show its unity to the world. We took from our ancestors a great dream. We here offer it back as a great unified reality." Waxing metaphysical, the President conjured up a "spirit" of the New World, and appealed to this noble abstraction to do double duty as the guardian of hemispheric security and as an inspiration for the "millions of human beings in other less fortunate lands."[38]

With a few exceptions among the extremist journals of the right and of the left, press reaction in the Argentine capital was highly favorable to the presidential visit; never had an American leader been the object of such panegyrics from the customarily ill-disposed Buenos Aires dailies. "Roosevelt passed through our city like a meteor," recounted the popular *Noticias Gráficas*. "For forty-eight hours he conquered the sympathy of our people . . . This 'Shepherd of the People' has the irresistible fascination of an apostle."[39] The cerebral *La Nación* spoke flatteringly of the great hope that the democratic president held out to mankind— and wished the Argentine government would take the hint.[40] *Crítica*, hammering editorially at the very nail Roosevelt had come to Buenos Aires to strike, declared: "At a time when the mad-dened world of the dictators is full of audacity and aggressiveness, Roosevelt . . . has set the antithesis of doctrines before the court of the world."[41]

La Razón interpreted the Roosevelt visit, indeed the Roosevelt presidency, as evidence of nothing other than a revolution in United States Latin American policy. Reminding its readers of the wrongs inflicted upon the Caribbean lands during the years of Republican rule in Washington, and of the economic woes that had befallen all of Latin America during the protectionist Hoo-ver administration, the journal rejoiced that the "old evil that caused the twenty republics of the continent to appear before the world as subject to a degrading guardianship has disappeared, and the United States has come to sit down with us at . . . Buenos Aires as one more brother, as an equal with no more rights than the most modest nations of Central America—with an open, cordial, and sincrely friendly mind."[42]

All of this was eloquent testimony to conceptions that Latin Americans, in this instance old rivals like the Argentines, entertained concerning the United States. Sumner Welles noted a "striking" contrast with views held a short time before, during World War I, when "hatred of the United States had been widespread throughout Latin America."[43] During the postwar decade, the image of the great North American republic continued to blacken in Latin eyes, as new interventions in the Caribbean area contributed to a further widening of an already all but unbridgeable gap between the two Americas. Such writers as Manuel Ugarte excoriated the very notion of a community of interests between the two dissimilar cultures of the Pan-American system. Convinced that so long as the United States remained a member the Pan-American Union would be "a congress of mice presided [over] by a cat," Ugarte urged Latin nations to seek closer ties with the League of Nations.[44]

On visiting Latin America in the late 1920s, Laurence Duggan (soon to become head of the State Department's Division of American Republics during the Roosevelt administration) learned to his discomfort that anti-Americanism was at epidemic proportions everywhere except in Brazil and Peru. Entering Rosario, Argentina, and finding the city shut down by a general strike, Duggan was surprised and dismayed to discover the reason for the stoppage. "The Argentines contemptuously reminded me that it was the second anniversary of the execution of Sacco and Vanzetti," and Duggan learned they were walking off the job to protest social injustice in the United States.[45]

The troubled relationship between the United States and Latin America reached its nadir at the 1928 inter-American conference in Havana, where all but four small states, clients of Washington, voiced their bitter opposition to American military intervention in the Caribbean. The issue had arisen the preceding year at Rio, where the International Commission of American Jurists solemnly resolved that "no state could interfere in the internal affairs of another." Delegates from the United States had reluctantly given their assent to the resolution, but only after it became obvious that the measure was headed for adoption no matter what they did.

When the resolution next came before an inter-American forum, at Havana in 1928, the United States mounted a tenacious defense of its "right" to intervene. The head of the American delegation, former Secretary of State Charles Evans Hughes, even went so far as to deny that the United States, then completing its thirteenth year of military rule over Haiti, was interventionist. Hughes did admit that his country sometimes exercised its influence over sister republics, but he termed these moments "interpositions of a temporary character." His stubbornness carried the day, and the nonintervention resolution was put in abeyance for five years. But it was Pyrrhic victory, for in reality Havana turned out to be, as Laurence Duggan put it, one of the "worst diplomatic defeats" ever suffered by the United States.[46]

Despite a sincere effort by Herbert Hoover to repair some of the damage done by the Latin American policies of the Coolidge administration, relations between the United States and its southern neighbors did not really improve much. Secretary of State Henry L. Stimson candidly told a nationwide radio audience in May 1931 that difficulties in Latin America had "damaged our good name, our credit, and our trade far beyond the apprehension of our peoples."[47] And though the Hoover White House was making an attempt to meliorate this state of affairs—for example, by scrupulously refraining from sending in the marines when a revolution broke out in Panama in early 1931—Latin Americans retained their profound distrust of Washington. Shortly after the Republicans were defeated in the 1932 election, the *Latin-American Digest* sadly admitted that inter-American relations had "come to such a pass that when the United States does not do a criminal act, it is pointed to with pride. It is as if I passed a neighbor in the street and expected him to give me praise because I did not stick a knife into him."[48]

Nor was the incoming Roosevelt administration initially any more satisfactory to Latin America; indeed, due to a clumsy interlude in Cuba, where American interference had a large hand in toppling two governments during 1933, United States policy seemed to be retrogressing.[49] Not until December 1933 did inter-American relations begin to improve. At the Montevideo conference of that month, the American delegation, led by Cordell Hull, did what Hughes had refused to consider five years before, and renounced intervention. Amid the huzzahing occasioned by the United States action, few seemed to notice—or care—that the nonintervention pledge was qualified by Hull appending to the appropriate article of the Convention on the Rights and Duties of States this caveat: that the United States was committing itself to observe both the noninterventionist promises made by Roosevelt before, during, and subsequent to the 1932 campaign, *and* the operative principles concerning intervention "in the law of nations as generally recognized and accepted." As some international lawyers were quick to point out, the law of nations recognized a right to intervene in certain cases.[50]

Although Hull later claimed that the parlous European situation had made a rapprochement with Latin America a necessity by the end of 1933, it is extremely doubtful that at this juncture security interests were in any meaningful way responsible for the decision to seek warmer relations with the southern neighbors.[51] A more credible explanation for the administration's action was that it wanted to protect those economic interests that Stimson had warned in his May 1931 broadcast were being jeopardized by a rising tide of anti-Americanism below the Rio Grande. As muckraking journalist Carleton Beals noted in the late 1930s, and as revisionist historians have reminded us more recently, a major impetus behind the early Good Neighbor Policy was the desire to safeguard and to extend American investments in Latin America.[52]

This is by no means to suggest that Roosevelt was staying awake nights during the latter months of 1933, in dread of what one recent writer has termed a "powerful and dangerous outburst of revolutionary nationalism in Latin America."[53] Far from it. The president had sent his closest aide, Louis Howe, to Hull with a bit of low-keyed advice for the latter, who was preparing to depart for the Uruguayan capital. "We don't think you need to undertake too much down at Montevideo," said Howe. "Just talk to them about the Pan American highway from the United States down through Central and South America."[54] Plainly, the Reciprocal Trade Agreements Program, which Hull introduced to the world at Montevideo, was not a top priority item for the president, as Hull himself admitted in his *Memoirs*, where he wrote— apropos his objection to a protectionist plank in the Democrats' l936 platform—"I do not know whether Mr. Roosevelt had given any personal attention to the tariff plank since he had shown interest in the trade agreements program only from time to time."[55]

The three years that intervened between the Montevideo and Buenos Aires conferences witnessed a major shift in the attitude of Latin America toward the United States. If by 1936 Uncle Sam was not yet regarded as the most reliable member of the inter-American household, still no one really expected him to make off with the silver every time he came to dinner. The rejection of the American proposal for a common neutrality policy showed that there was enough doubt about the wisdom of Washington's initiatives to discourage tighter bonds between the republics of the New World, but the drift toward warmer relations was nevertheless unmistakable.

In the United States itself there was developing a radically new understanding that, in a world that throbbed with danger, America's security was inextricably linked with the fate of the Latin republics. If, as seemed more and more likely, the Old World was slipping into a state of anarchy, it was becoming a matter of urgency for the administration to try to make of the New World a haven of peace. Although by December 1936 the great fear for the security of Latin America was only just beginning, it was clear that for Washington there could be no more talk of soft-soaping the Latin governments with highways, of blithely sweeping Latin problems under a mat—and especially of sweeping up Latin malcontents with the marines.

The adulation accorded him by the inhabitants of Rio, Montevideo, and Buenos Aires impressed Roosevelt greatly. He wrote his ambassador in Germany, William Dodd, that the peoples of the hemisphere were looking to the United States as their great hope for the future. "I wish you could have seen those South American crowds," exulted the president. "Their great shout as I passed was 'viva la democracia.' Those people down there were for me for the simple reason that they believe that I have made democracy function and keep abreast of the time and that as a system of government it is, therefore, to be preferred to Fascism or Communism."[56]

Although the man in the street was decidedly behind the American president, a few men elsewhere were not. As he was preparing to deliver his opening remarks to the Buenos Aires conference,

Roosevelt was greeted by the cry, "Down with imperialism," which was shouted out from the spectators' gallery of the Argentine Congress by a man who called himself Quebracho, but was in reality Liborio Justo, a leftist militant who also happened to be the son of the Argentine president.[57]

Far more annoying, if infinitely more polite, was the behavior of Saavedra Lamas. But even the Argentine foreign minister could not dampen Roosevelt's enthusiasm over the outcome of the conference. "There is no question of the excellent reaction in South America," he stated happily in a letter to his one-time running mate, James M. Cox, the Democratic candidate for president in 1920. "Three years ago Latin-American public opinion was almost violently against us and the complete change is, I hope, a permanent fact." The president did, however, confess to being "still most pessimistic about Europe."[58]

His pessimism prompted Roosevelt to suggest that perhaps the lessons of Buenos Aires might serve as a useful model for the nations of the Old World, stopping them in their gadarene rush toward war. "I still believe," he told a British statesman, "in the eventual effectiveness of preaching and preaching again. That is the method I have used in our Latin American relationships and it seems to have succeeded."[59] So taken was the president with this idea that for a short time he contemplated calling a European peace conference, patterned on Buenos Aires and other Pan-American conferences.[60]

Roosevelt pursued this notion in his 1937 address to the governing board of the Pan-American Union, which met annually in Washington to commemorate Pan American Day (14 April). The governors enjoyed hearing the president recount that his deepest impression of the Buenos Aires conference was "the potency of the unity of the Americas in developing democratic institutions in the New World and by example in helping the cause of world peace."[61] The Europeans, alas, refused to share in the joy and turned a deaf ear to Roosevelt's artless suggestion that he convoke a meeting of European leaders—a meeting that Roosevelt imagined would result, not in the signing of anything as formal as a treaty, but in the issuance of "a personal declaration of the rulers and a set of general resolutions."[62]

In a little more than a month, the president would be emphasizing a different theme when discussing the implications of Buenos Aires. When the treaties signed there by the secretary of state came up for Senate ratification at the end of May, Roosevelt concentrated upon the defensive and not the hortative features of that "spirit of solidarity" he had detected in the Argentine capital. Articulating a perspective that was to have tremendous importance for American foreign policy over the next four years, the President applauded the "determination of the American republics to keep lawless nations, and their habits, out of the Western Hemisphere."[63] Sooner perhaps than even he could have imagined, he would be watching that determination being put to the test.

3

A Deterioration
of the Pax Americana?

During the first three years of his presidency, Franklin Roosevelt had had the good fortune of being able to dispel, to a surprisingly large extent, the Yankee imperialist bogey that had dwelt within the collective psyche of Latin American intellectuals since at least the turn of the century. With his tour de force at Buenos Aires, he converted many of even the most die-hard anti-Americans to his side. For the first time—and, for that matter, the last—a president of the United States was finding supporters from, of all places, the Latin American left.[1] Early in 1937, the prominent yanquiphobe Manuel Ugarte announced that henceforth it would be neither necessary nor proper to attack the American government, for Roosevelt was above criticism. In a change of mind that paralleled Ugarte's, Socialist senator Alfredo Palacios of Argentina indicated that he, too, had become pro-American.[2]

For obvious reasons, the Latin left had early come to appreciate the trouble-making potential embodied in the sizable German and Italian populations of several South American countries. By the middle of the 1930s, these nuclei of what the left saw as Nazi and fascist oppression were held to constitute a challenge not only to such political ideals as socialism and democracy, but to the very sovereignty of some of the most important nations in Latin America. Although the left—the democratic left, above all—was not the only sector of society to harbor grave doubts about the ultimate intentions of Germans and Italians in the Western Hemisphere, it was the first one to give extensive and effective publicity to the idea that Latin America was imperiled by the Axis.[3] By the end of 1937 and the beginning of 1938 this publicity would bear its first fruits, as several Latin states launched drives to counter the growing influence of Germany and of Italy (and, to a lesser degree, of Spain and Japan).

Apart from the anti-Axis publicity generated by the Latin American left, the Roosevelt administration was also receiving, from its own sources, information of various shades of accuracy concerning Axis activities to the south. Regular diplomatic and military officers posted in major Latin cities; returning visitors eager to give their views, solicited or not, on the newest political developments; American newsmen; and, as of the end of 1938, agents of the Federal Bureau of Investigation—all these played a vital part in sensitizing Washington officials to subversion below the Rio Grande. A final, and by no means unimportant, element in the flow of information to White House sensory organs was British intelligence, especially the British Security Coordination office that Sir William Stephenson would direct from Rockefeller Center after the spring of 1940.[4]

For some years before the Buenos Aires conference, Washington had been receiving conflicting signals regarding Axis intentions in the Western Hemisphere; and though no one could divine the direction that political and military relations between Latin America and the European dictatorships might take, there was consensus among policymakers that, at the very least, Hitler was mounting a strong challenge to American economic interests in the southern part of the hemisphere. By 1936 Germany had surpassed Great Britain as the second leading exporter, after the United States, to Latin America, and had become the principal supplier of imports to the large Brazilian market.

In June of that year, Secretary of Agriculture Henry Wallace had sent the president some statistics documenting Germany's growing economic presence in Latin America. Roosevelt turned this information over to the man in charge of the administration's economic diplomacy, Secretary of State Cordell Hull, whose plodding and dogged efforts on behalf of free trade would later come under scathing attack from critics who feared that the Reciprocal Trade Agreements were an impotent response to the German challenge. But such attacks were still four years in the future; for the moment, the Hull program was considered an adequate solution to the problem of extrahemispheric economic incursions.[5]

While Henry Wallace's sense of worry was being whetted by German trade gains, there appeared at the White House a confidential report assessing the prospects of an invasion of the east coast of South America. This anonymous study concluded that, although Axis economic and political offensives could be expected in the coming years, there was only a slight chance that South America would actually be invaded—unless "complete accord" were to be reached among the four great naval powers of Europe: Britain, France, Germany, and Italy. Barring the extreme unlikelihood of the British fleet remaining at anchor while Axis ships steamed across the Atlantic, no military challenge could be mounted against the Monroe Doctrine. Until Munich no one in Washington would take seriously the possibility of an invasion of even the most tempting targets in South America: Argentina, Brazil, and Uruguay. As for the remainder of the continent, the report stated that "a challenge on the Pacific Coast . . . or on the Caribbean Coast seems impossible."[6] After Munich it would seem anything but impossible.

If by late 1936 American policymakers were becoming mildly concerned for the security of the hemisphere, there was as yet no cause for the alarm that would become general within a few years. Indeed, one cabinet officer, Secretary of Commerce Daniel Roper, persuaded himself that the international political system was stable enough to allow the United States to scrap the Monroe Doctrine altogether, replacing it with a policy built on the principle of the good neighbor. The secretary, whose main bureaucratic imperative was the furtherance of trade, was conscious of the fact that the Monroe Doctrine had given the United States a bad image in Latin America and that American business had suffered accordingly. Therefore he suggested to Roosevelt, shortly after the latter's departure for Buenos Aires aboard the cruiser *Indianapolis,* that the time would never be better to revise the Doctrine thoroughly, because Monroe's words had been uttered in response to a threat that no longer existed, a foreign invasion of the hemisphere.[7]

Cordell Hull was not as sanguine about the safety of the hemisphere, mainly because the State Department had been receiving a few disturbing reports from Latin American postings for several months prior to the Buenos Aires conference. It will be recalled from the previous chapter that the secretary of state had confessed to some uneasiness at the headway made by the Axis powers by the end of 1936. What Hull had in mind at this time was not an impending Axis invasion of any Latin country (although *that* fear would surface with a vengeance by 1940); rather, he was somewhat concerned about the potentially destabilizing presence of large German, Italian, and, to a lesser extent, Japanese communities in several major South American countries.

The Japanese presence was the least upsetting to Hull and other administration officials, although one popular journalist, Carleton Beals, was convinced that the heavy Japanese settlement in Peru posed a definite danger to the security of that nation and its Pan-American friends. For some unexplained reason, Beals believed that barbers were the most likely people to become spies; in Peru (where according to him there were 350,000 Japanese living in the most strategic parts of the land) "there is hardly a town, . . . however remote in the Andes or the jungles, in which the barber is not a Jap."[8] But policymakers like Under Secretary of State Sumner Welles inclined to a less conspiratorial view of Latin reality, and concluded that "the threat arising from Japan's activities in the hemisphere was slight."[9]

The same conclusion did not apply to the activities of Germans and Italians in Latin America. Although it is impossible to uncover anything like accurate statistical evidence on the size of the German and Italian population in Latin America, it is unquestionable that insofar as observers in Washington were concerned, far too many potential subversives were living below the Rio Grande. To get a rough understanding of what "too many" means, one need only consult some of the numerous, and more or less educated, guesses that were being made by official and unofficial witnesses of Latin political developments during the late 1930s and early 1940s.

The foreign wing of the German Nazi party, the Auslandsorganisation, claimed in 1936 to be well on the road to enlisting for the Fuehrer the more than one million *Volksdeutsche* (persons of German blood) and *Reichsdeutsche* (persons of German citizenship) that it counted as residing in Latin America. According to the AO, the vast majority (more than 800,000) of these potential converts to Nazism could be found in one country alone, Brazil; another 150,000 were in Argentina, and 30,000 lived in the third country of high German settlement, Chile.[10] For his part, Secretary of State Hull thought the AO estimates too low; he believed that the correct figure was one and one-half million Germans in all of Latin America.[11]

Others put the figure even higher. In 1942, an American political scientist, Karl Loewenstein, wrote that two and one-half million persons with some German blood were living in Brazil alone; and of this total, one million were of "pure" stock.[12] In the same year the FBI estimated that nearly five million people in South America were of German, Italian, or Japanese descent—and a significant minority of them were sympathizers with the policies of their fatherlands. Italians made up by far the largest group, some three million strong according to the FBI, concentrated chiefly in Argentina. Next came the Germans, two-thirds of whom (or about a million) were living in Brazil, particularly in the three southernmost states of Paraná, Santa Catarina, and Rio Grande do Sul. Finally there were the Japanese, numbered by the FBI at perhaps 300,000 in all of South America and, like the Germans, found mostly in Brazil.[13]

It was sometimes argued in Latin America and the United States, on remarkably little evidence, that Italians were politically more reliable than the Germans or the Japanese, because they were more easily assimilated into the Latin culture.[14] Not everyone shared this opinion, of course;[15] but it really did not matter in Washington whether or not the Italians were thought to be assimilable, for the sheer size of their communities in Latin America caused American policymakers not a little anxiety during the late 1930s, especially by 1938. Overt fascist propagandizing began there in earnest in 1935, as Rome sought to sway Latin opinion on the Ethiopian conflict. The outbreak of civil war in Spain in 1936 occasioned a redoubled Italian effort to influence Latin America, this time to generate support for the rebels of Francisco Franco. The net result of these campaigns is difficult to gauge, given the inclination of most Latin American governments (Mexico's and Colombia's being notable exceptions) to sympathize with Franco—thus making the Italian propaganda effort almost redundant. In any event, the Roosevelt administration would closely monitor Italian activity in the southern part of the hemisphere as the decade drew to a close.[16]

It was, however, the Germans about whom the White House would grow most concerned. Not nearly so numerous as the Italians, the Germans seemed to make up in zeal for what they lacked in size. For a government that incessantly remonstrated with Washington that it had no political or military interests in the American sphere of influence, Berlin spent an astounding amount of time and money trying to convert New World Germans to the cause of Nazism. It is not possible to state with any degree of accuracy whether the majority of Germans in Latin America were ultimately converted, but it is certainly the case that the AO persuaded or coerced tens of thousands to follow the party line.

Germany did not direct its propaganda solely at the Reichsdeutsche and Volksdeutsche; it also sought to sway the thinking of the "non-hyphenated" Latin Americans, and to this end huge sums were dedicated to shortwave broadcasting and to the print media, especially to newspapers and wire services.[17] To give substance to its messages, Germany devised various stratagems for capturing a larger share of the trade of Latin America—stratagems that did enable it to make substantial inroads into British and American markets in South America between 1933 and 1938.[18] Added to these considerations was the fact that only Germany, among the Axis powers, possessed the strength to pose a menace to the physical security of America's southern neighbors. And to the Roosevelt administration, a threat to the security of Latin America was tantamount to a threat to that of the United States itself.

But in early 1937 such a threat was still in the future. Notwithstanding the potential for danger in the southern part of the hemisphere, the *immediate* aftermath of the Buenos Aires conference was not an especially troubled time for the administration. A nimbus of good neighborliness lingered a while after the president's visit, leaving the impression (shortly to disappear) that all was well in the Western Hemisphere. By the end of February 1937, however, American policymakers would start to sense that things were not proceeding according to design. At that juncture, Sumner Welles invited his friend Adolf Berle, a member of the president's original brain trust, to succeed Jefferson Caffery as ambassador to Cuba. Berle, who later that year would join the government, did not feel that the time was right for him to take on the Latin assignment. He declined the offer, but he noted in his diary that the "influx of German and Italian Fascists to Havana is causing some worry."[19]

A few weeks later, news reached the War Department that some influential Argentines were beginning to express fears that Hitler might have aggressive plans for their country. In an Argentine lower house debate on the 1937 military budget, deputy Julio Noble read what he declared was an excerpt from a telegram sent by Germany's minister of economics, Hjalmar Schacht, in which the Nazi desire for Latin American lebensraum was adumbrated. Noble was alarmed by this cable, which had been passed along to him by an informer, and he made his feelings plain in declaring that "I confess my fears for our own Patagonia. I confess the fears that the men of Brazil also confess with respect to the great expanses of their territory." Argentina must quickly build up its armed forces, he continued, and join with all the neighboring republics in standing up to Hitler. "In normal times an invasion would be impossible, but the world is not living in normal times. . . ." In reporting these remarks to Washington, military attaché Lester Baker observed that Argentines were becoming less indifferent to events taking place across the Atlantic; referring to the sparsely settled Patagonian territories, he related that "now the legislators apparently look with some alarm at the possibility of a European power seizing by force a territory that could be the larder of the world."[20]

Aside from these brief flurries of anxiety, there had not really developed in the United States, through the first half of 1937, much sustained apprehension that Latin America was imperiled by the breakdown of stability in Europe. Perhaps a typical American view was that of New York businessman E. I. McClintock, who made what he termed an "extensive trip" through South America in the springtime, reporting in a lengthy letter to Roosevelt that, apart from the usual political squabbles in which Latin Americans were perennially involved, the continent was exceptionally placid, with hardly a trace to be found of Axis intrigue.[21]

In late June, a group of Latin Americanists, conferring at the University of Chicago, concluded that the United States had nothing much to worry about below the border. Professor Chester Lloyd Jones of the University of Wisconsin argued that the security picture was so bright that Roosevelt could easily get away with the nonintervention commitment the administration had made at Buenos Aires. For, Jones stated, "European and other non-American powers have their hands too full at home to adopt a strong policy in the New World."[22] The president himself evidently held a similar view; at about the same time he wrote to Charles Gilmore Maphis, of the University of Virginia's Institute of Public

Affairs, that the states of the Western Hemisphere seemed to be on the verge of achieving lasting peace.[23]

Roosevelt was alluding to the set of decisions taken at the Buenos Aires conference—decisions that tended to blunt the American sense of concern about the export of alien ideology to the New World. In this instance, it turned out that the administration had done its work too well at Buenos Aires; for, as long as American policymakers could satisfy themselves that a secure Pax Americana could reign in the hemisphere, thereby ensuring the safety of the United States, then so long would all arguments aimed at obtaining an American commitment to the defense of European democracy (i.e., Britain and France) fall upon deaf ears. No one appreciated this point better than Livingston Hartley, a member in excellent standing of what later came to be called the "foreign policy establishment" of the East Coast, a man who in the middle of 1937 drafted a reasoned plea for the abandonment of isolationist policy—a plea as noteworthy for its logic as for its prematurity.

Entitling his work *Is America Afraid?*, Hartley set out to convince his countrymen that the answer to this question could only be a firm negative, if the President would pay closer attention to the realities of international relations. One of the fundamental misconceptions under which the White House labored was the Three Musketeer-like aspiration for a hemisphere whose guiding principle was "all for one and one for all." It could never exist, Hartley argued, because the Latin American states were too pitifully weak to serve as an effective barrier to anything—let alone a totalitarian invasion of the New World.

Admitting that the hemisphere was not threatened yet, Hartley nevertheless warned of bad things to come if the United States did not act to halt aggression in Europe. Though his words were wide of their mark in that summer of 1937, in a short while they would ring with the resonance of prophecy, as the perceived appearance of a full-blown Axis menace converted what had been held to be only a possible threat to Latin America into a probable one. "The writing on the wall is not hard to read," Hartley stated, predicting that 130 million Americans would soon find themselves surrounded on the east and west by more than one billion totalitarians. "We are in a sense the ham in the world sandwich," he continued, making it plain that what was really keeping the meat from being devoured was the British fleet, not the existence of a large landmass toward the south filled with helpless buffer states.

Hartley's conclusion was straightforward: If the United States wished to preserve its security, it must henceforth align itself with Great Britain to stop the Axis, for, "as long as Great Britain continues to rule the European waves, we need have no fear of European attack." But let Britain either abstain from fighting Hitler or, far worse, go down to defeat before him, and the Latin American "firebreak" that so appealed to Berle and other policy makers would become worse than useless. "We would be better off if there were no Latin America south of the equator, since the South American republics would be quite unable to defend themselves."

Look at the map, suggested Hartley. There stood the naked bulge of Brazil, jutting into the Atlantic a mere eighteen hundred miles from Dakar, in western Africa. Rio de Janeiro was only three thousand miles from Cape Town. Should Germany attain mastery over Europe, Africa would fall to her as a matter of course. After that, the colors in Hartley's geopolitical canvas would not be difficult to fill in; within ten years the United States would be facing a "life-and-death struggle" for its national survival. "The Monroe Doctrine would then become the central issue in world affairs," Hartley declared. At best, Washington could look forward to the imminent eruption of civil conflict all over Latin America, patterned after the carnage in Spain; at worst, to the outright absorption of major South American republics into the Reich. In either case, Hartley concluded, "our present unrivaled strategic position would be fatally undermined."[24]

By a quirk of timing, Hartley's first scenario, envisaging the spread of Spanish-style civil war to the hemisphere, assumed real proportions simultaneously with the appearance of *Is America Afraid?* Raúl Díez de Medina, a Latin writer who frequently appeared in American publications under the pen name Gaston Nerval, was deeply troubled because the likely victory in Spain of Franco's Nationalists meant that "Spanish Fascism, abetted and supported by Berlin and Rome, would not take long to cross the ocean." Writing in the July 1937 edition of *Foreign Affairs,* Díez de Medina warned that the rise of a new Holy Alliance in Europe would lead not only to an upswing in totalitarian propagandizing in Latin America but also to an economic and political penetration of that region by European dictatorships. He chided:

ple of the United States realized the far-reaching impli-
this threat, not only in connection with the ultimate
Pan-Americanism, but with regard to their own interests, actually even their own safety, they might cease deceiving
themselves with the illusion of blissful isolation."[25]

Since the aftermath of her agonizing defeat by the United States
at the turn of the century, Spain had entertained the dream of
reinstituting at least a cultural imperium over her former colonies in the Western Hemisphere.[26] But it was only with the sweep
of Franco's forces through the Spanish countryside that a genuine interest in overseas expansion was rekindled. Early in 1937,
the Falange magazine *Fe* presented an article by Miguel Gran, a
writer who, sensing victory at home, was eager to commence settling some old scores with the United States. The moment had
come to unite the Latin American countries under the rule of
Madrid.[27] "We desire," declared Gran, "to put an end to 'Monroeism,' in order to put in its place our affirmation: 'The Spanish
world for the Spanish.' "[28]

Three years earlier, the Falange had drawn up a list of twenty-
seven points at a secret meeting held in the Spanish capital. One
of the items in the so-called Madrid Program was a demand that
the Spanish Empire in the New World be reconstituted.[29] Some
analysts in the Western Hemisphere took this demand seriously;
others did not. Among the latter was Enrique Gil, a professor of
political economy at the Universidad de la Plata in Argentina,
who argued that, with the exception of Argentina's, Franco would
have little influence on Latin American politics.[30] To Carleton
Beals, however, the significance of the war in Spain was vast
indeed: "Fascism is at our doors in bloody earnest. . . . Spain has
been the first big trench in the battle for our own continent."[31]

Despite alarums appearing in several American publications,
the White House tended toward the Gil view of the consequences
in the New World of the war in Spain. It was not persuaded that
the outcome of the war was likely to present a danger to the nations of the hemisphere. By insisting that the United States adopt
an impartial neutrality toward the belligerents, the administration was choosing to further one goal, isolation from European
wars, at the expense of another, the commitment (if only a ver-
bal one) to combat the spread of fascism. It was still possible, in
January 1937, to perform this feat of aspirational legerdemain,

because the president did not think that any major threat to the American position in the hemisphere would result from a victory on the part of the Nationalists, ably assisted by Hitler and (much less ably) by Mussolini. Two years later, however, at a time when the administration was only too aware that it faced a stern challenge in Latin America, Roosevelt would confess to his cabinet officers that the decision to embargo the Loyalists along with the rebels had been a "grave mistake."[32]

A second development of 1937 indicates that the perception of a security threat to Latin America had not yet—not even by early autumn—become articulated in Washington. Because of its important bearing on the issue of his abandonment of isolationist policy, the president's famous "Quarantine Speech," delivered in Chicago on 5 October 1937, is worth a word here. The address, in which Roosevelt made what has been widely interpreted as a call for a policy of international sanctions against aggressor states, is often seen by historians as a watershed in American foreign policy. "In effect," wrote two students of Rooseveltian diplomacy, "he broke with isolationism, discarded the policy of strict neutrality, and stepped forward as an advocate of collective security."[33]

This interpretation seems to have the hallmark of a *consensus gentium.* Indeed, Charles Beard and Basil Rauch, who could agree on little else, both concurred that the Chicago speech did, for better (Rauch) or worse (Beard), mark the end of an era.[34] I believe this view is erroneous, and I would argue that the administration did not abandon isolationist policy until nearly three years later, in the late summer of 1940. Elaboration of this point will follow in subsequent chapters; for the moment, let us look a bit more closely at what Roosevelt actually said in Chicago.

After some prefatory remarks on the providential fortune of Americans, who were among the few peoples of the world able to live in conditions of "happiness and security and peace," the president settled into his topic: to discuss and to decry the "present reign of terror and international lawlessness" that had begun in the early 1930s. Although citing no nation in particular, he deplored the fact that "without a declaration of war and without warning or justification of any kind, civilians, including vast numbers of women and children, are being ruthlessly murdered with bombs from the air." He also went on to criticize, again naming no names, governments that meddled in civil wars in foreign lands.

The world was being shaken to its very foundation by the forces of "international anarchy," and someone had to cry halt. Apparently, Roosevelt imagined himself to be that someone. Using a memorable metaphor from the domain of public health, he declared that "when an epidemic of physical disease starts to spread, the community approves and joins in a quarantine of the patients in order to protect the health of the community against the spread of the disease." *How* that protection was to be administered, the president did not say. What he did say was that the United States was doing its utmost to avoid involving itself in war, and that it would also strive to help other peaceful states restore "the principles of the Prince of Peace." However, unlike Jesus, Roosevelt made no promises.[35]

While there can be no doubt that the president would have wished his words to be taken seriously by certain high officials in the German and Italian governments, it is nevertheless the case that he was *mainly* addressing his remarks to Japan, which had recently begun an undeclared but quite real war against China. Both Hitler and Mussolini had been relatively well-behaved through 1937—if one could forget, as the leaders of Britain and France seemed to be doing, the dictators' aid to Franco. Since the reoccupation of the Rhineland, Germany had gone over a year without upsetting the European status quo; and Mussolini was contentedly digesting Ethiopia. But Japan was on the march in China, and some American observers believed that public opinion in the United States was, as Berle phrased it, "slowly but steadily crystallizing in favor of some kind of measures against Japan."[36]

Berle likened the national mood to that of the early months of war in 1914; acts such as the bombing of Nanking were causing the public to demand a harsher policy toward Japan. At the same time, Americans remained as determined as ever to stay clear of any European entanglements. Roosevelt evidently appreciated the popular mood, because for a very short time he contemplated making a bold move to dissuade Japan from plunging deeper into China. According to Sumner Welles, at whose Maryland estate the president spent several evenings during the sweltering summer of 1937, Roosevelt was toying with the idea of erecting an Anglo-American naval barrier in the Pacific, aimed at containing Japanese expansionism. He thought he could get away with this show of force because the Japanese economy, stretched to the breaking point by the fighting in China, could not support a war against the United States. To be sure, the president was also apprehensive about German intentions, but as Welles emphatically recalled, "I wish to make it unmistakably plain that in 1937 he was far more preoccupied with the threat represented by Japan."[37]

If some sort of anti-Japanese démarche was occupying Roosevelt's thoughts in midsummer, he hid it well. By early October it would have taken a soothsayer to figure out what, if anything, the president proposed to do, and what, if anything, he meant by the Quarantine Speech. Not being gifted with preternatural vision, those who attended Roosevelt's press conference on the day after the Chicago address were incapable of deciphering the strange responses they were getting to their questions. Could his remarks of the previous evening be interpreted as a repudiation of neutrality? the president was asked. Not at all, came the reply; they could mean an extension of neutrality. Was he calling for sanctions? "They are out of the window." How about coercive action on the part of the United States? Definitely not. "Moral" action, then? "No, it can be a very practical sphere." And so it went; by the time Roosevelt was through with this muddled Socratic exercise, none of the press was any wiser for having attended the news conference.[38]

Some students of the Roosevelt years have dissented from the interpretation that the Quarantine Speech signaled the demise of isolationist policy. Dorothy Borg has argued persuasively that the president's inability to elucidate his understanding of "quarantine" reflected his own deep uncertainty about which course the United States should pursue. She rejects the claim that Roosevelt was making his break with isolationism that night in Chicago; instead, she maintains that the speech indicated that "he was still pursuing a variety of nebulous schemes for warding off catastrophe." Of a similar mind is William Leuchtenburg, who has written that "the speech itself, often described as a turning point in American foreign policy, changed nothing at all. The degree to which the United States still pursued an isolationist line quickly became apparent."[39]

While we shall probably never know for sure if Roosevelt was engaging in anything other than rhetorical exercise at Chicago, there would appear to be *one* certainty in respect of the Quarantine Speech—Welles's contention that the president was concerned primarily with Japan. Berle's diary contains a revealing account of a meeting held at the State Department some two weeks before Roosevelt's speech. Secretary of State Hull, who had summoned the meeting, declared that the Far East was the nation's biggest worry, and suggested that the United States might have to stiffen its position toward Japan, perhaps going to the length of staging a joint naval demonstration in the Pacific with Great Britain. Berle said that he thought this could be accomplished safely enough, assuming that the United States would be able to appease Germany and Italy, without whose help Japan would be forced to give in.

At the end of the conference, Berle drew aside Hull and presidential adviser Charles Taussig, and suggested that concurrent with any naval move in the Pacific the administration make an inter-American démarche. He proposed having Washington monitor Latin American exports to Japan, allowing only the "normal" peacetime trade to take place; the balance, he suggested, could be diverted to Italy and Germany, as a kind of "peace credit" to discourage those powers from going out on the prowl. In short, Berle wanted to initiate a global game of appeasement, played in large measure with Latin American counters. Hull invited some follow-up memoranda on this idea, but he also expressed skepticism that it would work, not because it represented appeasement—he could support that—but because he doubted that Argentina and Chile could be induced to forgo a lucrative war trade with Japan.[40]

What is curious about this meeting is Berle's apparent lack of concern for Axis aggression in Latin America, as evidenced by his willingness to bind Latin economies to the future behavior of Germany and Italy. Coming from Berle, who would shortly become one of the champions of the hemisphere isolationists, this could only mean that as of September 1937 the administration was much more apprehensive about Japan than about the European dictatorships. Certainly this is how the Germans saw things: their ambassador in the United States, Hans Heinrich Dieckhoff, cabled the Foreign Ministry on 9 October that nothing in Roosevelt's Chicago speech should be alarming to Berlin, for it was "mainly, if not exclusively, directed against *Japan* and . . . the possibility of assuming a more active role in European questions was not contemplated."[41]

Advocates of collective security, both in the United States and Great Britain, drew a different—and mistaken—inference from the president's address. Shortly after the speech, Lord Lothian wrote in the *Observer* that "it will probably mark for the historian the point at which the United States definitely began to turn away from the isolation which had been its policy since the presidential election of 1920."[42] League of Nations devotees in the United States shared Lothian's joy. James T. Shotwell, president of the League of Nations Association, hailed the Quarantine Speech as a "milestone in the long march of nations" toward peace, while another member of the association, Clark Eichelberger, saw in it the "collective system manifesting new vitality."[43]

Within a month of his hope-inspiring speech, Roosevelt was to disappoint sorely these spokesmen of collective security. At the Brussels Conference of November 1937, convoked by the signatories (other than Japan) of the Nine-Power Treaty to discuss the Far Eastern situation, the United States made it clear that it would not support stern measures to make Japan live up to the commitments made in 1922. The president personally instructed the American chief of delegation at Brussels, Norman Davis, to avoid scrupulously even the mention of sanctions. Not surprisingly, Davis complained to Sumner Welles on his return to Washington that "he felt very keenly that he had not been properly supported by his own Government."[44]

October of 1937, then, was not a very significant month in the chronicle of American foreign policy, despite the much publicized Quarantine Speech. But November *was* important, for it was in that month that events in Latin America started to move in a direction that would eventually lead the administration to alter radically its policies toward Europe.

At a White House luncheon early in the month, the president confided to his friend and Dutchess County neighbor, Secretary of the Treasury Henry Morgenthau, that he was fearful Germany and Italy were beginning to act up again. Coming on top of recent dire economic forecasts, this observation was doubly troubling to Roosevelt, who was so downcast that he suggested to Morgenthau, in all seriousness, that big American industrialists might be tempted to stage a coup and install their own man in the White House. Now, in addition to problems on the home front, it looked as if fascism was spreading through the world, as demonstrated by Italy's decision of 6 November to subscribe to the Anti-Comintern agreement, which Germany and Japan had created the previous November. What was worse, continued the president, was that Brazil was "veering that way" as well.[45]

Two days after this luncheon, the president of Brazil, Getulio Vargas, made himself dictator of Brazil in a move interpreted on both sides of the Atlantic in a manner that corroborated Roosevelt's secret presentiments. Typical of initial American press reaction to the Brazilian coup of 10 November was this headline from the *New York Times:* "U.S. Fears Fascism May Spread Among Latin American Countries." The *Times* was not certain that Brazil had become an irreclaimable adherent to fascism, but all indications were that Rio had chosen to forsake democracy, which it had never embraced very forcefully anyway.[46]

In Europe, too, the Brazilians were big news, the Italians according the change in government an especially enthusiastic reception. *Il Messagero* welcomed the new fascist (or so it was called) regime with glowing praise for Vargas, "one of the greatest and strongest of contemporary statesmen," a man who "has ploughed the initial furrow for the new civilization and prosperity of his country in this fascist century." *Il Tevere* celebrated the renunciation of Good Neighbor Policy on the part of a "great South American country [that] has just rejected the democratic lie. There is no health in the democracy of Cordell Hull." Broad indeed were the grins worn by Italian leaders, as Mussolini's propaganda chief hailed the latest member of the "new Holy Alliance."[47]

In Germany, the reaction to Vargas's coup was somewhat more restrained—but only somewhat. American Ambassador William Dodd reported that Berlin's official response was to downgrade any presumptions that the new Brazilian dictatorship was linked to the totalitarian powers of Europe. But local American press correspondents had told Dodd that Nazi leading lights were walking around in a state of "suppressed elation." And in the German press, hosannas were sung to the newest recruit in what the *Berliner Zeitung am Mittag* called the battle against the "Red world pest."[48]

The British and French did not particularly like the news from Rio. From Paris, Ambassador William Bullitt notified the State Department that the city's principal dailies were handling the story as a clear-cut victory for fascism in the largest Latin American country. "Pertinax" managed, withal, to descry a silver lining in this storm cloud, believing that Vargas's action "makes it more than ever necessary for President Roosevelt to declare that the splendid isolation of the United States is a thing of the past." Fleet Street, on the other hand, was not prepared to consign Brazil to the fascist column, but it did worry that the coup of 10 November indicated, at the very least, that Rio was about to sign the Anti-Comintern Pact.[49]

Actually, there was something to these British fears. On 19 November, Referat Deutschland, a liaison agency within the Wilhelmstrasse dealing with matters of race and communism, recommended that Berlin seek not only Brazilian adhesion to its anti-communist manifesto, but Argentine and Chilean adherence as well. Reports from the ambassador in Rio, however, convinced the Foreign Ministry that although Vargas was definitely a foe of communism, he could not be expected to jeopardize relations with Washington and London by joining the Axis nations in combat against the red menace. Thus on 30 November the political division in charge of Latin American affairs at the Wilhelmstrasse suggested a different tack: that Germany dramatically step up its anti-communist propaganda offensive in Latin America, chiefly through the use of its Transocean news service.[50]

Brazil never did join in the Anti-Comintern Pact. Nor did events in Brazil have the immediate effect sought by "Pertinax": of forcing the United States to cooperate more closely with the European democracies. But they did constitute a giant step in that direction, for they jangled American security nerves and prepared the administration to accept psychologically that the awesome potential challenge which the Axis could mount against Latin America—the challenge that Hartley had recently sketched in all its austere dimensions—might well become an *actual* challenge in the near future.

Brazil made a determined and partly successful effort to assuage American concern that it had "gone fascist." Vargas held a press conference on 13 November to declare that, while his government did not intend to give the Bolsheviks any respite, it would remain "100 percent" loyal to American ideals. He denied that his regime was totalitarian; rather, he said, it sought to maintain "democratic dogmas within a social and nationalistic framework." Five days later, *O Jornal*, the capital city's most influential paper and an accurate guide to official thinking, ridiculed the rumor that Brazil was contemplating signing the Anti-Comintern Pact. "The axis of the Itamaraty's [Brazilian foreign office] international policy is Washington, to which government we are linked by identic democratic ideals, by a community of economic and political interests, and, still further, by sentiments of inter-American solidarity which were affirmed in such a definite manner at the Buenos Aires Conference."[51]

This kind of statement was welcomed indeed by Sumner Welles, who had been much disturbed by the sensationalist coverage the American press was according the constitutional changeover in Rio. Nevertheless, the under secretary did instruct Ambassador Jefferson Caffery to obtain reassurances from Vargas's own lips, *and* to place all State Department personnel in Brazil immediately on the alert "regarding any possible increased influence with the Government of the German and Italian Governments. . . ." Vargas told Caffery that it "was laughable" to imagine that Germans, Italians, or Japanese were in any way mixed up in the coup. On hearing this, Welles breathed a good deal easier, and took the opportunity afforded by a previously scheduled speaking engagement at George Washington University to deliver his and the State Department's benediction for the new Vargas regime, at the same time reminding his audience of the need to demonstrate a "spirit of tolerance in inter-American relationships."[52]

Although Washington was mollified to an extent by the official Brazilian justifications and disclaimers, there was no undoing the fact that the 10 November coup caused many people in the administration to begin worrying seriously about Latin America. And, in the manner of a self-fulfilling prophecy, the redoubled search for an Axis menace southward soon began to reveal the existence of one. It was at this juncture that American strategists commenced work on a plan that paid serious attention, for the first time since the end of the World War, to the danger of combat in the Atlantic. From 1919 until November 1937, general war plans had been based on the assumption that Japan constituted the principal menace to American security. In the nomenclature of the day, ORANGE plans referred to warfare involving Japan as the enemy, while RED plans singled out the British Empire. In their most febrile moments, the planners conjured up the peril of a Japanese-British alliance against the United States: notwithstanding the fact that an Anglo-Japanese entente had been renounced by Britain at the Washington Naval Conference of 1921–22, a RED-ORANGE contingency represented the summit of American theoretical war preparations from 1924 until the end of 1937.[53]

One of the men around the president who suddenly evinced a real interest in the hemisphere republics was Secretary of the Treasury Morgenthau. A month after the coup, he informed his department's director of monetary research, Harry Dexter White, that the economic and financial difficulties of many Latin states were forcing them to turn for assistance to the fascist powers, a development that Morgenthau considered fraught with peril for the United States. Specifically mentioning Cuba and Mexico, he suggested that the Treasury Department explore methods of reorganizing Latin finances, with a view to strengthening "democratic tendencies" in the southern part of the hemisphere.[54]

Coupled with the economic penetration that so bothered Morgenthau, Germany had been conducting an intensified propaganda campaign in Latin America. By "adopting" the Auslandsorganisation into its midst, the Foreign Ministry, formerly the Cinderella of the Nazi bureaucracy, was able to become an active participant in the competition for influence over Latin public opinion by the end of 1937.[55] The "growing propaganda of non-American countries in Latin America" was called to the attention of the president in December, in the form of a somber letter sent him by Samuel Guy Inman, a professor at the University of Pennsylvania and an old Latin hand who had been an unofficial observer at Buenos Aires the previous year. Roosevelt quickly put Inman in touch with Sumner Welles.[56]

It was not just the administration that was starting to feel uneasy about stepped-up Axis activities below the Rio Grande. On 15 December, *Foreign Policy Reports* published a study on fascist and communist movements in Latin America. Readers of the journal were apprised that if for the moment neither ideology appeared powerful enough to unseat a Latin government—with the possible exception of Brazil's—there was a good chance that fascism, the stronger of the two "isms," would develop soon into a danger to American security. It would not necessarily happen, reasoned author Stephen Naft, given that the fascist states of Europe did not have very much in common with the repressive regimes of Latin America. The former strove to exert total control over the political, economic, and cultural affairs of their peoples; while the latter were usually willing to settle for domination of only one sphere, the political. Moreover, mass support, a distinguishing characteristic of fascism, was lacking in every Latin land save one, Brazil. Still, the situation bore watching.[57]

Influenced perhaps by this sort of speculation, the German ambassador to the United States, Hans Heinrich Dieckhoff, penned in late December what was surely the most perceptive dispatch of his career. In his year-end summary of Washington diplomatic developments, written for State Secretary Ernst Weizsäcker, the ambassador went straight to the point: Berlin should be made aware, beyond the shadow of a doubt, that it was running a very serious risk that the United States would sooner or later cast off its isolationist policy toward Europe. And should America reenact its performance of 1917 by taking up the sword against Germany, it would do so in no small measure because "developments in Brazil and events in other South American countries have increased the apprehension that the ideology of the totalitarian state is reaching out from Europe to the Western Hemisphere." Dieckhoff closed by reminding Weizsäcker that the Nazi hierarchs seemed to be forgetting an important fact: American power had spelled the difference between victory and defeat in the World War.[58]

There is no evidence that the ambassador's warning ever reached Hitler. It most likely did not, for Foreign Minister Joachim von Ribbentrop rarely forwarded reports from the diplomatic fussbudgets in the American capital, whose "defeatism" annoyed him tremendously. On the other hand, the woefully inept observations of the military attaché, Gen. Friedrich Boetticher, who always placed German strength and American weakness in the most favorable juxtaposition, were eagerly passed on to Hitler by Chief of Staff Wilhelm Keitel. They were, noted Keitel, read "with the greatest interest" by the Fuehrer—certainly not a wise way for the latter to invest his time, for Boetticher was continually stressing that America would never get mixed up in European affairs, since it was hopelessly divided between a pro-German "General Staff" and a "Jew-ridden" press.[59]

The coming year was to reveal how prescient Dieckhoff could be.

4

"A Natural Field
for Greed and Conquest"

If Latin America was beginning to warrant the close attention of policymakers in Washington by the end of 1937, it was not due solely to the recent events in Brazil. All of Latin America was starting to appear susceptible to destabilization of one sort or another, and nearby Mexico certainly seemed to be highly vulnerable to Axis political and economic pressure. It was not that America's southern neighbor had large and potentially subversive Axis populations to contend with, as did the larger republics of South America. Only six thousand Germans were living in Mexico at this time, most of them tucked away in the far south, in the coffee-growing state of Chiapas. But Mexico had something perhaps even more dangerous than hundreds of thousands of disaffected Germans: it had a wealth of raw materials—materials that many in Washington feared would prove irresistible to a Germany vowed to break out of its "have-not" status in minerals. And minerals, then more so than now, had a major bearing on a state's power.[1]

It was no secret that Germany lacked the mineral resources to become a truly great power.[2] Time and again, Hitler had preached that the Reich would not allow itself to be choked to death by the well-endowed states, particularly by the Anglo-Saxon powers, who between them controlled two-thirds of the earth's mineral reserves, while Germany was self-sufficient in only two of the thirty-five raw materials necessary for modern warfare.[3] So persistent was this theme that there could indeed be said to exist, in the words of Robert Strausz-Hupé, "real claustrophobia in German national psychology."[4] To be sure, German chemists had made remarkable progress in synthesizing materials (gasoline was the classic example) that were indispensable to a nation bent on war, but such technological advances could not reasonably be

71

expected to supply the needs of an economy on a permanent martial footing.[5] Sooner or later, the contradictions embodied in *Geopolitik* were bound to result in expansionism. There was absolutely nothing irenic implicit in the German quest for self-sufficiency; for the Reich, deprived of most of the vital sinews of war, autarky could only mean imperialism.[6]

What had this state of affairs to do with Latin America? Depending upon whether one read certain authors or listened to certain speechmakers, very much indeed; for this area and its people—whom the German naturalist Alexander von Humboldt had so memorably described a century before as "beggars in rags, sitting upon mountains of gold"—were considered by many to be the most tempting booty on the face of the earth.[7] Not the least important of these observers was Hitler, who in the summer of 1934 had said that one Latin American country alone, Mexico, possessed enough raw-material wealth to guarantee German ascension to the ranks of the foremost powers. To Hermann Rauschning, a Nazi leader from Danzig who would later defect to the west, the Fuehrer enthused: "With the treasure of the Mexican soil, Germany could be rich and great! Why do we not tackle this task?"[8]

Whether Hitler had accurately assessed the potential of Mexico's mineral contribution to Germany's geopolitical future prospects is beside the point; what is important is that Mexico and many other Latin American nations were widely held, in the United States as well as in Germany, to be fantastically endowed with raw materials. One American business executive, John B. Glenn (president of the Pan American Trust Company), limned for a Washington audience in December 1937 the attractions of an area that was "without exception the richest in natural resources in all the world. . . . Latin America is the greatest potential producer of staple foodstuffs and raw materials in the world today."[9] Juan Trippe, head of Pan American Airways (not connected with Glenn's company), agreed that in South America, "as nowhere else on the globe, there are tremendous natural resources awaiting development . . ."[10] And Hubert Herring was similarly awed, if unnerved, by the knowledge that "Latin America is cut to the order of aspiring empire builders. She has room, millions of empty acres, untouched forests, untapped mines. Her soil and her veins yield or can be made to yield every foodstuff, every product, every mineral needed by an industrialized world."[11]

Latin Americans were only too aware that their natural wealth might prove to be a very mixed blessing. Manuel Seoane, a leader of the Peruvian Apra, feared that its mineral wealth, on the one hand, and its lack of defense, on the other, doomed Latin America to the fate of Belgium and Holland, traditional pawns in the power struggles of greater nations. In the dismal international environment of the late 1930s and early 1940s, Seoane considered the Latin republics to be "rich spoils of war, a natural field for greed and conquest."[12] Hugo Fernández Artucio, a Montevideo radio personality and anti-Nazi crusader, agreed that "the future of South America is in immediate and mortal peril. South America is, indeed, the most priceless booty which Germany, Italy, and Japan could obtain because . . . its mineral deposits, its vast virgin forests, its extensive, indented coastlines, comprise the products and mark the sites which, through their strategic value, may decide the outcome of the Second World War."[13]

Cordell Hull thought similarly. In the spring of 1939, the secretary told a Latin diplomat, Bolivian Minister to the United States Luis Fernando Guachalla, that "in this dangerous, chaotic world situation there was never such a ripe plum dangled before a hungry person than Latin America appears to be to . . . lawless nations, hungry as wolves for vast territory with rich undeveloped natural resources such as South America possesses."[14] At the time Hull made this remark, Latin American nations were the world's leading exporters (but not necessarily producers) of five of the fifteen most important industrial minerals: Chile was the principal exporter of smelter copper; Venezuela of crude petroleum; Bolivia of tin ore and concentrates; and Mexico of refined lead, as well as of zinc ore and concentrates. Moreover, for thirteen of these same fifteen minerals,[15] at least one Latin state was among the top ten exporters; and for four of them, at least three Latin republics were among the top ten.[16]

If, to revert to Hull's metaphor above, Brazil was regarded as the most succulent plum on the hemisphere tree by the end of 1937, there were a few policymakers in Washington who considered Mexico to be the ripest for plucking. Foremost among them was Henry Morgenthau, the secretary of the treasury, who in the middle of December appointed himself administration guardian of the pro-Mexico lobby in Washington. The Mexicans needed some friends in the American capital, for private interests in the United States had been injured by recent land expropriations carried out by the reformist government of Lázaro Cárdenas, and they were mounting an anti-Cárdenas offensive in Congress and in the press.

Roosevelt was in sympathy with Mexico's objectives, but because his political stock was at a low point, he did not wish to alienate potential congressional supporters by making his views public. Roosevelt considered Cárdenas one of the tiny group of Latin leaders who was actually preaching and trying to practice democracy. In addition, he was keenly aware of Mexico's important role in inter-American politics. In the words of a contemporary political analyst, the country was, "if not the keystone, at least an essential block in the arch of the Roosevelt-Hull Good Neighbor Policy. The threatening trend of world affairs has made the political factor of Latin American friendship outweigh at Washington the economic importance of United States investments south of the Rio Grande."[17]

But if Roosevelt could not afford to champion the Mexican position, Morgenthau could—and did. On 16 December the treasury secretary assembled his top aides to discuss ways in which the administration might assist a team of Mexican negotiators who had recently come to Washington to obtain support for the plummeting peso. Morgenthau was taken aback at the meeting when his assistant secretary, Wayne Taylor, remarked of the Mexican delegation: "My recommendation is that the boys cool their heels for quite a period." Recovering his composure, the treasury chief responded: "And give the Japs and Germans and Italians a chance to go in there?" Warming to the opportunity of making some points at the expense of the State Department, Morgenthau told Taylor and his other associates that, with the exception of Sumner Welles, everyone at that department was plumping for a hard-line policy that could only end in disaster for American interests in Mexico.[18] "They're not going to get anywhere," he said of his enemies at the State Department. "We're just going to wake up and find inside of a year that Italy, Germany, and Japan have taken over Mexico. I'll put money on it that those boys—it's the richest—the greatest source of natural resources close to the ocean of any country in the world. I mean it's perfectly amazing what they've got. They've got everything that those three countries need—everything."[19]

Morgenthau's labors on behalf of Mexico were crowned with success at year's end: Welles informed him that he had secured Hull's consent to a Treasury Department plan for the purchase of 35 million ounces of Mexican silver, valued at 16 million dollars; in addition, the Treasury Department would continue to make its regular monthly purchase of 5 million ounces.[20] To his top assistants, Morgenthau expounded on 31 December upon the wisdom of having the administration unite behind his policy of "brotherly love" toward the Latin republics. "I think it's terribly important to keep the continents of North and South America from going fascist. I don't know anything more importantly politically." Even more important than France? asked one of the aides, Herman Oliphant. "Oh, sure," Morgenthau replied. "Well—I mean—I'll put it this way. I think Mexico is the key to the situation of North and South America right now, and I think France is the key to the situation in Europe. Then, I say, but I think the American continent is more important to us than the European continent."[21]

The United States effort to bail out Mexico's economy came not a moment too soon, as far as Morgenthau and some other Americans were concerned. In the last few weeks of 1937, reports of Axis espionage rings hard at work in Mexico had reached Washington.[22] And rumors were afoot in both North American republics that Berlin was intriguing to overthrow Cárdenas, replacing him with the congenital rebel, Gen. Saturnino Cedillo. A Democratic congressman from Montana, Jerry O'Connell, was convinced that Germany was stirring up trouble below the Rio Grande, and said so publicly in January 1938, at the same time "warning" Hitler of the folly of meddling in the affairs of the hemisphere.[23]

All the while, overly enthusiastic Axis luminaries were continuing to gloat over their accomplishments in Latin America, much as Ambassador Dieckhoff had feared they would. In January Rome's *Corriere Diplomatico e Consolare* relayed the refreshing information that Il Duce's example was being emulated by no fewer than eleven nations on the other side of the Atlantic; basking in the glow of Mussolini's "triumphant light" were, according to this source, Argentina, Brazil, Bolivia, El Salvador, Guatemala, Honduras, Nicaragua, Paraguay, Peru, Uruguay, and Venezuela. In Berlin, the School of Advanced Political Studies was hosting a gathering of the cream of the Hitler Youth crop, instructing them that vast stretches of Latin America were populated by Germans crying out for the protection of the fatherland.[24]

On 28 January President Roosevelt confessed to the nation that he feared it might no longer be immune to the spread of extra-hemispheric political and military contagions. Accordingly, he was asking Congress to increase the defense budget, primarily because the United States could no longer enjoy the luxury of thinking that all it had to do was to lie in wait off its own coast-line to pick off any and all invading forces. From now on, Roosevelt declared, the country would have to employ its military and naval might to safeguard areas "many hundred miles away from our continental limits." Roosevelt even dared to suggest that the sanctum sanctorum of America's strategic position, the Panama Canal, might no longer be inviolable.[25]

His fears for the safety of the Canal were not without foundation, for American naval maneuvers in the Caribbean during the previous decade (in 1923 and 1929) had demonstrated its vulnerability to air attack. The maneuvers might even have had an effect on Hitler, who in any case believed that the United States could never be a serious impediment to his European plans because, as he explained to Ernst "Putzi" Hanfstaengl, "you would only have to blow up the Panama Canal and they would not be able to exert pressure either way with their navy."[26] Just two days before Roosevelt addressed Congress the Buenos Aires paper *Crítica* indicated that Hitler had exactly this in mind, for according to its sources, Axis airfields were being set up in Guatemala and in Nicaragua.[27]

Charles Beard, an historian who had taught himself the inef-faceable lesson that Europe was completely beyond redemption, did not wait long to accuse the president of trumping up a bogus scare story that the "fascist goblins of Europe are about to take South America . . ."[28] Testifying before the House Naval Affairs Committee in February, Beard drove the opening wedge into what had been an isolationist consensus by charging that Roosevelt was perverting a hallmark of the noninterventionist credo—the idea of the separation of the two spheres—for the purpose of involving the United States in the moils of Europe. From this point on, the isolationist camp would be split into two factions over the question of security in the hemisphere: one group would take refuge from Old World troubles behind an imagined wall of hemisphere invulnerability (the "Fortress America"); the other faction would come, ever so slowly, to the realization that the nation's southern neighbors must finally succumb to totalitarian pressure unless the United States used its strength to tip the European balance of power in favor of Britain and France—although by the time this realization had been reached, France was no longer an independent nation.

Beard's accusation that the White House was creating out of whole cloth a threat to the hemisphere was to be a recurring feature of the great debate on foreign policy that took place over the next three years; indeed, it has continued to enjoy long life in the works of many postwar historians and political scientists, revisionist or otherwise. It *is* possible to support the theory of a fabricated security threat, but only if one believes not only that the president was inordinately devious and untruthful in his public and private statements, but also that he refused to give credence to the numerous confidential reports reaching his desk from observers in Latin America—reports that gave serious consideration to what was, after all, the most likely manner in which United States security could be menaced in an era before the advent of sophisticated weapons and delivery systems caused a radical change in the nation's strategic position.

I believe that it is much more convincing to regard the president as a man who, in his own words, had to maintain the vigil of a "fire chief,"[29] constantly on the lookout for an outbreak of the conflagration that could destroy the geopolitical edifice within which was contained the core of his own understanding of America's global position. Roosevelt shared with the isolationists—whose ranks he did not abandon finally until the late summer of 1940—the idea that the security of the United States was synonymous with the security of the Western Hemisphere. He differed from them in that he, the man bearing ultimate responsibility for that security, had access to an information flow that was of necessity denied to his critics; and the sweep of intelligence reaching him from 1938 on became, as regards Latin America, an almost continual stream of bad tidings.

But one did not have to be an "expert" on Latin America to imagine, by a process of worst-case (but nonetheless logical) analysis, that the Axis had designs on the hemisphere. Indeed, the perceived *potential* threat to Latin America always far outdistanced the perceived *actual* threat—an indication, perhaps, of paranoia, but one occasioned, as most paranoias are, by a well-grounded fear. Thus, Assistant Secretary of State George Messersmith, writing to Hull in February 1938, was not engaging in scaremongering when he predicted that Hitler would soon be on the move again, while Britain and France would remain inert. The consequences of German expansionism in Europe, the most immediate of which would be a deep erosion of London's influence, troubled Messersmith greatly. "I am confident," he said, "that in the end we would have our troubles in South America, where Germany, Italy, and Japan are already so active and where they have their definite objectives—particularly Germany. With England and France in a purely secondary position and with the Empire disintegrated, we in this country would stand practically alone, and that our troubles would come a little later does not give me any comfort."[30]

At the same time as Messersmith was making his dire forecast, the State Department, working from "data from the field," was preparing a memorandum on the growing Axis menace in Latin America. Echoing Messersmith's prognosis, the State Department attempted to measure the degree to which the American republics had fallen prey to subversion. In accordance with departmental policy, it was conceded that recent events such as the Vargas coup were not to be taken as ipso facto evidence of fascist expansion. The Good Neighbor Policy would have screeched to a halt if Washington had been forced to condemn dictatorship per se in Latin America; there simply was not very much of what could be even loosely construed as "democracy" among the southern neighbors. "Nevertheless," stated the memorandum, "even a superficial totalitarianism if established in this hemisphere would have most serious consequences," bringing in its train not only the demise of whatever remained of Latin democracy, but also facilitating the economic and political extension of the Italian and German systems of government. Already, eight Latin nations were showing signs of having been exposed to unhealthy amounts of Axis influence: Argentina, Bolivia, Brazil, Chile, Guatemala, Paraguay, Peru and Uruguay.[31]

One of the developments that most disturbed the State Department was Berlin's apparently successful campaign to widen its influence over the numerous and sizeable German communities in South America. The struggle, at times violent, between local Nazis and anti-Hitler Germans for the allegiance of the German colonies was being won nearly everywhere, as far as Washington could determine, by the wrong side. But Washington was not the only capital in the hemisphere where this observation was being made; early in 1938 the governments of Argentina and, especially, Brazil, began to crack down with vigor on what they construed as a threat to the integrity of the state itself—a threat represented by the myriad cultural and educational institutions subsidized by Berlin for the purpose of converting the Volksdeutsche to Nazi ideology.

What was particularly galling to Buenos Aires and to Rio was Berlin's claim not only to the minds and souls of the Volksdeutsche, but to their bodies as well; for Germany, insisting upon the validity of the feudal premise known as the *jus sanguinis*, which held that blood determined citizenship, was considering Latin-born Germans to be citizens of the Reich. Latin Americans, sensitive to this affront to their sovereignty, countered by championing the authority of *jus soli*, which held that place of birth determined citizenship. Reflecting the mounting public anger in this matter, *Crítica* thundered in late March: "It is not sufficient to hinder attempts at Nazi interference in this continent, it is necessary to put an end to them once and for all."[32]

This goal was never reached, at least not before Pearl Harbor in the majority of Latin countries, and certainly not even after December 1941 in the case of Argentina. But there can be no doubt whatsoever that the Roosevelt administration heartily seconded *Crítica's* appeal for a continent freed from Nazis. It is clear that by the spring of 1938 the United States was at last on full alert against Axis intrigue in the hemisphere. The nagging uncertainties that had surfaced at the time of the Vargas coup seemed to have become dreaded realities. By the end of the first few months of 1938, it had become hard for anyone familiar with developments in Latin America to entertain the belief that the Western Hemisphere enjoyed an automatic invulnerability in conditions of collapsing world order.

If one month could be singled out as a turning point in American perceptions of the danger to the south, it would be April 1938.

It was at this moment that the hemisphere, north and south, began to react to both real and apprehensible Axis inroads in several New World republics. An early and consistent opponent of these incursions, Argentine writer Ernesto Giudici, who had begun his anti-Axis crusade in the pages of *Crítica* at the time of the Vargas coup, recalled that at first his warnings were received with general skepticism and indifference; but by April the disbelievers had become a minority, for "the Nazi danger now became understood by all."[33]

From London, Ambassador Joseph Kennedy expressed his anxiety over the spread of German propaganda—especially radio propaganda—to the Western Hemisphere. He feared that the Axis, led by its strongest member, was proving itself to be a "stiff opponent" of the United States in the latter's sphere of influence. Kennedy—later considered by some, especially in England, to be a man who was indifferent to (or even secretly pleased with) the increase of German power—urged the president to impress upon every American diplomat the value of the radio as a political weapon in the struggle against Nazism.[34] He recommended that the administration adopt some of the tactics of Berlin's shortwave propaganda campaign, particularly its "news bulletins into South America. [which] have done more than anything else to stimulate German propaganda throughout the southern hemisphere."[35] What was worrying the ambassador was by now a familiar fear to the president, whose own sense of concern for the Latin American republics had been stimulated by the events of the previous November. Thus it was more a coincidence of timing than anything else that the White House, at about the same time as Kennedy was making his suggestions, decided to commence what the German foreign office rightly regarded as an anti-Axis offensive in the southernmost republics of South America.[36]

It was not just German propaganda that troubled Roosevelt. At a Washington news conference, held for members of the Associated Church Press on 20 April, he indicated clearly that events overseas might have serious military implications for the United States and its Latin neighbors. When a reporter asked how much territory the enlarged navy sought by the White House would be required to protect, the president responded with some questions of his own. "Suppose," he replied, that "certain foreign governments, European governments, were to do in Mexico what they did in Spain," that is, organize a "Fascist revolution." Suppose that those foreign powers were to arm Mexican rebels, and that the rebels were victorious. "Do you think that the United States could stand idly by and have this European menace right on our borders? Of course not. You could not stand for it."

Roosevelt hastened to assure his listeners that he himself did not think that Mexico was about to turn into a second Spain; he was merely citing it as an example of the kind of situation that could develop anywhere in Latin America. Did he not believe, he was asked, that three thousand miles of water was a sufficient safeguard of American security? He answered that, admittedly, the Atlantic was a wide ocean, but "we would not be attacked from across the ocean . . . if they came from Mexico." Could he explain why a European power would wish to foment revolution in Mexico? "They did it in Spain," the president replied, adding—so as to leave no room for doubt about who "they" might be—that Spain was three days' traveling time from Germany, and Mexico but seven.

The questions continued: Would the United States resist a European challenge mounted not against Mexico, but against a country in a more distant republic, say one down in South America? Roosevelt could see no logical reason to refrain from defending Venezuela, which was, after all, only "an hour and a half by some of these modern planes" from Cuba, and everyone knew that the United States would fight for Cuba. Anticipating the next question, the president brought up Brazil. "It is half way to Europe. Brazil—Would we do it [fight] in the case of Brazil? Well, you have a principle established. . . . We are trying to keep an independent continent, north and south."[37]

Roosevelt's determination to isolate the hemisphere from war could hardly have drawn a quibble from even his most vitriolic critics; no one, including and especially Charles Beard, wanted the New World to become the scene of a conflict fomented in Europe. The staunchly isolationist governor of Wisconsin, Philip La Follette, was in total accord with the White House on this point. In April, La Follette launched a political movement, the National Progressives of America, which he hoped to develop into a viable third party by enticing disenchanted liberals away from the Democrats. There was, however, no disagreement with the president or with his party on foreign affairs. At an organizing rally held 28 April on the campus of the University of Wisconsin, the Progressives issued this forceful policy pronunciamento: "From the Arctic to Cape Horn, let no foreign power trespass!"[38]

Spring of 1938 was a more worrisome time in Washington than the spring of 1937 had been. Not only had Hitler resumed his restless expansionism, annexing Austria in March and immediately turning a receptive ear to the cries of the Sudeten Germans for an *Anschluss* of their own;[39] Latin America was intruding upon America's consciousness as it never had before. On 17 May the Washington-based Council on International Relations addressed itself to the problem of fascist penetration in the southern part of the hemisphere, an area where, as Samuel Guy Inman pointed out, a "tremendous effort" was being made to implant totalitarian ideology. The council urged the administration to waste no time in creating an effective program of counterpropaganda, recommending that that fullest use be made of radio in spreading the message of democracy throughout the hemisphere.[40]

Ironically, at this very moment of heightened insecurity in Washington, Berlin was taking a long second look at its own efforts in Latin America. Reluctantly, the chief of the Auslandsorganisation, Ernst Wilhelm Bohle, sent out orders to party enthusiasts in the Western Hemisphere to put a damper on their activities on behalf of local German communities, for their zeal was stirring up reaction throughout Latin America, jeopardizing the gains the Reich had made there in the previous half decade.[41] Bohle's biggest and most recent concern centered on Brazil, where on 11 May a predawn opéra-bouffe attempt had been made on the life of Getulio Vargas—an attempt launched by native fascists (the Integralistas) who the Brazilian leader suspected were serving as pawns of Hitler.

Among the dozen or so indigenous fascist groupings of Latin America, the largest and most influential was in Brazil—the Ação Integralista Brasileira. Established in October 1932 by a Mussolini devotee named Plínio Salgado, this party drew its inspiration from the twin fountainheads of anti-communism and anti-Semitism, both of which were so nourishing to the radical right of the Western world during the interwar years. Not only did the Integralistas rely on European models for ideological purposes (although it must be said that Salgado articulated many nativist aspirations), they also copied the garb and mannerisms of the Old

World fascists. If nothing else, an Integralista parade was always sartorially impressive, as hundreds, and at times thousands, of green-shirted zealots tramped along Brazil's streets, sporting sigma armbands, black trousers, and leather boots, while flashing the familiar stiff-armed salute and murmuring the fraternal greeting, "anauê"—which was one of Salgado's nativist touches, derived from a word in Tupí, a Brazilian Indian tongue.[42]

The Integralistas, champions of Getulio Vargas in November 1937 when the Brazilian president erected the Estado Novo, soon became disenchanted with their erstwhile hero, and they tried to depose him the following May. Although there is no evidence to support the view, accepted at the time, that Germany had instigated the putsch, it is clear that Berlin would not have been displeased by a change in government in Rio, even though German statesmen themselves had serious reservations about the ultimate goals of the Integralistas. What is significant is that in Washington, as in Rio, the gunplay at the presidential residence was initially interpreted as a case of Nazi aggression in the Western Hemisphere.[43]

When an indignant Vargas demanded the recall of the German ambassador in the wake of the incident, relations between Rio and Berlin, heretofore increasingly cordial, reached their lowest point in years. A typical American view of the putsch was expressed by a prominent political scientist and student of Latin America, Karl Loewenstein, who wrote that "most responsible observers agree that the Integralist movement had become a serious danger to Brazil" by May 1938.[44] The Office of Strategic Services, in a report issued during World War II, claimed that the Integralistas had been closely linked to the German and Italian governments, and further that Berlin had even supplied the weapons and ammunition used in the attempt on Vargas's life.[45] Germany vehemently and publicly protested its innocence. Privately, Ambassador Karl Ritter admitted to Foreign Minister Joachim von Ribbentrop that Germanic elements in the southern states of Brazil had "bungled" in 1937 by getting mixed up in an Integralista plot, but he denied that any Germans were involved in the recent incident.[46] Not surprisingly, few in the United States believed the public German disclaimers when they were uttered, although American scholars are now agreed that, in this instance, Berlin was telling the truth.[47]

It was in this same month of May that segments of the American reading public got their first exposure to the kinds of worries besetting Washington policymakers, in the pages of the sensationalist book by Carleton Beals, *The Coming Struggle for Latin America.* Beals, a foreign correspondent and somewhat of a muckraker, was a seasoned chronicler of Latin affairs and the bane of the State Department throughout much of the 1930s; a nemesis of his, Assistant Secretary of State Adolf Berle, blamed Beals's book for stimulating the "fear that South America was about to fall prey to Fascist ideology on a large scale."[48] Coming from Berle, this was an interesting criticism, for he, more than any other Roosevelt adviser after 1938, was on a continuous alert for Axis encroachments in Latin America. A Brazilian analyst of international relations, Helio Lobo, considered *The Coming Struggle* to be an invaluable lesson for Americans, showing them for the first time what really was taking place below the Rio Grande.[49]

Beals was no comfort to his readers, most of whom were discovering to their dismay that a contest of the first order was raging in Latin America, where the stakes were none other than the security of the United States itself. The large German communities in several South American republics were almost totally converted to Nazism, and were an indispensable element in Hitler's dream of conquest. But even nations with insignificant German populations could not be trusted; for, with the exception of Mexico and Costa Rica, the rest of the Latin countries were "frankly Fascistic and pro-Franco." So, unless Franklin Roosevelt stopped truckling to Latin dictators and started supporting the masses in their fight for social justice, the southern half of the hemisphere would be as good as lost. Thus wrote Beals.[50]

No one in the United States—including Carleton Beals and Franklin Roosevelt—could have known it, but by the summer of 1938, high-ranking German representatives in Latin America were also worrying about the Reich's position in the hemisphere. Anti-German activities, particularly those taking place in Brazil and Argentina, had made a significant impression on German envoys to the major Latin states—significant enough to induce them to hold a special meeting to try to resolve their problems. This meeting took place in Montevideo at the end of July, lasted two days, and was intended by the diplomats to be a showdown over who was to exercise ultimate authority for the government in Latin

America—the accredited ambassadors and ministers, or the interlopers from the Auslandsorganisation.

Inasmuch as there were no AO officials at the conclave, the diplomats reached the decision that they, and not the party operatives, would have the power to settle all major matters of policy, unless Berlin decreed otherwise. It was also agreed that Berlin would be advised to limit German aspirations in Latin America solely to cultural and economic ends, meaning that "aims of power" were to be explicitly renounced. Failing such a renunciation, it might well prove impossible to prevent the United States from exploiting fears of German imperialism and consequently solidifying Latin America behind its leadership, a development that would result in the "crush[ing of] Party organizations all over South America."[51]

Upon his return to Buenos Aires, Edmund von Thermann, the German ambassador to Argentina and spokesman of the Montevideo conclave, met with AO officials from both Argentina and Germany, in order to inform them of the decisions taken by the diplomats. He was able to persuade his adversaries to temper their propaganda activities and to modify their recruiting techniques, according to guidelines laid down by Bohle in his directive of 18 May. These guidelines stated that the AO men should switch from overt to "internal indoctrination"; that they should segregate in their organizing efforts the Reichsdeutsche from the Volksdeutsche, in order to remove an outstanding source of Latin grievance; and that they should build separate cells within the party for the Reichsdeutsche.[52] These things the AO officials agreed to do, even though they insisted that "there is no reason for nervousness."[53]

Thus by the late summer of 1938 there had arisen the interesting spectacle of two major powers, each perceiving its rival to be making gains in Latin America at its own expense; it was a zero-sum game in which both players considered themselves losers. The ingathering of the foreign German tribe, an event held annually in Stuttgart, was not the lively occasion in 1938 that it had been the year before. No shower of decorations from the Fuehrer fell upon Reich diplomats from South America this time; instead of garnering happy tidings of continuing success, Berlin was gleaning from its observers in the New World the disturbing news that "America is already fighting against us today in Latin America

. . . The fight becomes comprehensible when it is realized that there are many influential American politicians who claim to have proof that the totalitarian states, Germany among them, aspire to the acquisition of Latin American soil. . . ."[54]

The mood among American policymakers was no lighter. On 18 August Roosevelt journeyed to Kingston, Ontario, where he told a convocation at Queen's University that the United States would guarantee the security of Canada. At the same time, he directed the attention of his listeners from America's northern to its southern border, remarking that 1938 had been a year of rude awakening from a position of security that had once been regarded as impregnable. "We in the Americas," said the president, "are no longer a far away continent, to which the eddies of controversies beyond the seas bring no interest or harm. Instead, we in the Americas have become a consideration to every propaganda office and to every general staff beyond the seas."[55]

Some writers detected in the Kingston address, just as others had in the Quarantine Speech, clear evidence of an abandonment of isolationism and an undertaking of entangling European commitments. Charles Callan Tansill, for example, accused Roosevelt of betraying the faith in Canada: "Since 1932 [he] had been lustily singing in a chorus of isolationists but had been furtively eyeing the exotic wench of collective security who waited in the wings for the cue that would inevitably come." To the metaphorical Tansill, Kingston was Roosevelt's lascivious wink, his inevitable "cue" to the European democracies.[56] In fact, it was no such thing; it would be another two years before the president would truly start batting his eyelashes at England, and then the fluttering would be a function of fear and not of romance.

Shortly after the Kingston speech, the long-simmering controversy over the fate of the millions of Germans in the Sudeten region of Czechoslovakia reached a climacteric, at a moment when American eyes were fixed apprehensively on German expansionism in the Western Hemisphere. Assistant Secretary of State Berle, anxious that Roosevelt keep European events in the proper (i.e., isolationist) perspective, sent the president a policy memorandum on 1 September advising against letting any anti-Hitler feeling lead the United States into the same kind of mess it had been led into by anglophilic advisers during the World War. Berle was afraid that, in the event of war, British propagandists would exploit

American sentiment as effectively as they had two decades before; and although "we have not yet developed a Walter Hines Page or a Colonel House," there was no way to guarantee that pro-British advisers, such as Page and House had been in 1917, would not appear in the future.

German territorial acquisitions in Central Europe, however distasteful they might be, were facts of life to which we had better adjust, said Berle, adding that no vital interests of the United States would be imperiled if Hitler annexed the former constituent elements of the Austro-Hungarian Empire. Washington need only tend to two concerns: staying out of European war and making the Western Hemisphere invulnerable. "It seems to me," he concluded, "that we should be developing a north-south axis, and not be swung off base by either diplomacy or emotion."[57]

Berle's memorandum had not been on Roosevelt's desk very long before something happened in South America to stimulate the administration's desire to make that "north-south axis" a reality. On 5 September, in the heat of the bitterest presidential campaign in recent Chilean history, several dozen young Nacistas (members of the Chilean National Socialist movement) launched a coup against the conservative government of Arturo Alessandri. As the leader of the Nacistas, Jorge González von Marées, later explained, it was feared that if the October elections were held as scheduled, the winner would certainly be Alessandri's candidate, Finance Minister Gustavo Ross. And to the troubled González von Marées, a self-designated Spenglerian "socialist" who hated both liberalism and Marxism (and who liked Hitlerism), a Ross administration would have meant that "the republic would have fallen into a veritable orgy of materialism, and the citizenry would have been reduced to the status of spectators."[58]

To avert this evident catastrophe, González von Marées ordered his followers to seize two buildings in the heart of Santiago and to use them as a rallying center for antigovernment forces. This action, intended to serve the youthful rebels as a springboard to power, brought death instead, as scores perished in a bloody suppression of the coup. The surviving Nacistas, one of whom was their leader, sought solace in the knowledge that the sacrifice had not been in vain. "As objectionable as were the Naci[stas]," Frederick Nunn has concluded, "the summary execution of sixty-two young citizens turned opinion against the Alessandri administration," and toward the candidate of the Popular Front, Pedro Aquirre Cerda—whose first official act upon becoming president would be to free González von Marées from the dungeon in which he had been awaiting execution.[59]

In the United States, observers of Latin American politics tended to see a relationship between the Nacista uprising and the attempt made in May by the Integralistas to remove Getulio Vargas from power in Brazil. The *Nation* reported in late September that "with a new world war tragically imminent, the Third Reich is bending every effort to establish itself on the South American continent. . . . When the Brazilian putsch failed, Germany turned to Chile as the next best possibility." The authors of this article suspected that Germany wanted Chile because of its geopolitical potentialities: "Just as Spain was invaded because of its strategic importance in a possible war of the fascist powers against France and Great Britain, so Latin America is being contended for as a base of operations from which Germany's military, naval, and air forces might launch a decisive attack on the United States and the Panama Canal in the upcoming world war."[60] Besides being indispensable to a would-be conqueror of South America, Chile had an additional strategic value: it controlled the Strait of Magellan, which, as John Whitaker explained, would in the event of the Panama Canal being knocked out "become overnight the key to American security."[61]

This of course was skirting the fantastic, and it is highly unlikely that the White House was tremendously concerned, one way or the other, with the Strait of Magellan. But it is very likely that the administration was indeed worried about the political stability of Chile, and since its worries stemmed from perception rather than fact, it did not really matter that the Nacistas were as little connected with Berlin as had been the Integralistas. What did matter was that American diplomats believed that the Nacistas, with forty thousand partisans—all undoubtedly stroked by the same malign wand that had touched the German Nazis— possessed the potential for destabilizing Chile, and therefore indirectly threatening the security of the United States. Although the Nacistas were not as numerous as the Integralistas, it must be remembered that Chile, with fewer than five million inhabitants in 1938, had only one-tenth the population of Brazil. On the whole, the Nacistas received sympathetic coverage from the Chilean press, especially after the September bloodshed, and they were lauded by such prominent intellectuals as the novelist Carlos Keller.[62] They were, in the words of an American writer who visited Chile in 1941, "fearless, determined, ruthless, and ready for any act of violence."[63]

In early 1939, Ambassador Norman Armour cabled the State Department that as far as he could determine, the Nacistas were being directly subsidized by Berlin, despite some recent claims of González von Marées that his party's national socialism was sui generis.[64] Armour was referring to an interview that the Nacista leader, out of prison and a hero, had had in December with Freda Kirchway, editor and publisher of the *Nation*. He had, at this time, proclaimed his party's total independence of Germany (which was true) and its refusal to have anything to do with spreading anti-Semitic propaganda (which was false).[65] He also maintained that the Nacistas were closer in ideology to the Socialists than to any other Chilean party, and that if ever given the opportunity, they hoped to govern Chile in the way that Lázaro Cárdenas was governing Mexico.[66] Clearly, the Nacista leader's remarks seemed tailored for his audience, in this case, Kirchway, an admirer both of Chile's Socialists and Mexico's Cárdenas. But Armour and policymakers in Washington were less inclined to believe that the Chilean National Socialists were not intimately connected with Nazis in Germany, and the prevailing view in the United States of the failed coup of 5 September was that it constituted yet further evidence of, as *Foreign Affairs* put it, "totalitarian inroads in Latin America."[67]

By September 1938 it was becoming plain to the Roosevelt administration that it must look more seriously to the creation of the "north-south axis." And this implied even less likelihood that the White House would seek any effective political and military links with the democracies of Europe, who were on the verge of succumbing to German pressure over the Sudeten question.

5

Good Intentions
on the Road to Lima

In the midst of the Sudeten crisis of September 1938, a book appeared in the United States bearing conclusions identical to those advanced by Assistant Secretary of State Adolf Berle in his policy memorandum of 1 September. Maj. George Fielding Eliot's *The Ramparts We Watch* urged Americans not to let themselves be swayed by their emotions into another disastrous crusade in Europe; instead, wrote this Army reserve officer turned strategic analyst, the nation would be well advised to stay on its own side of the Atlantic and to solidify its hemisphere defenses. Eliot was not so much worried that a war would erupt in Europe over Czechoslovakia as he was concerned that one would *not;* for if fighting broke out, he—like most Americans—was confident that Britain and France, joined possibly by Russia, would easily defeat any German-led coalition. On the other hand, if London and Paris refused to meet Hitler's challenge and continued to acquiesce in German continental expansionism, then the consequences for American security could be momentous.

For example, postulated Eliot, once Hitler's puppet Franco gained his inevitable victory in Spain, what would keep Germany from taking control of Portugal? And once Germany established herself there, she would be able to set up bases in the Azores, just two thousand miles from New York, as well as in the Cape Verdes and Portuguese Guinea, only sixteen hundred miles from Brazil. "These Portuguese outposts, in German possession, might become foci for German efforts to assume a more important and dominant status in Brazilian affairs; or to be a menace to our Caribbean security."[1]

Although Eliot, like Livingston Hartley the year before, was aware of a threat to the hemisphere, he did not draw the same conclusion as Hartley: that the administration should immediately discard its policy of isolation and line up beside Britain and France. Eliot reasoned that the only conceivable chance the Axis had would be if it won a very short war, in which event American aid would arrive too late to make a difference; in a long war, American aid would be superfluous, since the defeat of the Axis would be sealed by its mortal shortage of raw materials. But had Eliot seen a book that was appearing at the same time as his own, he might have reconsidered what such a raw-material shortage could augur for the security of the Western Hemisphere; for a young Latin writer, Adolfo Tejera, had just demonstrated that Germany would turn toward Latin America precisely because it needed the minerals that were to be found there, and nowhere else, in such abundance.[2]

But Roosevelt did not really need Eliot's advice, for he like most Americans wanted above all else to keep the United States out of the next European war. On 9 September he met the press in the study of his Hyde Park home, where he emphatically denied the suggestion that he was about to align the nation with Britain and France, calling such an idea "about 100 percent wrong." The president was especially eager to quash the rumor that his ambassador to France, William C. Bullitt, had recently stated that the United States would support the democratic powers.[3] Bullitt had, in fact, said nothing of the sort; indeed, he was as adamant as Berle that the administration should steer clear of Europe. He wrote Roosevelt later that month that "the prospects for Europe are so foul that the further we keep out of the mess the better. The moral is: 'If you have enough airplanes, you don't have to go to Berchtesgaden.' "[4]

To be sure, the president was appalled by Europe's month-long vigil on the brink of war. He took comfort, however, from the presumption that Hitler would be no match for the combined forces of the democracies, with Russia possibly thrown in for good measure. At a cabinet meeting in late September, he predicted that an outbreak of fighting over Czechoslovakia would quickly strip Germany of her allies. According to Secretary of the Interior Harold Ickes, who attended the meeting, Roosevelt said that "if war came the French would speedily mop up the Italian colonies in northern Africa and would promptly liquidate Franco in Spain."[5]

When the news reached Washington that Hitler had issued, and

Neville Chamberlain had accepted, an eleventh-hour invitation
to come to Munich for a final attempt at a peacable solution to
the Sudeten question, Roosevelt was genuinely relieved, and wired
the British prime minister a warm "Good Man" message.[6] He
would shortly send a similar note to Ottawa, telling Canadian
prime minister Mackenzie King that "we in the United States
rejoice with you, and the world at large, that the outbreak of war
was averted."[7] But as happy as he was at the prospect of a contin-
uance of peace in Europe, the president had now to consider that
Germany might be able to focus its attention on Latin America
without having, at the same time, to worry about its European
flank. The scenario that White House strategists had dismissed
as being highly improbable in mid-1936—namely that the hemisphere could be confronted by a German military challenge if the
European naval powers were to remain on the sidelines—now
loomed as a possibility.

Ironically, Munich, in averting the prospect of war in one
hemisphere, had made it appear conceivable in another. Throughout the drama of September 1938, the administration had been
contemplating the ramifications that the Czech crisis could have
in Latin America. On 22 September, the day Chamberlain was
making the second of his three peace voyages to Hitler, who waited
nervously in the Rhine resort town of Godesberg, another meeting was quietly taking place in Washington. At the State Department a high-level "Europe watch"—consisting of Secretary of State
Cordell Hull, Adolf Berle, and political advisers James Dunn, Jay
Pierrepont Moffat, and Norman Davis—had gathered. All those
present, even the anti-isolationist Davis, agreed that the wisest
policy for the United States to follow was one of total abstention
from the Czechoslovakian conundrum. But policymakers are
rarely content to advocate sheer do-nothingism, and this meeting was no exception to that rule.

It fell to Berle to suggest some active steps that the administration could and should be taking. "I raised the point," he said, "that
it seemed now that our true line was north and south, [and] that
this called for swift action to counter weight the inevitable and
immediate growth of movements along the lines of the German
and Italian idea . . ." The United States had to meet head-on the
Axis challenge to the hemisphere, commencing in Mexico and
Cuba, lands where subversive elements were already dangerously

at work.[8] Berle had rehearsed this argument the previous day with the American minister to the Dominican Republic, Harry Norweb, who had agreed with him on the urgent necessity of bolstering the United States position throughout the hemisphere, "since it is probable that the immediate result of Hitler's move [in the Sudetenland] will be to strengthen the Nazi propaganda there [i.e., in Latin America]. We ought to be ready to defend."[9]

Three days prior to his meeting with Norweb, Berle had advised Hull to end the State Department's campaign of pressure against the Mexican government, which in March had caused a furor in the United States and Great Britain by nationalizing oil holdings of the two countries valued in the hundreds of millions of dollars.[10] In response to what one commentator described as "the most severe test yet offered to the Good Neighbor Policy,"[11] certain elements in the State Department, among them Hull and his economic adviser Herbert Feis, launched a poorly conceived diplomatic offensive designed to get Lázaro Cárdenas to satisfy American demands for prompt and adequate compensation, not only for the oil properties but also for some American-owned land that had been previously expropriated. The oil controversy could not have come at a worse time as far as the White House was concerned, and from the wings the president gave his quiet support to Secretary of the Treasury Henry Morgenthau and Ambassador to Mexico Josephus Daniels, who were together doing their utmost to sabotage the hard-liners' bid to bring Cárdenas to book.[12]

By the middle of the summer it was plain that the secretary of state was getting nowhere; even worse, it was becoming a matter of some concern that the Hull-Feis tactics might drive Mexico into German hands. At the end of August the administration learned to its dismay that Mexico was bartering her oil (which American and British oil companies were refusing either to buy or to transport) for manufactured goods from the Axis powers. Apropos of this barter, Daniels pointed out to Hull that "we know from experiences in some South American countries that trade influences other associations."[13]

Germany had moved quickly to take advantage of the oil expropriation. Three days after Cárdenas issued the nationalization decree of 18 March the German minister in Mexico City cabled to Berlin his suggestion that Germany avail itself of the opportunity to build up its stockpile of oil.[14] The ensuing oil purchases notwithstanding, Berlin did not suffer the misapprehension that by getting Mexican crude it would at the same time be obtaining Mexican goodwill. The champion of Republican Spain in the Western Hemisphere, Mexico under Cárdenas was regarded by the German minister as "belonging to the Communist bloc," a nation so out of sympathy with fascism that it "would hardly be able to maintain a neutral attitude in case of armed conflict."[15] Minister von Rüdt did not attempt to hide his feelings; to the American naval attaché in Mexico City, Comdr. W. M. Dillon, he remarked that Mexicans frankly did not like Germans, and that, in Dillon's words, "he had no faith in them whatsoever."[16]

Policymakers in Washington also had little faith in the Mexicans. Mexico's oil might yet prove to be a "balm of hurt minds." Not only was it enhancing the military potential of America's probable enemies in the next war, but the very exchange of this commodity promised to bind Mexico economically to the Axis, whether Cárdenas liked it or not. Thus when the American military attaché in Mexico City informed the War Department that a shipment of fifty commercial aircraft, all convertible to military use, was due to arrive soon from Axis Europe, Berle decided that the administration had better mend its Mexican fences.[17]

On 19 September Berle told Hull that the latter's hard-line stance was becoming increasingly untenable, for Mexico was "already trading oil for German planes, which would undoubtedly mean German instructors, as well, and we had better get to work towards a solution."[18] A similar plea for detente reached Hull a few days later, from Daniels, who wrote that "the compelling reason which has caused me to urge a course of reconciliation, even of some sacrifice, is that I believe the Good Neighbor Policy must be undergirded if this hemisphere is to escape the contagion that threatens Europe."[19] The arguments were effective: Hull, eager to prevent Daniels's apprehensions from becoming realities, and faced with the dismal spectacle of a Europe on the brink of war over Czechoslovakia, agreed to cease pressuring the Cárdenas government for a settlement favorable to the companies, a decision that he would later justify on the grounds that "nothing could have been more unhappy for the forthcoming Lima Conference than an acrimonious diplomatic battle between our southern neighbor and ourselves."[20]

Daniels, Hull, and Berle were not the only men in Washington to perceive an intensifying danger to the hemisphere after Munich. On 14 October, the president announced at a press conference that, contrary to the reporters' expectations, he would not be making a statement on the budget for the coming fiscal year, "for the reason that the new developments in national defense require such a complete restudy of American national defense that it will defer, necessarily, any budget comments for some time."[21] During the same week, *New York Times* reporter Anne O'Hare McCormick concluded after interviewing Roosevelt that insofar as recent developments in Europe were concerned, the president believed that the "outstanding fact of the present hour is that all signs point home."[22]

Statements like these were music to the ears of some close presidential advisers. The most enraptured listener of all was Henry Morgenthau, who quickly offered Roosevelt his own thoughts on the kind of new defense posture the United States would have to assume. Above all other considerations, said the treasury secretary, who was one of the cabinet's foremost anti-Nazis, the administration had to look after the Latin American states; for "unless we assist them, they will become a helpless field for political and economic exploitation by the aggressor nations." Morgenthau remarked that the totalitarian powers had already made "some inroads" in Latin America. "Now, after the Munich agreement, we may expect that Germany, Italy, and Japan will become bolder and more effective in their attempts to establish areas of economic and political support to the south of us."[23]

A few days later, Roosevelt told Morgenthau how he would like to see the nation rearm, starting with the production of an incredible fifteen thousand planes for the coming year. (The president subsequently scaled this figure down to a still-impressive, and seemingly unattainable, target of ten thousand.) Upon hearing this, Morgenthau became "tickled to death," and confided to his diary his hope that Roosevelt would make the United States "so strong that nobody can attack us. . . . We want enough planes to take care of the whole South American continent, too."[24]

British observers were as pleased as Morgenthau that the president was at last talking of rearmament. The *Economist* expected great things from America's discovery that its own security was being menaced from abroad for the first time in more than a century, anticipating that finally the United States would real-

ize the folly of its policy of isolation and join the Western democracies in a collective resistance to aggression.[25] While this is what
would ultimately, by the summer of 1940, come to pass, for the
short run the administration's heightened sense of insecurity led
it to withdraw even further into an isolationist hemispheric shell,
devoting its resources to what would come to be considered, by
mid-1940, an impossible task: making the American half of the
globe totally safe from domination by an Axis that was all but
triumphant in Europe.

It is true that in 1939 the White House would work for and
obtain (in November) the repeal of the arms embargo, thus allowing Britain and France (and legally even Germany and Italy) to
purchase war supplies in the United States. But it is not the case
that lifting the arms embargo constituted a repeal of the isolation policy. Certainly, Roosevelt sympathized tremendously with
the European democracies. However, his decision to sell them
arms was entirely consistent with traditional (pre-1935) American neutrality policy, and to insist that by 1939 the administration was no longer isolationist because it was doing even *less* than
the isolationist Wilson administration had done for the Allies from
August 1914 to April 1917 is, at the very least, to distort the meaning of words. As I noted in chapter 1, isolationism as a policy
simply meant a refusal to support the European status quo with
American military power, or to enter into a European alliance.
By reverting to traditional neutrality, Roosevelt was neither committing the United States to a course of intervention, nor com-
pacting with Britain and France. Contrary to the prediction of the
Economist, American foreign policy at the end of 1938 would be
characterized by an even greater obsession with the Western Hemisphere, which meant, conversely, an even greater reluctance to
have any substantive ties with Britain and France.

The most visible manifestation of the administration's determination to construct what Berle termed the "north-south axis"
came during the Eighth Inter-American Conference, held in Lima
at the end of the year. With the American republics preparing to
meet in their first regular Pan-American session since Montevideo in 1933, the White House was laboring to build the walls of
isolation in the hemisphere so high and thick that no conceivable European power could ever topple them. Roosevelt was in total accord with Berle on the pressing need to create, with economic
and political tools, a hemispheric "firebreak." Even more urgent

was the business of rearming the hemisphere's guardian state; and to this end, the president announced on 14 November that he would seek to triple the Army Air Corps, to an astounding ten thousand planes (from fewer than three thousand), while increasing to the same figure the yearly productive capacity of the nation's aircraft industry. By doing this, he said, the United States would be helping to make the New World secure "from Canada to Tierra del Fuego."[26]

The following day, Roosevelt elaborated for the press his new policy of continental defense. He said that the past five years had witnessed a stream of events in Europe that were fraught with significance for the nations of the New World, leading them to seek security in an unparalleled display of solidarity. "The first thing we realize is the fact that any possible attack has been brought infinitely closer than it was five years or twenty years or fifty years ago," primarily because of technological advances in aerial warfare. From now on, he said, the United States, in cooperation with the other American republics and with Canada, would be guarding the air and water approaches of the hemisphere against European invaders. At this point, the president was asked by a newsman what the White House would do in the event that the solidarity of the hemisphere was shattered by the defection to the Axis camp of an important Latin American nation. Roosevelt refused to consider this even within the bounds of possibility, declaring imperiously that there was "a good deal of reason" for him to have unequivocal confidence in the fundamental and lasting unity of the inter-American family.[27]

The president was whistling in the dark before the reporters; they might not have known it, but he certainly did. Despite what he had told them, the menace of air attack was only one, and not the greatest, of his worries. Far more troubling was the possibility that a Latin government would be overthrown or subverted by Axis intriguers, in which case the hemisphere would find itself harboring a veritable Trojan Horse. As we have already seen, there was no shortage of suspect regimes in Latin America; indeed, there were few, if any, governments below the Rio Grande that warranted the kind of confidence that Roosevelt demonstrated at his press conference. It was by now apparent, as Carleton Beals expressed it, that "territorial conquest is no longer the only European danger with which we have to reckon in Latin America."[28]

Critics of the president, both at the time and in later years, have charged that he was dragging the red herring of an endangered hemisphere across the trail of his increasingly interventionist European policy. Postwar revisionist historiography is studded with accusations that Roosevelt was generating "fear-provoking stories" with the ulterior motive of preparing public opinion for an eventual war against Germany. A typical revisionist allegation is Frederic R. Sanborn's statement that "Mr. Roosevelt was convinced at that time [autumn 1938] that America would get into war."[29] And even objective chroniclers of the administration like Robert A. Divine have concluded that, by the autumn of 1938, the president was concerned primarily with aiding Britain and France, but that "he carefully masked this objective, emphasizing instead the need to strengthen the armed forces in order to defend the Western Hemisphere."[30]

It is possible that Franklin Roosevelt did manipulate events in Latin America to suit his own "internationalist" predilections. Indeed, after mid-1940 he would appear to be doing just that. But where is the evidence to show that by late 1938 the president had decided to abandon his isolationist policies? It is rather more likely that the president was sincerely impressed by the danger of Axis encroachments in the Western Hemisphere, and that this danger was magnified by his essentially isolationist world view, which emphasized to an exaggerated degree the position that Latin America occupied in relation to the military, political, and economic well-being of the United States. Shortly before recommending that the air corps be expanded, Roosevelt received an urgent letter from Rep. A. J. Sabath, an Illinois Democrat, who thought that the administration could be doing much more to protect American interests in Latin America. "Within the last ten days," the congressman reported, "I have received so much information relative to the activities of Nazis in those countries that unless we act immediately, they will undermine our standing and destroy our commerce in those lands."[31]

A message in the same vein came to the White House the following week, suggesting that the president make a personal appearance at Lima, just as he had done at Buenos Aires two years before; otherwise, feared Leo R. Sack, former American minister to Costa Rica, the rising tide of Nazi propaganda would roll unmolested across the continent. "These anti-American drives have increased in intensity," said Sack, "and are at last beginning to concern Latin American officials who would preserve their democratic institutions."[32] For Roosevelt, who had been since late 1937 extremely conscious of Axis involvement in the hemisphere, warnings like these served to confirm his own determination to make the New World impervious to intruders from the Old World. Notwithstanding the tacit community of interest that the United States shared with the European democracies, there can be no mistaking the fact that, after Munich, Roosevelt's main anxieties centered not around Britain and France, but on a hemisphere that he believed to be imperiled; as he wrote his minister to Portugal, Herbert C. Pell, the "dictator threat from Europe is a good deal closer to the United States and the American Continent than it was before."[33]

This perception of incipient danger was held by policymakers in other branches of the administration. On the same day (14 November) that Roosevelt asked for a tripling of the Army Air Corps, the Standing Liaison Committee was discussing the latest disquieting news from southern South America. Under Secretary of State Sumner Welles informed his counterparts from the War and Navy Departments, Chief of Staff Malin Craig and Chief of Naval Operations William Leahy, that State Department officers in Brazil were expecting German-instigated rebellions to occur soon in Uruguay, Argentina, and Brazil—all "as part of a large Nazi movement to obtain control of those countries." What Welles wanted to know was, if these fears turned out to be real, would the navy be capable of heading off any "filibustering" activities on the east coast of South America? Leahy thought so, assuming it could use Brazilian ports.[34] For the next month, the administration studied Brazilian developments closely. According to Harold Ickes, the cabinet devoted much of its meeting of 16 December to the "very serious situation in Brazil. The Nazis there are up to mischief, undoubtedly with the encouragement, if not with the active backing, of Hitler. They are also very active in Uruguay."[35]

This flurry of excitement about an impending Nazi coup in a strategic part of South America had been generated by a secret report that Breckinridge Long had sent the president in early November. Long had been dispatched south on a special fact-finding mission, and what he found was disturbing. In the Brazilian capital, he had been informed by President Getulio Vargas and Foreign Minister Oswaldo Aranha that an insurrection was

almost certain to take place soon in the four states of Brazil with
the heaviest German settlement: São Paulo, Paraná, Santa Catarina, and Rio Grande do Sul. Relations with Berlin had been at
the point of rupture ever since the May attempt on Vargas's life,
for which the Brazilians had held Germany responsible. Now Rio
wanted help from Washington. Aranha requested that the German embassy in Washington, which he was positive was the hub
of all Nazi intrigues in the Western Hemisphere, be placed under
the closest surveillance. In addition, the foreign minister wanted
the United States to assign FBI agents to Brazil, to serve as advisers to the countersubversive agency being set up by Rio.[36]

From Brazil, Long traveled to Argentina, where he discovered
the government of Roberto Ortiz to be somewhat less worried
about an imminent Nazi putsch. It was not political but economic
subversion that was troubling the Argentine president; for unless a satisfactory trade agreement could be reached between the
United States and Argentina (the two states had not concluded a
formal commercial pact since the Treaty of Friendship, Commerce
and Navigation of 1853),[37] Ortiz was fearful that his nation would
inevitably be brought into the orbit of European economic and
political powers.[38]

In the middle of November 1938, with everyone in Washington policymaking circles talking about the prospect of Nazi aggression below the Rio Grande, the president received a clamant
telegram from his friend Archibald MacLeish, the poet whom he
would soon appoint Librarian of Congress. It was not literature
that MacLeish had on his mind, but Latin America. He wanted
to make sure that Roosevelt fully understood the terrible effect
that the administration's refusal to lift the Spanish arms embargo
was having in that part of the world. MacLeish had spent time
there the previous spring, doing some reporting for *Fortune,* and
he was convinced that it was "critically important" for the president to be briefed by someone like himself, with extensive South
American experience, who could explain how a Franco victory
in Spain—a victory made possible in part by United States arms
policy—would redound to the detriment of the administration,
depriving it of the Latin goodwill that it had worked so hard to
gain. Moreover, said MacLeish, a fascist triumph in the former
mother country of most of Latin America might cause a chain
reaction of fascist coups in other lands of the hemisphere. "Re-

actionary groups in certain republics," he concluded, "would warmly welcome [a] demonstration that our attachment to [the] republican form of government is not so great that we can be counted on to protect South American republican governments against fascist adventurers of European origin."[39] Four days after receiving this cable, Roosevelt summoned MacLeish to the White House to find out what the writer knew about the growing Nazi danger to Latin America.

As MacLeish had suggested, the Spanish arms policy of the administration was turning out all wrong, despite the seeming wisdom, back in January 1937, of an arms embargo on both sides in the civil war, to prevent the spread of fighting to neighboring lands. The president was by now as aware as anyone that a fascist victory in Spain was bound to be harmful to his Good Neighbor Policy, to say nothing of American security. But in this instance, the administration's concern for the security of the hemisphere took precedence over its desire to spread democracy throughout Latin America. As much as he would have wanted to lift the Spanish embargo, Roosevelt wanted even more to preserve the unity of the New World; and he realized better than most that the majority of Latin America's leaders wanted Franco to defeat what they considered to be the atheistic, Marxist forces of Loyalist Spain.[40]

Confronted with a Hobson's choice over Spain, the administration sought other ways to counter the Axis penetration of the hemisphere; and it was precisely this problem that vexed Roosevelt and his advisers as they turned their attention to the upcoming Eighth Inter-American Conference, at Lima, the most important meeting of American republics that had ever taken place. As he had done twice before (at Montevideo in 1933 and at Buenos Aires in 1936), Secretary of State Cordell Hull would lead an American delegation to South America. But unlike the previous trips, made in more peaceful times, the voyage to the Peruvian capital was being made in an atmosphere fraught with extrahemispheric complications. The *New York Times* reported in early November that the European powers, "especially the totalitarian states, are closely watching developments at Lima as they have never watched any other American parley."[41]

German agents, some of whom had arrived in Lima shortly before the conference opened on 10 December, seemed to be everywhere. One of them, a professor from the University of Munich,

delivered a passionately anti-Roosevelt lecture at the National
University of San Marcos, iterating what was to be a German
propaganda refrain for the next two years: that any thought of
Germany's invading South America was a ludicrous Yankee
fabrication, amusing but malign.[42] Professor Ubbelolide-Doering's
lecture of 5 December was only one of several attempts by Axis
emissaries to influence Latin opinion, thereby bringing pressure
to bear on Lima delegates to oppose the United States in its bid to
strengthen the defenses of the hemisphere.[43]

Having observed in Europe that German protestations of injured innocence were peculiarly short-lived, the White House did
not put any stock in what Ubbelolide-Doering or any other German had to say on that matter. Instead, American policymakers
believed that the Axis was intensifying its efforts to subvert the
republics to the south. As Hull later insisted: "The threat was
no mere conjuring by an excited fancy; our diplomatic representatives in Latin America had given us literally hundreds of concrete instances. . . . To me the danger to the Western Hemisphere
was real and imminent."[44] Fully endorsing this view was Laurence
Duggan, head of the State Department's Division of American
Republics, who stated that "the Lima Conference was confronted
not with theoretical dangers but with the very real prospect that
the Nazis, Fascists, and Japs might include the American republics in a world war of conquest."[45]

Illustrative of the fears of Hull and Duggan was a message that
the American minister to Venezuela, Antonio González, sent to
Roosevelt in late November. González reported a marked increase
of Italian influence upon certain military leaders in Caracas. Not
only were Italian pilots training Venezuelan air cadets, but the
government, on the urging of the pro-fascist ministers who held
the armed forces portfolios, had just contracted to purchase some
Italian planes.[46] To Washington, the danger below the Rio Grande
was not confined to the possibility of military aggression. Far more
worrisome was the likelihood that Germany would seek to desta-
bilize the hemisphere in the same fashion that it had destabilized
parts of Europe, through ceaseless propagandizing, overt Nazi party
activities, and economic pressure. "We had seen the method employed with great success in Austria and in the Sudetenland,"
wrote Hull. "The same technique was obvious in Latin America."[47]

In a way, Lima was an appropriate site for the United States to try to rally the hemisphere against the Axis. Host country Peru had attained notoriety in some American minds because of its close ties with Italy and the swelling volume of trade that it had been carrying on with Germany over the previous five years. Dictator-president Oscar Raimundo Benavides was enjoying the fifth year of a reign that was noteworthy for the way in which it mixed an abundance of repression with a handful of splashy public work projects, a combination of the mailed fist and the WPA. A year and a half before the Lima conference, the departing American ambassador, Fred Morris Dearing, had written Roosevelt that Benavides was proving to be a "poorer and poorer neighbor every day."[48]

Nothing in the intervening months caused the White House to revise Dearing's assessment of the Peruvian strong man. Indeed, it was agreed to by all that, if anything, Benavides was changing for the worse. In the first place, it was being recollected in Washington that Benavides had been a diplomat in Rome in 1917, and hence was undoubtedly still an Italophile. Secondly, it was evident that Benavides had allowed Italy to attain a commanding position over the finances of his nation, the command being principally exercised by the Banco Italiano and its gregarious director, Gino Salocchi, whom *Fortune* considered to be, "next to the president, Peru's most important man."[49] According to journalist Carleton Beals, Benavides had struck up a warm friendship with Benito Mussolini while in Italy during the World War; later, while minister to Spain, he had spoken publicly and glowingly of the virtues of fascism, leaving Beals to conclude early in 1938 that "today, Peru . . . has largely been integrated into the fascist column."[50]

Discomforted as it was by Italy's powerful influence over the economic and military affairs of Peru (Lima having recently purchased six Italian bombers), the Roosevelt administration was even more concerned with the ominous increase in trade between Peru and Germany. From 1932 to 1936, German exports to Peru had risen 400 percent in value, while her imports from that nation had increased by 300 percent. Although the United States retained its ranking as the leading supplier of Peruvian imports, it was clear that it had suffered great absolute losses in the past few years.[51] Making matters worse was the nagging fear, which was never completely dispelled until the middle of World War II, that

Berlin had acquired secret access to a submarine base in the northern city of Trujillo.[52]

It is unlikely that Benavides even thought of making port facilities available to German U-boats, but it is known that he, along
with other heads of state in Latin America, did request armaments
from Germany. Just nine months before the Lima conference he
had ordered some 88-mm antiaircraft guns from the Krupp munitions works. The order delighted the German minister in Peru,
who implored Berlin not to ignore this hand outstretched in
friendship, but to get the weapons to Lima as quickly as possible.
"It is a question," remarked Minister Schmitt, "of demonstrating at the Pan American Conference to be held in December that
in case of necessity Peru is not defenseless even against the North
American air force."[53]

It was not the American air force that Benavides wished to train
these German 88s on, although he probably would have liked to
bring down to earth the high-flying American ambassador, Laurence Steinhardt. Assistant Secretary of State Adolf Berle was upset over the "bad situation" that had arisen in Peru as a result of
the many social improprieties committed by Steinhardt and his
"pretty, spoilt and socially ambitious" wife. The ambassadorial
couple clearly did not fit into the humble-diplomacy mold that
the Roosevelt administration was attempting to create for its Latin
American representatives—the sort of good-neighborly, plain-folks
role that Josephus Daniels was playing so well in Mexico. Berle
was afraid that unless Steinhardt were sent elsewhere, prefera-
bly Moscow, "where he can do relatively little damage," United
States relations with Peru would continue to deteriorate.[54]

Although relations between the United States and Peru were
strained, it was not the host country that dominated the thinking of the American delegates as they steamed southward aboard
the SS *Santa Clara*. Everyone was concerned instead with the position that Argentina might adopt at the conference. Would the
self-appointed leader of Spanish America repeat its performance
of two years before at Buenos Aires, and serve as the paladin of
universality in contradistinction to the hemisphere isolationism
of the United States? Hull and the rest of the delegation feared
that it would,[55] for State Department officials, during the month
preceding the Lima conference, had been sending home disturbing reports about the new foreign minister, José María Cantilo,

who was said to be intending to "out-Saavedra" Hull's antagonist at the Buenos Aires conference, Carlos Saavedra Lamas.[56]

From military intelligence, the American delegation received further unpleasant news. According to Col. Lester Baker, the military attaché in Argentina, the ruling class in Buenos Aires would not tolerate at Lima any deviation from Argentina's traditional policy of transatlanticism, nor would it accept any United States proposal of alliance that might endanger Argentina's "wheat and meat market." Baker forwarded an article that had appeared in a recent edition of the Buenos Aires daily, *La Nación*, whose columnist Fernando Ortiz Echagüe reported that Argentina would steadfastly resist an anticipated Brazilian attempt to "wave the phantom of continental danger in the face of the Conference." Argentina, said Echagüe, did not have the same kind of problems with *its* Germans as Brazil seemed to be having with its.[57]

The Roosevelt administration did not have to wait long before discovering how perceptive were its rapporteurs, not to mention Echagüe. Despite his not being an official delegate, Cantilo addressed the Lima assembly on its first day, 10 December. Tearing a page from an old Saavedra Lamas script, he adjured the American republics not to take rash action against any "theoretic threat and offend the sensibilities of friends in Europe." Cantilo recognized the fundamental unity of the hemisphere, even rendered it lip service, but he reserved his best eloquence for the bestowal of praise where praise belonged, on Europe. In a burst of ecumenicism, he paid tribute to all the major powers of that continent (and to a few of the smaller ones as well), declaring that "if to the mother country [that is, Spain, Portugal, or England] we owe the basis of our literature, then to French culture we owe the basic formation of our intellectual life, and to Italy and Germany all the vital aspects of our evolution."[58]

Back home in Buenos Aires, the foreign minister's speech was the object of warm praise from the Italian-language newspaper, *Il Mattino d'Italia*, a pro-Mussolini daily that interpreted Lima's first round as a victory for the "Latin and Mediterranean conscience," represented by Cantilo, over the "Anglo-Saxon, Protestant, Quaker, atheist, brutal" civilization personified by Hull.[59] In Lima, the target of this vituperation was mulling over the remarks of his Argentine counterpart. What annoyed the secretary of state most was not the tenor of Cantilo's speech—no one in the American delegation really expected the foreign minister to plead the case for tighter hemisphere unity—but the fact that the Argentine statesman quit the conference the following day for a vacation in the Chilean lake district, leaving the delegation of his nation, after the United States one of the two most important at Lima, in the hands of a relatively inexperienced legal counselor attached to the foreign office, Isidoro Ruiz Moreno.[60]

Hull, who had developed a keen antipathy to Argentine statesmen after his frustrating encounter with Saavedra Lamas at Buenos Aires, saw Cantilo as a sort of Saavedra reincarnated. In fact, the new foreign minister might prove himself more of a nuisance than the old one, since it was suspected that he had come under the sway of fascism while serving a recent tour of duty as ambassador to Italy. It was Hull's conviction that "Cantilo had run away from the conference in order to kill it."[61] A correspondent for the *Chicago Daily News*, John T. Whitaker, concurred, terming Cantilo's hasty departure a deed that "outdid the Nazis for diplomatic boorishness."[62] But some Americans were prepared to give Cantilo the benefit of the doubt. Samuel Guy Inman, for example, asked him why Argentina refused to get behind the United States and to help make the hemisphere safe from Hitler. Cantilo replied that, in the first place, his government did not consider Germany a threat to the New World, and secondly, that Washington never seemed able to grasp that Argentina had strong cultural and economic links with Europe. "How can we expect," said Cantilo, "to forget all about the people who give lifeblood to our nation and buy our products?"[63] One historian has even discerned in Cantilo's behavior evidence that the foreign minister was really sympathetic to the United States; unlike Saavedra Lamas, whose oratory at Buenos Aires had taken Hull completely by surprise, Cantilo repeatedly, in the months before the Lima conference, tipped his hand for all to see.[64]

However one chooses to interpret Cantilo's actions, there can be no denying that they certainly complicated Hull's job. The American delegates had decided before the conference opened that any accords dealing with the vital subject of defense in the hemisphere must obtain unanimous approval at Lima; accordingly, this meant that they would have to cater to Argentina's opposition and attempt to satisfy her grievances—even at the cost of a greatly weakened anti-totalitarian declaration. In instructing the delegation prior to its departure for Lima, Hull emphasized that the avoidance of controversy was to be a top-priority item. He also reminded his colleagues that "among the foreign relations of the United States . . . the Pan American policy takes first place in our diplomacy."[65]

Sumner Welles, who Berle suspected had been left behind by Hull "because in previous [inter-American] negotiations [he] had taken so much of the laboring oar that the secretary felt he himself was not in control of the situation,"[66] was also worried about dissension at Lima. As the ship carrying Hull and the other American delegates drew near the Peruvian coast, Welles cabled Robert Scotten, the American chargé d'affaires in Rio de Janeiro: "I consider that it would be disastrous for any open break to take place at the conference which would make public to the rest of the world any wide divergence of views between the American republics at this moment." If, said Welles, the United States must temper its own aspirations to get Argentine cooperation, so be it; the reward would be well worth the sacrifice.[67]

For two long weeks the American delegates juggled as best they could the demands being made at Lima by the northernmost Latin states, led by Mexico and Colombia, who wanted the conference to adopt a strong anti-Axis statement and the opening toward Europe *qua* Europe, which was the hallmark of the Argentine position. At times the juggling act appeared on the verge of collapse; and when John White of the *New York Times*, who was busily working his way to the top of the White House enemy list of hostile reporters, wrote from Lima that by abdicating leadership on the question of solidarity the United States was losing the respect and support of the smaller republics, the State Department took angry notice.

In an agitated mood over the "defeatist stories" being filed by White and some other American correspondents, Welles suggested to Hull, in a cable of 16 December, that the secretary do something to stifle such criticism.[68] Hull doubted that there was anything either he or Welles could do—after all, one had to consider that freedom of expression was guaranteed by the Constitution. Welles, however, was not as able as Hull to grin and bear such journalistic impudence. Later that week, after reading another White story in the *Times*, this one predicting that the United States was on the brink of losing the "first skirmish in this hemisphere between democracy and totalitarian ideology," Welles became depressed enough to lament to Jay Pierrepont Moffat, chief of the State Department's Division of European Affairs, that it was a "black day indeed."[69]

Fortunately for Welles, his period of anguish turned out to be a short one. On Christmas Eve, the United States was given an unexpected gift: the Lima conference, hitherto hopelessly deadlocked on the question of what sort of statement to make about the situation in Europe, arrived at a compromise, entitled the Declaration of Lima. By giving their unanimous consent to this declaration, the American republics did two things: they reaffirmed their "continental solidarity" (whatever that might mean in operational terms); and they agreed to set up consultative machinery in the event that an extrahemispheric power tried to threaten that solidarity.[70]

On the surface, it looked like a clear-cut victory for Washington. This was the interpretation that President Roosevelt chose to give the declaration when, at a press conference on 27 December, he hailed it as a "very, very great success."[71] Hull was only slightly less enthusiastic, remarking of the outcome at Lima that "although not all I had wanted, [it] was not far from it." Certainly, he would have preferred a treaty to a declaration, since the former (if ratified) would have substantially more binding force than a mere statement of good intentions. And it would have been a nice touch if the Axis states could have been singled out by name in the Lima declaration. But on the whole, Hull was satisfied that the Christmas Eve pronouncement was a sound piece of work, which made it plain that the Western Hemisphere would be prepared to defend itself against Hitler and his cohorts.[72]

Others thought so, too. Samuel Guy Inman, who had been an unofficial observer at the conference, called the declaration "a fighting platform for American democracy. It was a new continentalized Monroe Doctrine in its guarantee of the 'American System.' "[73] Some years later, historian Alton Frye would write that "the hemispheric unity achieved at Lima was genuine."[74] But was it really? Was Inman justified in claiming that, at long last, the Monroe Doctrine had been multilateralized? It would seem not: for the final draft of the Declaration of Lima watered any commitment to collective security by reminding the declarants that "it is understood that the Governments of the American Republics will act independently in their individual capacity, recognizing fully their juridicial equality as sovereign states."[75]

In short, while the republics of the hemisphere were prepared, in a general way, to denounce aggression against any of their number on the part of unspecified powers from some other region of the world, they were not yet ready to formulate any specific plan of action against Germany, Italy, or Japan. "Translated into simple language," observed a skeptical Nicholas John Spykman, "the Declaration of Lima announced that the American states were concerned about the safety of the hemisphere and that in common defense each would protect its own territory." The results of Lima, said this international relations expert from Yale, "fooled nobody, least of all the Germans."[76] Others dismissed the Lima declaration as an "extravagently loopholed declaration of good intentions,"[77] and as "another Argentine triumph for innocuity."[78] Duncan Aikman even likened the declaration of solidarity against a nebulous danger to a response that Calvin Coolidge is alleged to have given a questioner who wanted to know what the president's minister had said that day about sin: "He said he was against it."[79]

As weak as the Declaration of Lima was, it was still better than no declaration at all. But the Roosevelt administration would discover, over the next eighteen months, that it would take much more than good intentions and fine phraseology to get the Western Hemisphere united behind its leadership. It would take a show of resolve on the part of the United States sufficiently forceful to convince the nations to the south that it would and could act to protect them from Axis economic, political, and military pressure. This was the challenge that awaited the Good Neighbor Policy as 1939 began.

6

"As Safe as a Kitten in Its Basket"

In the aftermath of Lima, some Americans had extreme difficulty in bringing themselves to agree with the White House position on the Declaration of Lima—that it would constitute an
effective weapon in the struggle against the totalitarian states.
But in Germany, there was consensus among political observers
about the purport of the declaration; Nazi officialdom, from Hitler on down, claimed to be both surprised and hurt that Washington or any other capital in the hemisphere could think that
the Reich had any designs on the American republics. "Germany
wishes to live in peace and friendship with all nations, including
America," said Hitler on 30 January 1939. "We refuse to intervene
in Latin American affairs, and we reject with the same energy U.S.
intervention in German affairs."[1]

Other German officials echoed the hurt, yet defiant, words of
the Fuehrer. Werner Rheinbaben, a researcher with Berlin's Ibero-
Amerika Institut, contrasted the recent conference with the 1936
Buenos Aires conference. The earlier assembly had been above
all a peace conference, while Lima had unfortunately been allowed
to develop, "in accordance with the intentions of United States
leaders, into a conference for the preparation of war."[2] The Institut
director, Wilhelm Faupel, pursued this line of argument in a May
1939 propaganda piece aimed at Latin American readers. Faupel
adduced four reasons to show why the United States had been
conducting an odious campaign against Latin America's great and
good friend Germany: (1) the U.S. needed to capture or recapture
Latin markets; (2) Franklin D. Roosevelt had a warped personality;
(3) "Judeo-Masonic" elements had a stranglehold on American
political and economic life; and (4) Washington bureaucrats had
deep-seated imperialistic pretensions. Faupel, who knew Latin
America well, having served as a military adviser in Argentina,

Peru, and Brazil for nearly twenty years, concluded by observing that "to arouse distrust against Germany, North American propaganda has invented the danger of a supposed German attack on Ibero-America."[3]

Needless to say, German assurances that the Western Hemisphere would be respected as a United States sphere of influence—assuming that the United States refrained from meddling in purely European affairs—did not register too well in Washington. In his annual message to Congress, on 4 January 1939, President Roosevelt reaffirmed the intention of his administration to preserve the freedom of the entire hemisphere, declaring that "we, no more than other nations, can afford to be surrounded by the enemies of our faith and our humanity." To ensure adequate defense, Roosevelt told Congress that he would need 2 billion dollars for military spending.[4]

Later that month, the president received a visit from his ambassador to Mexico and old friend, Josephus Daniels, who had been secretary of the navy and Roosevelt's chief during the World War. In a memorandum made shortly after this White House meeting with Roosevelt, Daniels recorded that the latter was convinced that the Luftwaffe, with thirteen thousand "effective combat planes," constituted a serious threat not just to the European democracies, but also to the United States. The president foresaw the likelihood of an American war against Germany, stemming from the nation's obligation under the Monroe Doctrine to defend Brazil. Was this, asked Daniels, because there were a million Germans living in that South American land? A million and a half, replied Roosevelt, who then proceeded, in an excited manner, to depict for the ambassador a probable scenario for the German conquest of Brazil.

For the next few minutes, Daniels was treated to the awesome spectacle of armadas of bombers swooping down upon Brazil in support of a Volksdeutsche insurrection in the four southern states. Daniels was taken aback by the lively illustration, partly because the thought of an actual Nazi invasion of Brazil was new to him, and partly because he was surprised to find that the president of the United States should consider such an invasion to be a serious possibility. He left the White House not completely convinced that Hitler would in fact do what Roosevelt said he would do. Daniels was, however, convinced that the president was positive Brazil was endangered, and he noted with some amazement that his former subordinate actually "spoke as if that might be the real danger to the continent."[5] Stopping next door at the State Department, Daniels found Cordell Hull to be "in a more pessimistic mood about Pan America than I had expected after his public report of the Lima Conference. He thinks Germany is trying to get footholds there by barter transactions and otherwise."[6]

Roosevelt's request for an increase in the defense budget drew some angry comments from political opponents who, fearing that the administration was about to commit the United States to the protection of Britain and France, maintained that the present size of the armed services was sufficient to handle any conceivable foe. The president responded to these criticisms at a press conference on 3 February, where he forcefully denied that he was thinking of abandoning isolationism. United States policy, he avowed, had not changed one iota; the order of the day was still "no entangling alliances." Admittedly, stories to the opposite effect had reared their ugly heads, but they were all—and here he slowed down for the benefit of reporters who had orthographic problems—"pure bunk—b-u-n-k,bunk, . . ." Roosevelt was especially annoyed by a report that he had told a group of senators that America's frontier henceforth would be on the Rhine. That allegation he called a "deliberate lie" propagated by "some boob."[7]

The Rhine statement had ostensibly been made at a secret meeting convoked by the president on 31 January for the purpose of briefing a select group of senators on the latest developments in American foreign policy. He felt that he had to comment upon a story that had been making headlines across the nation—a story about a French air mission that was in the United States shopping for planes. The mission, which the French government wished to remain top secret, was brought into the open on 23 January, when an experimental Douglas twin-engined bomber crashed in California, killing its American pilot and injuring a French officer who was on board. The presence of the French flier aboard the doomed craft, and the secrecy surrounding the mission, touched off an uproar in the United States, one that Roosevelt hoped to quell by explaining to members of the Senate Military Affairs Committee that America had a strong interest in helping France rearm.[8]

While it is impossible to determine whether the president actually said that the nation's frontier was now on the Rhine, it is important to stress that the Neutrality Act was not being contravened by this instance of Franco-American collaboration, however clumsily it might have been conducted. In January 1939, France, not yet a belligerent, was legally free to purchase implements of war from private American manufacturers. After the war began in September, the White House increased its efforts to have the arms embargo lifted, which Congress agreed to do in November. But (as stressed in the previous chapter) even this action of the administration did not annul its policy of isolationism; for by working to have the embargo removed, the president was simply seeking to have the United States revert to its traditional neutrality policy, insofar as the export of arms and ammunition was concerned.

One writer who suspected that Roosevelt was up to something far more complicated and more dangerous than traditional neutrality was Quincy Howe, an England-hater who would, after the outbreak of war in September, receive subsidies from the German embassy in Washington for his anglophobic publications. What brought Howe to the attention of the Germans was the appearance, in February 1939, of his *Blood Is Cheaper than Water.* This critique of Rooseveltian foreign policy compared the president's jeremiads on the Axis menace to the hemisphere with the recent Orson Welles broadcast of *War of the Worlds,* and concluded that, like the radio play, Roosevelt's description of an imperiled Latin America was nothing but a hoax. Howe conceded that Berlin might indeed be attempting to perpetrate hostile acts in some South American countries, but he did not think that much would come of such attempts; after all, Germany had tried the same sort of thing during the World War, and no one had ever proved that American security had been threatened as a result. With a proper preparedness budget of, say, a billion dollars a year, the United States could make the hemisphere entirely secure, even without a two-ocean navy.[9]

Unfortunately, continued Howe, the nation was being led into war by two diametrically opposed factions: imperialistic interests who wished to pursue manifest destiny in Asia and Latin America, and liberal anti-fascists who would fight to preserve the European status quo from totalitarian revisionism. Both groups were benefitting from the catchword "hemispheric defense," as

evidenced by the growing enlistment into their ranks of quon-
dam isolationists, and no matter which faction came out on top,
Howe was afraid that the "American way of life was over and
done with." Nevertheless, a choice had to be made between the
two war parties, and to Howe the imperialistic faction was the
lesser evil, because if the United States was bound to fight anyway,
it might as well fight for its own empire and not for those of Britain and France. Besides, he added, an American war for empire
would not be taking place in the Europe that Howe so despised.[10]

However inaccurate Howe might have been in claiming that
Americans were aligning themselves into two equally bellicose
camps, he was correct in perceiving the beginning of a marked
exodus from isolationist ranks. Prior to Munich, public opinion
polls had regularly shown that 95 percent of the nation was firmly
against participation in another European war. By February 1939,
however, even before Germany annexed the rump of Czechoslovakia, Gallup was finding that a large minority (17 percent) would
be willing to give military support to Britain and France. And by
late August, nearly half the American public (46 percent) would
aid the Allies militarily if it appeared that Germany was about
to win a European war. They would extend this aid primarily because they feared that America's own security would be jeopardized should Hitler eliminate the armed forces standing between
himself and the Western Hemisphere.[11]

Howe was in error on two counts: his misperception of the
United States as a nation divided into two war-hungry factions,
and his confident assessment that the Western Hemisphere was
inviolable. Every day that passed in 1939 brought with it new
evidence of increasing Axis pressure on the lands below the Rio
Grande. Even Roosevelt's ambassadors to Britain and to France,
Joseph P. Kennedy and William C. Bullitt, both of whom had coun-
seled strict noninvolvement in the Munich crisis, were quick to
understand the implications that Germany's European successes
would have for Latin America.

On 3 March 1939, Kennedy informed the president that a German victory in the Old World would force the United States to
become a garrison state simply to ensure its own survival. While
the nation would probably remain safe from direct invasion, a
"simultaneous attack on both the Atlantic and Pacific fronts, with
Latin America under totalitarian influence, might well be more

than the Navy could handle alone." Three weeks later, Bullitt cabled Hull that he had been informed by a reputable source (Otto von Bismarck, the German chargé d'affaires in London) that Hitler had been boasting of taking Czechoslovakia as a prelude to a conquest of all Europe. As a sequel, sometime in 1941 Hitler was expected to try to "conquer the United States by a joint attack with Japan on North and South America." Bullitt said he was certain that Hitler had made these statements.[12]

Another prominent American who did not like the way in which Latin America was becoming involved in world politics was Henry Stimson, whose Washington career dated back to the beginning of the century, when he had been secretary of war under William Howard Taft. On 7 March, the veteran policymaker (he had also served as Herbert Hoover's secretary of state and would, in a little more than a year, replace Harry Woodring as Roosevelt's secretary of war) wrote a letter to the editor of the *New York Times,* in which he urged the president to discard isolationism and assume a stance of open military support for Britain, France, and China. Not only was this the only noble thing to do, Stimson said, it was also the only sane thing, for "if we should stand idly by . . . our own hemisphere might become economically so affected and militarily so endangered that it would be neither a safe nor a happy place to live in. . . ."[13]

In the following week came the denouement of the Czechoslovakia problem, as Hitler annexed the Czech portion of that unhappy land and converted Slovakia into a Nazi satellite. On 16 March, one day after Prague was occupied, Acting Secretary of State Sumner Welles (Hull was on vacation) called a meeting to discuss whether American relations with Germany should be broken off. Department militants Norman Davis and George Messersmith thought they should, but overriding these two men were James Dunn, Jay Pierrepont Moffat, and Adolf Berle, all of whom argued that apart from the symbolic value of a diplomatic rupture, the United States would gain nothing by such a move. None of the above officials, on the other hand, advised passivity when Welles raised the matter of the likely consequences for Latin America as a result of Hitler's latest piece of aggression; instead, all agreed, in Berle's words, that "if we did nothing German prestige would probably rise."[14]

The assistant secretary of state had some thoughts about the ongoing crisis in Europe. Berle wanted every action that the administration took in the future to be premised on two assumptions: that Britain and France were not to be trusted, for they were "frightened and unfrank"; and that American interests were greater in the Atlantic than in the Pacific. "This is because the Atlantic is no longer wide enough to be a defense against attack; the Pacific still is."[15]

Had there been, at this juncture, absolute political tranquillity in Latin America, policymakers in Washington would still have had ample cause for concern about that part of the world, given their prevailing three-fold assumption that Hitler was an insatiable expansionist, that Britain and France could not be counted upon to stop him, and that the Atlantic Ocean was eminently bridgeable by the technology of modern warfare. In sum, Latin America was as natural a spot to expect Nazi encroachments, perhaps even military incursions, as it was possible for the isolationist planners of the Roosevelt administration to envision. But the early spring of 1939 was not a placid time in South America, least of all in Argentina, which was now fated to taste the sort of fear that Brazil had been experiencing for much of the preceding year. In late March the news exploded of a Nazi plot aimed at fomenting the secession of a large portion of southern Argentina, with the goal being its eventual union with the German regions of southern Chile in a new Teutonic republic.

For over a month, the War Department had been receiving reports from intelligence officers in Buenos Aires that the rich Patagonian territories figured prominently in a German plan to split Argentina in half. For some time there had been active in Patagonia a movement seeking to get the territories upgraded to provincial status. In February 1939, the leader of the provincialists, Alberto J. Grassi, announced that Nazis had been infiltrating his movement, in hopes of instigating the secession of Patagonia and its eventual linkup with parts of southern Chile.[16] Grassi's allegations were given dramatic apparent confirmation on 30 March, when the Buenos Aires daily, *Noticias Gráficas*, reported that it possessed a two-year old despatch, obtained from the files of the German embassy, that discussed plans for what the document labeled the Patagonian "no man's land," which was to be annexed by the Nazis. The newspaper published a photostatic copy of the highly offensive communiqué, which bore the signatures of the leader of Argentina's Nazis and a counselor of the German embassy in Buenos Aires.[17]

Germany reacted quickly to the exposé, denouncing it, in the words of Chargé d'affaires Erich Otto Meynen, as a "clumsy falsification."[18] German diplomats around the hemisphere got busy trying to show that the whole affair had probably been concocted by the Americans or by the British (in this case, it seems to have been the latter). Willard Beaulac, an official at the United States embassy in Havana, was told by the Cuban secretary of state that Berlin had conducted a full investigation of the incident and had concluded that the Argentine charges were absurd. "So far as Germany is concerned," said a German diplomat in Havana, "there is no Patagonian question."[19]

Germany's ability to convince people in the hemisphere that the document was a forgery, the annexation menace a sham, was severely damaged by the credibility chasm the Nazis had created for themselves by recent statements and actions in Europe. Although a subsequent Argentine investigation would cast doubt on the veracity of the *Noticias Gráficas* charge that Patagonia was the object of a Nazi plot, for the moment Argentine policymakers were treating the allegation very seriously indeed. Foreign Minister José María Cantilo, who had been so unimpressed with talk of an Axis menace at Lima, informed the American chargé d'affaires, S. Pinkney Tuck, that his government, after carefully examining the documentary evidence, had concluded that the threat to Patagonia was genuine.[20] The Argentine ambassador in Washington corroborated Cantilo's statements a few days later, indicating to sources inside the State Department that Buenos Aires had all but ruled out the possibility that the document might have been forged.[21] Tuck himself was uncertain whether forgery might have been involved, but he was sure that the Ortiz administration was convinced of the authenticity of the plot.[22] So convinced was it, in fact, that in early April it launched a nationwide anti-subversive roundup, ranging from Patagonia in the south to the Misiones territory in the northeast. Among those apprehended in the sweep was Alfred Müller, the Nazi leader whose signature appeared on the incriminating document.[23]

In Washington, as in Buenos Aires, officials were taking the threat to the hemisphere seriously. Although some policymakers shared Tuck's doubts about the authenticity of the document in question, none knew at the time that it had been fabricated—almost certainly by the British.[24] Obviously, London would not have given out this information, for that would have defeated the whole purpose of the Nazi-scare in Patagonia—assuming, of course, British responsibility for that scare. British propagandists of the late 1930s were well aware that Americans were not about to believe the kind of atrocity stories, for a Second World War, that had had such credibility during the early years of the First World War. The great revisionist awakening that had swept the United States in the mid-1920s convinced the American public that it must never again let itself be "suckered" into a European war as it had been in 1917. Official British statements made in the 1920s, indicating that London had frequently (but not always) lied about German atrocities during the Great War, had a sobering effect on opinion in the United States.[25] As the editor of the *Richmond Times-Despatch* pointed out in December 1925, "in the next war, the propaganda must be more subtle and clever than the best the World War produced. These frank admissions of wholesale lying on the part of trusted governments in the last war will not soon be forgotten."[26]

By the end of the 1930s, Americans had become, in the words of two youthful social scientists, "prisoners of memory." As Harold Lavine and James Wechsler wrote, in a study undertaken in late 1939 for Yale's Institute for Propaganda Analysis, "the greatest obstacle to Allied propagandists in World War II was the propaganda that preceded American entry into World War I. Skeptics are not crusaders, and disbelief was the chief inheritance of America from the last war."[27] British propagandists knew better than to try to resurrect any of the old calumnies with which they had assailed the kaiser's Germany—even if, in Hitler's Germany, they had an infinitely more deserving target for atrocity allegations. Instead, London heeded the advice of Capt. Sidney Rogerson, who wrote an influential book in 1938 predicting that Americans would only allow themselves to enter another European war if they perceived that their national security would be imperiled by a German victory.[28] One did not have to be a military strategist to realize that, as far as the Roosevelt administration and most of the public were concerned, the most vulnerable part of the nation's defense system was its "soft underbelly," Latin America. Accordingly, from the late 1930s on, London began to emphasize the great and imminent danger that would confront the republics be-low the Rio Grande should Hitler ever defeat Great Britain.

There is no question that in the wake of the Patagonia affair Washington was more sensitive than ever to events in Latin America. More nervous than most of the president's advisers was Adolf Berle, who drafted a revealing aide-mémoire for Roosevelt in early April, arguing that the United States had only three feasi-ble choices in the event that a war broke out in Europe. It could attempt to achieve a strict isolation, which would require it to be rigorously neutral toward all belligerents. It could develop a neutrality policy tilted in favor of the European democracies. Or it could intervene diplomatically, in hopes of bringing the bellig-erents to the peace table. Berle favored the first course of action, recognizing fully that it would mean making the hemisphere vir-tually airtight by sealing it off to all the warring states, including Britain and France. "Both European contesting groups," he warned, "would seek to establish footholds in this hemisphere, partly for political reasons and largely to assure supplies of materials, food and munitions. Any such foothold, no matter by whom estab-lished, would be unfriendly to us."[29]

Roosevelt was not as confident as Berle that it would be possi-ble to seal off the hemisphere from the currents of war, even it if was desirable. Nor did the president regard British activity in Latin America with the distrust manifested by his anglophobic adviser. But he did not completely rule out Berle's first option; instead, Roosevelt decided that there was something worth trying in all three suggestions. In September 1939 the administration would, in the Declaration of Panama, signify that it was serious about segregating the hemisphere (south of Canada) from all belliger-ent actions. Two months later, it would achieve a revision of the neutrality legislation, in effect tilting American neutrality toward the Allies. Finally, the White House would attempt to implement Berle's third option—to try to get the warring powers to talk peace.

This option was actually the first of the Berle proposals to be explored. In his Pan American Day address of 14 April 1939, Roo-sevelt offered to host an international conference that would ar-range for the peaceful revision of the European and Asian status quo. The United States would, he said, be prepared to act as an intermediary, but it would expect the totalitarian powers to guar-antee, in return, that none of thirty-one nations (which the president named) would be attacked for a period of at least ten years. This speech made up in audaciousness for what it lacked in sagacity, and apart from giving Hitler a chance to sharpen his wit at Roosevelt's expense, it accomplished absolutely nothing; not only did the Fuehrer bluntly deny that any of *his* neighbors were threatened, but he took time to point out that none of Roosevelt's were either. "I should not like to let this opportunity pass," said Hitler in a sarcastic tone, "without giving above all an assurance regarding those territories which would, after all, give [Roosevelt] most cause for apprehension, namely the United States and the other states of the American Continent."[30]

If Washington's offers of mediation were obviously not going to lead to European peace, then perhaps war might be averted if the president could convince Congress to eliminate the more noxious features of America's neutrality legislation. In early spring, Roosevelt and Hull decided to remove the stalled neutrality revision bill from the feckless leadership of Key Pittman, the Nevada Democrat who chaired the Senate Foreign Relations Committee and who had been, since 20 March, orchestrating the upper house battle for revocation of the arms embargo. The proposed revisions did not represent a rejection of isolationist policy, for at the same time as the White House was seeking some means to help the democracies rearm, it was also attempting to design safeguards that would obviate a recurrence of the kind of maritime incidents that had brought the United States into the World War. It hoped to attain this latter goal by tightening the cash-and-carry provisions of the 1937 neutrality law, which required belligerents to transfer title of their American purchases before leaving the United States and to remove them in their own ships. Needless to say, arms and ammunition could not be purchased by a belligerent under any terms, according to the legislation passed between 1935 and 1937.[31]

The foremost underlying consideration in the administration's campaign to have the embargo lifted, an action that would give badly needed encouragement to London and Paris, was the worry that Germany would be able to devote its full attention to the Western Hemisphere after finishing off the under-armed democracies—assuming, that is, that Britain and France bothered to resist Hitler at all. This was a prospect that was becoming easier for many informed Americans to imagine, as was revealed by testimony that the Foreign Relations Committee recorded in April and May on the subject of neutrality revision.

At the opening hearing of 5 April, Henry Stimson set the somber tone for revision proponents by telling the crowd of legislators and spectators who had jammed into the caucus room that the United States simply could not afford the luxury of refusing to aid the European democracies. "We have only to read about some of the occurrences to the south of us," he said, "to realize that even we are within the zone of [the Axis] orbit."[32] A few days later, the elder statesman's warning was echoed in the nationally syndicated column written by Drew Pearson and Robert Allen, "Washington Merry-Go-Round." Pearson and Allen reported that suspicious Nazi movements were being revealed in vital regions of Patagonia, especially in the oil-producing zone located near the port of Comodoro Rivadavia. The United States was now faced with the prospect of the strategic Strait of Magellan passing over to German control. And, to make a bad story worse, it was apparent that the Argentine Nazis were receiving timely assistance from their brethren in Chile and Brazil.[33]

A witness who testified after Stimson explained to the committee how the security of the Western Hemisphere was contigent upon the British and French being allowed access to American arms in the event of war. Raymond Leslie Buell, president of the Foreign Policy Association, charter member of the internationalist elite, and reputedly anti-isolationist, told the senators on 20 April that the United States must help the democracies rearm for its own selfish reasons. He admitted that "a few years ago it was possible to argue that the Axis powers would never threaten the Western Hemisphere, even though they did defeat France and Britain." But no one who had seen such recent developments as the Patagonian affair could honestly believe that Germany was sincere in abjuring imperialistic ends in Latin America; it would be sheer irresponsibility for the administration to make plans that did not take into account a probable violation of the hemisphere in the near future.

Nor was the defeat of Britain and France, added Buell, the only danger confronting the United States. As had been the case since Munich, one could never discount the possibility that the two nations would just stand aside and let Hitler take what he wanted. He reminded his listeners that a recent article in the Berlin *Boer-*

sen-Zeitung had even invited Britain and France to join with the
Axis to counter American imperialism in Latin America. At this
point, the witness was interrupted by California's Hiram Johnson,
who asked whether the alarums of the present time concerning
Latin America were really any different from those of the World
War years. Buell thought that they were, adding that "I am as
sure as I can be of anything that the Western Hemisphere, a part
of Brazil if not Patagonia, could be attacked, and it would be extremely difficult for us, if we chose to do so, to resist attacks
there." Under Johnson's prodding, Buell admitted to doubting that
Germany could ever establish itself in Mexico—the United States
would never tolerate that. But further south, he said, the chances
of resisting Axis imperialism would be greatly lessened, an opinion with which the California Republican concurred.

Was Buell, then, advocating American military involvement
in Europe? wondered the next questioner, Idaho's William Borah,
who was like Johnson a firm anti-interventionist. Not at all, was
the reply; the United States had no business in sending troops
across the Atlantic. Instead, Buell would dispatch an expeditionary force southward, to Brazil, and order the fleet to Patagonia if
an emergency arose. The best course, he continued (sounding not
all unlike the isolationists to whom he was allegedly anathema),
would be for the United States to take up strong positions around
the hemisphere, then wait for attackers to come to it. Borah remarked that he was "certainly delighted to hear that."[34]

On the same day, a mile away on Pennsylvania Avenue, the
president himself was explaining why the Neutrality Act was in
desperate need of revision. As the situation now stood in Europe,
it was an "even money bet" which side would win if war broke
out. The horrid prospect of a totalitarian victory would have to
be confronted, whether one wished to or not. Consider this, said
Roosevelt to the American Society of Newspaper Editors: The
Axis had fifteen hundred planes capable of hopping the Atlantic
(with a stopover in the Cape Verde Islands) and reaching Brazil
the next day. To oppose this air armada, the United States had
only eight interceptors capable of reaching South America in time.
Scary, to be sure, continued the president; but this was only one
aspect of the Axis threat to the hemisphere, the overtly military
challenge.

There were other, no less dangerous, implications of a totalitarian victory in Europe—a victory that would lead to "virtually, political slavery, economic slavery, the end of real independence on the part of the Argentine." Brazil and Mexico were similarly vulnerable, which would mean that these important republics would also slip from economic and political subservience into a condition of outright military domination by the Axis, because in a battle with the latter, the Latin Americans "would not last a week." Obviously, the United States would be stripped of the protection that the Atlantic moat had once afforded in happier times; for while German bombers could not hit American targets from Europe, they could easily find their mark from bases in Latin America. "I think," Roosevelt said, gesticulating in the direction of the Kansas editor, William Allen White, "I am a lot safer on the Hudson River than I would be if I were in Kansas."

The president agreed that this kind of talk did not seem believable or even rational. But he wondered whether anyone back in 1933 would have believed that within four years two nations in Europe, Germany and Italy, would be strong enough to jeopardize the independence of every country on that continent. In any case, when it came to defending the hemisphere, the stakes were simply too high for him to assume anything but the worst. After all, "it would take planes based at Yucatán, modern bombing planes, about an hour and fifty minutes to smash up New Orleans." Of course, he said, the Army Air Corps would try its hardest to halt them before they reached the Louisiana shore, "but we do not know. It is a very small world."[35]

For all his talk about bombs falling on American soil, the president was not prepared to go beyond revoking the arms embargo as a means of ensuring that the Allies would be better equipped to fend off the Axis in Europe. Roosevelt at this juncture was trying to get American neutrality law rewritten with a view to preventing United States ships and citizens from going into any future war zones. He was not about to jettison the set of lessons that he had culled from the nation's allegedly disastrous experience in the World War. "We have to try everything that we can to prevent messes in the war zone," he told the editors, reminding them that this was what William Jennings Bryan had been pilloried for in 1915. "The country said at that time, and perhaps I said it,

'Any American has any right to go anywhere in the world and fly the flag and it will protect him.' Now, we have progressed a long ways. Mr. Bryan was right.''[36]

It has been argued that Buell, Roosevelt, and all the other advocates of neutrality revision were merely conjuring up the phantom of hemisphere danger in order to stimulate Congress to lift the arms embargo. According to this view, "nobody could have rational grounds before May 1940 for expecting that [the French army or the British navy] could be broken or bypassed. The threat of aggression from across the Atlantic . . . simply did not exist for reasonable men.''[37] This interpretation is widely held, notwithstanding the existence of much documentary evidence contradicting it. The documents seem to compel the conclusion that any reasonable policymaker getting the kind of information that Franklin Roosevelt was receiving in early 1939 would have been forced to take seriously the proposition that the New World might indeed be imperiled by the totalitarian powers. For example, just one day after Roosevelt and Buell made their comments to the press and to the Foreign Relations Committee, the White House received a top secret report from the Joint Planning Committee, the planning forum of the army and navy.[38] Unlike the Roosevelt and Buell statements, this report was most definitely not intended to sway public opinion; rather, it was intended to impress upon policymakers the gravity of the Axis challenge to Latin America.

This JPC study, which the committee had been working on since the previous autumn, was premised upon the assumption that "not only are the interests of the United States affected by fascist penetration into Latin America, but its actual and immediate security is threatened by the approach of this penetration toward the Panama Canal and the Caribbean." For the moment, Axis incursions in the most distant parts of South America were seen only as detrimental to American interests, not immediately dangerous to national security. Nevertheless, the planners predicted that it would be in just such areas as Patagonia that the United States would have the toughest job rooting out Axis subversion.

The JPC did not think that a genuine challenge to the Monroe Doctrine could be mounted unless Britain and France were somehow removed from Hitler's path—either through defeat in, or abstention from, war. Regardless of how the removal of the European democracies was accomplished, the planners considered it unlikely that the Axis could launch a substantial offensive against the hemisphere for at least one year, or until the spring of 1940 at the earliest. This did not mean that the United States could afford to sit back and watch the Axis carry on its successful trade and propaganda campaigns in many important South American nations. Nor could the White House blink the presence of the numerous German and Italian airlines flying to and within Latin America.[39] For the JPC analysts were convinced that it was not direct military assault that constituted the principal Axis menace to the hemisphere, but rather the possibility that Germany and Italy would succeed, by virtue of their support of subversive elements in several republics, in destabilizing much of the New World.

As the JPC somewhat clumsily put it, "the most likely form of violation of the Monroe Doctrine which would call for employment of Army forces in South America would be the attempted establishment by Germany of a Nazi regime in Argentina, Uruguay, or with less likelihood in Brazil, in which areas the spearhead of German colonization and influence affords the most likely area for such a German effort." Should Hitler seek either to subvert a Latin government or aid a totalitarian revolutionary movement in this task, then the United States would have to respond with force. If force was met with force, the planners expected that the Axis would be able to send nearly half a million men to fight below the Rio Grande.[40]

The United States, of course, would not be without allies in the struggle for the southern continent. The planners could report that, with a few notable exceptions like Mexico, "the present outlook is that the United States can rely on the cooperation of nearly all Latin American states to oppose any German or Italian violation of the Monroe Doctrine. . . ."[41] But the cooperation offered by the Latin neighbors would be limited to the political sphere, for militarily the nations to the south could not be relied on at all. Brazil, with an army of a third of a million (larger than that of the United States), was a case in point. In March 1939, a month before the JPC presented its findings to the president, the

Army War College completed a top secret study of its own, concerning the fighting capabilities of the hemisphere's second largest country.

The War College report was not totally negative. The Brazilian soldier did possess some good qualities. He was an ardent patriot. He was "not uncourageous physically." And he was obedient. Unfortunately, these three attributes exhausted the positive features of native soldiery, and the War College analysts proceeded to detect a torrent of flaws that, taken together, would seriously handicap Brazil's ability to contribute to the common defense. "The lack of moral stamina is [the Brazilian's] principal weak point. He succumbs easily to temptation and is *quickly thrown into deep dejection by severe reverses.* With the crowd and winning he is capable of sustained intensive effort and he is capable of a grave, spectacularly instantaneous sally against great odds. But to maintain a stout and prolonged fight in an apparently hopeless cause would probably exceed his limits of morale."[42]

Nor was morale the Brazilian warrior's only liability; his physical shape matched his psychological condition—indeed, poor health was cited as the principal cause of poor morale. "The average Brazilian is a poor physical specimen, and . . . particularly subject to certain diseases. His morale tends to disintegrate if he falls ill. . . ." Moreover, he was highly susceptible to the enticements of the mob, and while tractable, he lacked the "mental resources" to handle any but the simplest changes in his orders. Compared with the average GI, the Brazilian was a physical, intellectual, and moral wreck. But his sorry state was not the fault of the individual soldier, for "fortitude is not a Brazilian characteristic."[43]

After this review of Brazilian fighting potential, the War College experts concluded predictably that "against an external threat of any magnitude, Brazil would be helpless." This situation, however, was not entirely the fault of the Brazilian army. The navy was just as pitiful: its aging, decrepit fleet of two battleships, twelve destroyers, two light cruisers, and four submarines was famous for doing "very little operating at sea" and too much operating in the corridors of political power. Said the War College report: "The senior naval officers play politics. Their loyalty to a cause may be doubted. They may be expected to follow a leader and consequently their loyalty to the established government in case of rebellion is doubtful." With potential allies like this, the War College analysts must have wondered, Who needed enemies? Drily, they recommended that "if the Army has not now the so-called Hemisphere Defense Force required, the War Department should take steps to create it."[44]

The War College writers were particularly annoyed that the Brazilian general staff persisted in regarding Argentina, and not the Axis powers, as the principal threat to national security. While the eyes of American strategists were glued to the map of north-eastern Brazil, planners in Rio were mesmerized by the regions bordering on Argentina. And wisely so, in the opinion of one officer (unidentified) who read the War College report and penciled in this comment next to a passage predicting that Argentina would withhold assistance from Brazil if the latter were attacked by a European state: "Argentina would probably take advantage of the opportunity to increase her own power in South America at the expense of Brazil."[45] But the military attaché in Argentina, Col. Lester Baker, dismissed all talk of Argentine aggression against Brazil as the "fantastic" creation of the Vargas regime, which hoped to divert the attention of Brazilians from the nation's serious internal problems.[46]

Back in the United States, men who knew nothing and cared little about the state of Brazil's (or any other republic's) defenses were continuing to challenge claims made in the wake of the Patagonian affair that American security was imperiled by developments below the Rio Grande. Suspecting ulterior—and interventionist—motives, the military affairs expert from the *New York Times*, Hanson W. Baldwin, was certain that Roosevelt wanted to build up the Army Air Corps to fifty-five hundred planes for the sole purpose of being in a better position to aid Britain and France. Everyone knew, said Baldwin, that "no air threat of comparable magnitude can arise against the United States in the near future, or even against any part of the Western Hemisphere."[47]

And a Dartmouth College professor, L. D. Stilwell, testified at the Senate neutrality hearings that talk of Germany turning her guns on the United States was nothing but "plain fancy nonsense" spouted by overexcited jingoes; any power that managed to beat the mighty combination of Britain and France would be so worn out that it would need twenty years to recover. Stilwell ridiculed the very idea of an invasion of the United States, ranking it after an attack from Mars in credibility. "The United States," he declared, "is as safe as a kitten in its basket—entirely safe."[48]

Notwithstanding the comforting simile, it was clear that even as Stilwell was speaking, a large part of the American public was coming to share in the administration's apprehension that the United States might soon be anything but safe. A Gallup poll conducted at the end of April showed that a sizable majority (62 percent) felt that the security of the nation would be endangered by a totalitarian victory in Europe. At the same time, the number of Americans who would approve of arms sales to Britain and France in the event of war had increased from 34 percent before Munich to 57 percent.[49] Evidently, reports of Axis machinations to the south were having an effect on public opinion. So, too, were the statements made before the congressional neutrality hearings (there was one in the House, as well) by anti-embargo witnesses. For every Stilwell there were half a dozen articulate exponents of the position that if the United States was like a kitten in a basket, it was a basket that was being eyed expectantly by a nasty dog.

On 2 May 1939, an Argentine who taught Latin American culture at Sarah Lawrence reminded the Senate Foreign Relations Committee that even as he, David Efron, was standing before them, the Axis was stealthily advancing in the hemisphere, especially in those three crucial South American republics, Brazil, Argentina, and Chile. Perhaps there was some truth, Efron conceded, to the rumor that Hitler did not believe Latin America could be taken militarily; but that was immaterial, for the greatest danger was not invasion but internal subversion. (This was exactly what the JPC analysts had concluded a few weeks before.) Still, Efron thought it would be foolhardy to rule out an invasion, given that Franco, an Axis minion, had bases not too distant from the Western Hemisphere, in the Canary Islands, Ifni, and Spanish Guinea. What was happening in Spain, he added, was an object lesson for the American republics: Hitler and Mussolini were acting according to plan in backing Franco—a plan that "was all of a piece with their already extensive fascist penetration of Latin America."[50]

Efron was followed to the witness stand the next day by the vice-president of Georgetown University, the Reverend Edmund Walsh, who made all the senators uneasy by posing, in good Jesuitical fashion, a question that no one could answer: What do we do, given the nonintervention promises made by the administration at recent Pan-American conferences, if a Latin American republic invites in the Nazis? The dilemma was sharpened by the knowledge that the Monroe Doctrine could no longer be interpreted, as it had been earlier in the century, so as to sanction the invasion by the United States of a Latin American nation. The senators tried to wrestle this problem to the ground, but it was obviously beyond their strength that day. The hearing broke up on a depressing note. Hiram Johnson reminded his colleagues, Walsh, and the gallery spectators of recent unsettling events in Bolivia, where it seemed that the Nazi cause had just gained a new adherent in the person of dictator Germán Busch, who had announced he was converting his nation into a totalitarian republic. Germán Busch: the name alone was ominous.[51]

7

War in Europe,
Peace at Home?

Throughout the intensifying heat and humidity of the Washington spring of 1939, the White House continued its drive to get the nation's neutrality legislation revised. On 19 May, President Roosevelt again spelled out the consequences to the hemisphere of an Axis victory in Europe, this time telling a group of skeptical House leaders that there was at least an even chance that Britain and France, deprived of the opportunity to draw on American arms suppliers, would lose the war that the administration regarded as being almost inevitable. An Axis triumph would be attended by an easily predictable chain of events: the seizure of the British fleet; the strengthening of trade ties between Germany and Latin America; and the dispatching of Axis advisers to Latin general staffs. Assisted by Japan, the totalitarians would have a two-to-one naval superiority over the United States. "Therefore," Roosevelt concluded, "the temptation to them would always be to try another quick war with us, if we got rough about their South American penetration."[1]

Despite the president's efforts, America's neutrality laws would not be altered that summer; not until after the outbreak of war in September would Congress finally see fit to lift the embargo on arms sales to belligerents.[2] It would be wrong to see in the initial failure of the revision campaign incontrovertible evidence of congressional insensitivity to the plight of the European democracies, just as it would be wrong to assume that Congress was fundamentally more "isolationist" than the executive branch.[3] In truth, neither branch of government, by the summer of 1939, was contemplating a radical shift in American foreign policy. What can be said is that Congress was not convinced of the imminence of European war, while the White House was. To Congress, it was plain that the absence of war meant the absence of belliger-

130

ents, and without the legal stigma that attached to the status of belligerent, Britain and France would be perfectly free to continue purchasing weaponry from private American arms manufacturers.

It is also incorrect to imagine that the administration's attempt to reveal the existence of a Latin American security menace was a complete failure. Although there existed a large body of legislators who undoubtedly believed that the United States *was* as safe as Stilwell's kitten, it is nonetheless the case that a growing minority in Congress was beginning to sense a real peril to the Western Hemisphere. This does not mean, however, that this minority was ready to underwrite the survival of Britain and France; for even among those Americans who did perceive a threat to national security, wide circulation was given to the view that America could best be defended if it shunned Europe and redoubled its efforts to make the New World impregnable. Roosevelt himself was unwilling, after the war began, to tie the United States irreversibly to the fate of the European democracies—although, to be sure, a tiny minority of interventionists was urging him to make an immediate declaration of war. The removal of the arms embargo in November, a step away from isolationism, was accompanied by the solidification of the provisions requiring that cash-and-carry be the basis of all war trading, a move that has been called the "very epitome of American isolationism."[4] Not until the survival of Britain seemingly hung in the balance would the administration drop the policy of isolationism, which in large measure had been born of a repugnance of war, and take concrete actions that risked getting the nation into war. The repeal of the arms embargo was not such an action.

This, then, was the dilemma with which the president struggled during that spring and summer of 1939. On the one hand, he was as sincere as most Americans when he declared his abhorrence of war, and he was as ready as any to try to keep the country out of it; on the other hand, he saw more clearly than most the billowing clouds of danger gathering below the Rio Grande. All the potential for trouble in Latin America that Roosevelt had been warning about was just that, potential only, so long as Great Britain remained undefeated across the Atlantic. So long as the British were strong enough to handle Germany, the United States would have little to fear (by the summer of 1939, no one close to the president any longer doubted that Britain would fight if challenged).[5] If Britain could take care of Germany, the United States would not have to. But if Britain could not defeat Germany, the United States might not be able to. Roosevelt hoped to be able to solve the problem of sheltering the hemisphere from the furies of war while at the same time assisting in Hitler's defeat by allowing Britain and France access to the arms that, it was fervently hoped, would allow them to succeed in the coming conflict.

No one, of course, could be certain that this aid would be sufficient, but if it did not prove to be a decisive element in rectifying the European balance of power, the administration was not as yet willing to redress that balance through American military intervention. Having tried mediatory initiatives and pro-Allied neutrality, the White House could always fall back on Berle's first option and build an impregnable defense in the hemisphere. With the powers of Europe once again shambling off to Armageddon, the stability of Latin America became more important than ever to American policymakers. Indeed, it is quite likely that of all the regions of the world, none was of such importance to the continuation of the administration's policy of isolationism as the southern part of the Western Hemisphere.

Every chance he got, Franklin Roosevelt sought to emphasize the connection between Latin America and the retention of isolationist policy. His public lectures on the consequences for the New World of an Axis victory in the Old have been interpreted by many observers as audio-visual trickery designed to illustrate a different lesson, namely that the United States must join the European democracies in the fight against totalitarian evil. But the evidence is strong that Roosevelt really did believe what he was saying about the danger to the hemisphere. Not only in his public addresses, but also—and more importantly—in confidential conversations with important advisers, he showed himself to be a man with a keen interest in Latin American developments.

For instance, on the afternoon of 25 May he discussed the possible outbreak of war in Europe with Assistant Secretary of State Berle. As he had done on other occasions, Roosevelt assessed the chances of an Axis triumph at fifty-fifty. Should the worst happen, Berle could expect to see taking shape an unpleasant series of events, which the president, in a litany that was by no means novel for either himself or Berle, proceeded to detail: first, the seizure or neutralization of the British fleet; then, an intensified

German trade campaign in Latin America; ultimately, the infiltration of Axis advisers in Latin American military establishments.
"At the end of a very short time," Roosevelt continued, "we should
find ourselves surrounded by hostile states in this hemisphere."
Most likely the Japanese, "who always like to play with the big
boys," would join Germany and Italy in aggression, should the
United States resist the penetration of the hemisphere. The president pointed out that all this was only a possibility—"but a
possibility," noted Berle in his diary, "no far-sighted statesman
could afford to permit. His job was to make sure that that kind of
a possibility could not happen."[6]

These words weighed heavily on Berle, who was (in the ideological sense) the most isolationist member of Roosevelt's inner
circle of advisers. In late June, the assistant secretary recorded in
his diary a continued distrust of British imperialism, and a belief
that adjustments in favor of Germany would have to be made in
the Central European status quo, as a simple matter of historical
logic, if not of justice. At the same time, Berle realized that the
control of the Atlantic must remain with the British; for the moment it was lost, "we shall be meeting imperialistic schemes in
South and Central America, not on a paper basis, as we do now,
but backed up by extremely strong naval and military force." And
should this come to pass, the American way of life would be ended,
brought to a close by the imperatives of the garrison state.[7]

Although Roosevelt had Berle persuaded about the gravity of
the Axis challenge to the hemisphere, the same could not be said
about Congress. Not only did that body continue to refuse to lift
the arms embargo, but it rejected, in June, a measure that the
White House believed urgent for the cause of good relations with
the Latin Americans: a 500 million dollar credit (both short- and
long-term) to enable them to combat their acute financial difficulties. A principal theme of the congressional opposition to the
credits was that they represented a prodigal expenditure of tax-
payers' money on Latin "boondoggling."[8] The White House,
however, considered that 500 million dollars was just the first of
several measures designed to eliminate one of the biggest impedi-
ments facing the Good Neighbor Policy, the Latin Americans'
shortage of foreign exchange.

From Washington's point of view, the greatest danger stemming
from the Latin exchange shortage was that it made them more

likely to direct their trade toward European countries with similar exchange difficulties, especially Germany (but also Italy). The Axis economic challenge to the hemisphere was of the utmost importance to the White House, as revisionist historian William Appleman Williams has perceptively shown.[9] But notwithstanding the insightfulness of Williams's argument, I remain convinced that the president's concern was primarily with the military and political implications of Axis economic penetration. The Axis economic challenge was seen first and foremost as a political threat to the hemisphere, and only secondarily as a purely economic threat. And rightly so, for as Albert O. Hirschman has demonstrated, Germany was explicitly developing trade policies that enhanced its power capabilities.[10] If the United States had to choose its enemies on the basis of their purely economic competitiveness in Latin America, then it would have had ample cause to be opposing Britain, not Germany.[11]

Early in 1939 a Department of Commerce memorandum raised the point that unless the United States intervened economically below the Rio Grande, Latin America would become even more dependent on Germany and other European trading partners. The Commerce Department proposed a scheme whereby the United States would purchase the surplus agricultural production of several important Latin republics, and then resell this surplus to Europe. Should the scheme turn out to be a money-loser, the Commerce Department argued that the political gains would far outweigh the financial losses. "The effect of it would be to deprive Germany and Italy of the whip hand they now hold over those governments through their control of the export and import trade of those countries, and to eliminate them as major political factors and trouble makers in internal affairs there."[12]

The Commerce Department proposal was rejected as being politically impossible, but no one in the White House was overlooking the department's concern with the extensive inroads that Germany had been making in Latin America. The Reich's trade drive had begun in September 1934, under the aegis of Minister of Economics Hjalmar Schacht, the financial "wizard" who, as head of the Reichsbank, had been widely credited with extricating Germany from the monster inflation of late 1923.[13] In a world that had become chronically short of free exchange, Schacht believed that Germany's wisest course would be to copy the bilateral trade techniques that had been developed in recent years by Great Britain and other European states.[14]

On 24 September 1934, Schacht's "New Plan" went into effect. Over the next four years, Germany would conclude bilateral agreements of one sort or another with twenty-five nations, mostly in the Balkans and in Latin America. More than half of German trade by 1938 would be carried on with these twenty-five lands, with Latin America alone accounting for 15 percent of the Reich's total imports.[15] The Schacht plan depended on four major methods of steering trade into bilateral channels: clearing agreements, compensation agreements, payment agreements, and the use of the *askimark.*

Clearing agreements consisted in each of the trading partners establishing a special fund for the purpose of servicing their two-way commerce. Each state's importers would make their payments into the fund, and from it each state's exporters would receive their remuneration; accounts, handled on a bookkeeping basis that obviated the need to transfer funds from one state to the other, would be periodically balanced to keep imports in harmony with exports. Similar to clearing agreements, in that no transfers of currency were involved, were compensation agreements, which required that each lot of imports be "compensated" by a shipment of exports of equal value, thus making trade a de facto form of barter. A third aspect of the Schacht plan was the payment agreement (which Great Britain pioneered): one state would agree to set aside, for the purposes of purchases and debt service, most or all of the foreign exchange that it earned in trade with the other state, with the actual discharge of payments being left to international money markets. The askimark (an acronym for Auslander-Sonderkonto-fuer-Inlandszahlungen) was a special currency used only in external trade, spendable only in Germany, and even then only in ways specified by Berlin.[16]

It was this last arrangement in particular, the sui generis askimark system, that most bothered the Roosevelt policymakers. As a Commerce Department memorandum of early February 1939 observed, "there is a tendency to attribute all of our difficulties in meeting German competition to the use of the askimark." Although the memo went on to state that this was not in fact the case—American exporters simply being unable to "meet German competition on an economic basis"—it remained true that the administration contemplated with discomfiture the spread of askimark trading throughout Latin America.[17]

Here is how the askimark was employed. Germany would agree to purchase a Latin commodity, Brazilian coffee for instance, to be paid for not with the ordinary mark, but with the special askimark, an undervalued currency used for external transactions only.[18] Since it was trading with a depreciated mark, Berlin could afford to pay an attractive price for the coffee. But the price was deceptive, for unlike typical blocked currencies, the askimark could be used by its recipient only for the purchase of selected items, whose prices were fixed arbitrarily by Germany. Thus Berlin was able to recoup most of whatever loss it had incurred in offering the premium for the coffee originally.[19]

If the askimark system was no blessing at all to the Roosevelt administration, it was but a mixed one at best to the Latin Americans. To be sure, it did offer the prospect of a market for otherwise unsalable goods. As a leading Brazilian agriculturist, Olavo Egydio de Souza Aranha, explained in June 1936, "compensation marks are worth much more to us than ashes."[20] (He was alluding to the Brazilian government's program, begun in 1931, of burning coffee in order to halt the downward slide of prices.)[21] However, the cost of such a market was often steep; for not only would, say, Brazil find itself forced to purchase goods that in many instances it neither needed nor wanted, but it would sometimes discover to its chagrin that Germany had been dumping on the world market coffee that it had purchased from Brazil with askimarks, thereby earning free exchange at Brazil's expense.[22]

Brazil would sometimes find itself on the horns of another dilemma caused by askimark trading. Importation of German manufactured goods interfered with the market for native producers of the same items; yet to refuse to make the stipulated German purchases would have left the treasury stuck with a veritable mountain of unspendable currency, an obviously untenable financial situation.[23] A final drawback of the askimark system was that it tended to make Brazil, or any other Latin country, dependent economically—therefore, potentially, dependent politically—on Germany. Two Brazilian opponents of the Vargas regime, writing from exile in 1938, condemned their nation's trade link with Germany, not only because of the economic costs involved, but "because it binds Brazil to a fascist power that takes from it raw materials for its rearmament program. It is to be condemned by Brazilians because it is prejudicial to Brazil."[24]

Whatever the hidden costs to the German consumer,[25] and despite the obvious drawbacks to Latin America, it is plain that Germany made significant economic gains in the southern part of the hemisphere through its bilateral trade strategy. By 1938, it had become the market for 10.5 percent of all Latin exports, and it was supplying 17.1 percent of all Latin imports. In comparison, Great Britain accounted for 16.8 and 11.1 percent, respectively, of Latin exports and imports. This was a far cry from 1932, when Britain had absorbed 26.1 percent of Latin America's exports, and had furnished 14.3 percent of the area's imports; while Germany had been a market for 9 percent of Latin exports, and a supplier of only 7.3 percent of imports.[26]

In spite of the relative decline in its own exports to the other republics in the hemisphere, the United States was never in any real danger of being surpassed as the leading supplier of imports to Latin America, and officials in Washington knew this. Early in 1938, a top-level Treasury Department report had noted that Germany, despite all the impressive gains it had registered in the past half decade, still had a very long distance to cover if it hoped to overtake the United States, which had outsold the Reich in the Latin market by two and one-half times in 1937. Nevertheless, cautioned George Haas, author of the report and head of the Treasury Department's research division, the United States could not afford complacency, for Germany had made substantial headway in five states—Brazil, Mexico, Peru, Venezuela, and Chile—and had, with the last three nations, doubled her trade between 1928 and 1939.[27]

Admittedly, United States exports to Latin America were not of overwhelming magnitude, averaging between 500 and 600 million dollars yearly in the late 1930s. In fact, in 1935–36, American exports to all of Latin America were of lesser value than sales in the United Kingdom market alone. Nonetheless, for certain industries in the United States, sales to Latin America were very important. For example, in 1935 the Latin market took 54.1 percent of cotton-manufacturers exports, and 55.3 and 22 percent, respectively, of steel mill and automotive exports.[28] But even if the American economic stake in Latin America had been increased tenfold, it would not have altered the fundamental reality that underlay the administration's concern for the Latin nations, namely that they constituted the principal agency whereby a challenge could be mounted against the security of the United States itself.

A man who appreciated this reality was Bernard Baruch, who had been a fairly influential figure in the policy process during the First World War, but whose influence had greatly diminished by the late 1930s.[29] In the wake of the Mexican oil expropriation of March 1938, Baruch wrote the president that the Cárdenas government's action, legal though it might be, "brings near to our shores the questions or war, Nazism and Fascism." Baruch feared that the expropriation would both strengthen Mexico's trade relationships with the totalitarian powers and serve as an example for every other government in Latin America with a resource sector in foreign hands. This sequence of events, he hastened to add, would be extremely dangerous to the United States, for "not alone does this threaten American assets, but American markets and prestige south of the Rio Grande, *and above all, America itself.*"[30]

This was a point on which the president and his close advisers needed no prodding; however great may have been Baruch's anxiety, administration policymakers were miles ahead of the old man in anticipating a danger to the security of the United States. Roosevelt never seemed to tire of explaining the political and strategic consequences that would attend Germany's possible economic domination of parts of Latin America. At a meeting on 23 June 1939 with the Editors of Trade Publications, the president described how Hitler could get control over South America without violating the Monroe Doctrine in any overt way. Since Europe constituted the only market for important exporting nations like Argentina, the Fuehrer would have overbearing economic and political leverage should he defeat the European democracies. He would set the conditions of trade, paying for imports of food and raw materials with manufactured exports of his choosing. "It is," said Roosevelt, "a perfectly open and shut thing and, if you have the complete, physical power to do it, you win. Isn't that right? It sounds like a crazy picture, but it is perfectly obvious, it is so sensible."[31]

But it was not only German economic potential that troubled the administration by June 1939. In the middle of that month, the

Standing Liaison Committee (which had been set up in April 1938 to enable the State, War, and Navy Departments to coordinate their activities in respect to Latin America) was busily investigating a rash of "suspicious activities along the coasts of South America and Central America, within flying distance of the Panama Canal."[32] The White House was extremely nervous about anything that even remotely offered a menace to the Canal, the lifeline of American naval defense.[33] In the middle of June, when legislation designed to upgrade facilities in the Canal Zone became bogged down in the bureaucracy of the House, Roosevelt grew angry. He ordered his secretary of war, Harry Woodring, to get Speaker of the House William Bankhead and Majority Leader Sam Rayburn moving on the legislation, which would have provided funding for a new set of locks—locks that would have made the Canal less vulnerable to sabotage, if not to aerial bombardment as well. "I consider," he told Woodring, "the provision at the Panama Canal of all facilities necessary to insure the uninterrupted passage of our fleet from one ocean to the other is urgent. . . ."[34]

Apart from the special strategic difficulties associated with the fact that the Canal happened to be located in Latin America, that part of the hemisphere furnished additional cause for concern for political reasons. Over the past year and a half, several Latin states had begun to show distressing signs of friendliness toward the Axis powers and their system of governance. In June, it seemed as if Paraguay were about to be added to an unstable line of political dominoes that already included Argentina, Brazil, Chile, Uruguay, Peru, and Bolivia. On the first of the month, the president's former law partner, Basil O'Connor, drew his attention to a *New York Times* report (filed by *bête noire* John White) that hinted darkly at Germany's increasing economic leverage over Paraguay—leverage that could soon have great political significance. O'Connor wanted Roosevelt, who would shortly be receiving a visit from the Paraguayan president-elect (and hero of the Chaco War), Gen. Felix Estigarribia, to keep Paraguay independent.[35]

Roosevelt was more concerned with keeping Paraguay out of the Axis camp than with preserving whatever freedom of maneuver it might have; and when he welcomed the Brazilian chief of staff, Gen. Pedro Aurelio de Góes Monteiro, to Washington on 7

July, he suggested that Rio might consider taking Paraguay into its sphere of influence, in the interests of stability in the hemisphere. The president made this suggestion in hopes of persuading Góes, and through him Vargas, to continue demonstrating the kind of *froideur* Rio had been showing Berlin since the May 1938 Integralista putsch. If making the Guaraní republic a virtual satellite of Brazil would keep it out of German clutches, then so be it. For the important thing, said Roosevelt to his guest, was to keep Hitler on the other side of the Atlantic. And the best guarantee of that would be if Britain and France firmed up their resolve to resist the German dictator, for "if Hitler succeeded in subjugating the Old World, he would immediately turn against the New with all the weight of his armed forces, in hopes of dominating the Americas."[36]

In contemplating the political situation to the south, American policymakers could take some (minimal) consolation from the fact that, by mid-1939, the most disturbing news had been coming from the republics that were farthest away from the United States. This situation began to change in late July, however; for according to the American naval attaché in Mexico, not even that country was safe from Axis depredation. Comdr. W. M. Dillon had discovered—from an Italian consul in Mazatlán who Dillon said had had too much to drink one evening—that Germany planned to make Mexico the keystone of a reconstructed Spanish Empire, under the nominal tutelage of Franco, but actually controlled by Hitler.[37] It was becoming easier, by this time, for Americans to imagine that what was going on in Spain might indeed have serious implications for the Western Hemisphere. As one writer in *Foreign Affairs* explained it, it was not necessary to establish that Franco was in fact a puppet of the Axis, for even if he was a truly independent tyrant he would still be seeking conquests in the New World. With European expansion prospects foreclosed by the imperialistic aims of his German and Italian tutors, Franco would be forced to turn abroad, and "no matter which policy he pursues in the end, it will be at the expense of Pan Americanism, for the reconquest of the Empire must always be the goal of Spanish Fascism."[38]

Given his perception of an Axis menace to the hemisphere, and in light of the numerous troubling incidents that had taken place in Latin America in the past few years, it came as no surprise that the president should speak to the urgency of sheltering the New World from strife when, on 3 September 1939, the suspense finally ended and the European powers went to war. In a fireside chat delivered on the first evening of war, Roosevelt promised that he would take the strongest measures to safeguard the security of the Western Hemisphere. At the same time, he reaffirmed his determination to keep the United States out of the war. The safety of the nation, he declared, "is and will be bound up with the safety of the Western Hemisphere and of the seas adjacent thereto. We seek to keep war from our own firesides by keeping war from the Americas." The job would not be easy, nor would it be possible to remain neutral in spirit. Alluding to Woodrow Wilson's attempt to encourage impartiality in 1914, Roosevelt pledged that "this nation will remain a neutral nation, but I cannot ask that every American remain neutral in thought as well. . . . I have said not once, but many times, that I have seen war and that I hate war. I say that again and again. . . . As long as it remains within my power to prevent, there will be no black-out of peace in the United States."[39]

Europe was, or soon would be, in flames, and that was a tragedy. But at least the White House could draw encouragement from the fact that, this time, Britain and France were most definitely resisting Hitler. Even the American public began to sense, after the first few weeks of fighting had passed, that perhaps the Nazi menace could be disposed of once and for all, without spilling any American blood.[40] Roosevelt's friend, Josephus Daniels, voiced the prevailing national hope that both isolation from war *and* the defeat of Hitler could be achieved. In a letter to the president on 12 September, Daniels declared himself to be "100 percent against our participation in this criminal war, but, of course, I trust that Europe will be delivered from totalitarian governments and the scourge of force." In any case, he concluded, the Western Hemisphere would be "vaccinated against the European war miasma."[41]

Charles Beard was hoping for the same things. In a pamphlet written in the middle of September, the isolationist historian applauded Roosevelt's promise to keep the hemisphere out of war. But when it came to keeping war out of the hemisphere, Beard had some thoughts of his own. He believed that it was "sheer folly to go into hysterics and double military and naval expenditures on the rumor that Hitler or Mussolini is about to seize

Brazil, or that the Japanese are building gun emplacements in Costa Rica."[42] Of course, by this juncture Roosevelt was not paying too much attention to anything that his nemesis, Beard, was writing; but the president behaved, nonetheless, as if he too were convinced that the start of the European war had eliminated, or at least greatly reduced, the danger of German penetration in Latin America. When, for example, he decided in September to strengthen the army and navy, he did not even consider it necessary to bring both services up to the rather low personnel ceiling set by Congress—280,000 men for the army, 180,000 for the navy.[43] Instead, as he explained to the press on 8 September, Roosevelt was seeking to "fill in the chinks, enough men to man certain defenses such as the Panama Canal, enough men to Puerto Rico, enough men to fill up certain arms of the service. . . ."[44]

In a manuscript completed just as Hitler was disposing of Poland, Thomas Russell Ybarra captured the prevailing American confidence that things were looking up in the New World. Ybarra wanted to assess the impact of the European war on the future security of the Western Hemisphere; and although there was no way to guarantee that Germany would not, in the coming years, resurface as a political and military menace to Latin America, it could safely be said that for the moment the Reich would be forced to confine its activities in Latin America to the economic sphere. Ybarra's *America Faces South* was, to say the least, much more soothing than Carleton Beals's *Coming Struggle for Latin America* had been the year before.[45]

But, by the summer of 1940, it would be Beals who would have the last word on the question of an Axis menace to the hemisphere. Already, in September, there were some presidential advisers who were beginning to have disquieting second thoughts about the new European war and its implications for the New World. To be sure, one *could* muster sufficient evidence that would all but prove the inevitability of an Allied triumph. The problem was that evidence could be found to "prove" the contrary as well. As always, the alleged facts contained enough ambiguity to allow of interpretation in any variety of ways, more or less at the pleasure of the person doing the interpreting. And when that person was an influential presidential adviser like Assistant Secretary of State Berle, the results could be interesting.

The day after London and Paris issued their declarations of war,

Berle engaged in some searching geopolitical calculus, and arrived at the disturbing deduction that "we cannot . . . count on a military victory of Britain, France, and Poland." Assuming the worst, Berle reasoned that the administration would then have to make a very hard decision: either enter the war to preserve these "outlying defense posts"; or cut them loose, triple the U.S. Navy, and get ready to meet the onslaught of a power-mad "Russo-German Europe" somewhere in the middle of the Atlantic Ocean. Rather than advocate American military involvement in Europe, Berle preferred his second option of meeting the totalitarians in mid-ocean. He recognized that this was perhaps a "brutal" recommendation, but he defended it on the grounds that it was based squarely on a "consideration of national interest."[46]

Berle was not hallucinating when he envisioned the Soviet Union joining Germany in a scheme to conquer the world. The Russo-German Pact of 23 August 1939 took everyone in the West by surprise, all the more so because it was made between two states who held such passionate hatred toward each other. The assistant secretary was far from being the only policymaker to assume that if Hitler and Stalin could suddenly agree to forget their mutual loathing, they were quite capable of pulling in harness against the fragile pillars of world peace. Thus, when the Russians, too, invaded Poland (in mid-September), Berle's worst fears seemed to be materializing: the world now had before it the prospect of a German-Russian division of the Eurasian landmass, "from Manchuria to the Rhine"—a dominion of such expanse that it would be doubtful if the West could ever liberate it.

Glumly, Berle noted that the United States had either to aid the Allies in this massive and uncertain liberation effort—a thought that he did not find appealing—or else retreat to the Western Hemisphere behind a strong naval defense line. Neither alternative was promising, "for the next phase [of digging in behind the Atlantic barrier] is simply this: the Western world is besieged on the two Americas; and the rest of my life, or at least most of it, will be spent trying to defend various parts of this world from the economic, military and propaganda attempts to establish domination over it."[47]

On the evening of 19 September, Berle went over to the White House to discuss foreign policy with a "very sleepy" Roosevelt, who agreed that Hitler and Stalin would "keep on going while the going was good." A drive to the west could be expected, the ultimate aim of which, both men knew, would be the acquisition of bases on the shores of the Atlantic and on certain Atlantic islands, probably the Azores and the Cape Verdes.[48] There was no doubt in the mind of either man why Germany wanted these bases. As Berle put it a few days later, "when the German-Russian propaganda battery gets started in Latin America, we shall be in for the fight of our lives to prevent the continental solidarity from disintegrating; after which, one presumes, that unless the American Navy is brought into action some of these countries will be ripped up and taken over by the methods now familiar in the Balkan countries."[49]

On the afternoon of 20 September, Berle and Roosevelt continued the conversation they had begun the previous evening at the latter's bedside. They were joined by presidential speechwriter Samuel Rosenman and Secretary of State Hull. Hull, who had his eye on the 1940 Democratic nomination for president, wanted Roosevelt to issue a public declaration that, no matter what happened in Europe, the United States would never declare war. For a moment the room was, in Berle's words, a tomb of "dead silence," a stillness that was broken only when the president turned and asked Hull, "Can you guarantee that? Can I guarantee that?" The answer, obviously, was no. No one present could guarantee much of anything under current international conditions. "Having in mind the discussion of the night before," recorded Berle, "in which the president had indicated that there could be no question of our going to war unless the sweep of German arms finally indicated the establishment of a naval base in the Atlantic islands, say the Azores, there was not much question what was in the president's mind, or anyone else's." No statement such as Hull wanted could be made. All the White House could do was adhere to the position that "until the Atlantic line is seriously threatened or crossed, we will not go to war. . . ."[50]

The next day, 21 September, Roosevelt appeared before a joint session of Congress to ask that the arms embargo be revoked, so that the United States, for the sake of its own security, might supply Britain and France with the arms they would need to keep Hitler from reaching the "Atlantic line." Once again, the president underscored his firm desire to keep the nation at peace; once again, he stressed his determination to keep the hemisphere out

of the clutches of the totalitarians. To the legislators and spectators who crowded into the House chamber to hear him, Roosevelt explained the awesome responsibility that had devolved on
the nations of the New World. "Destiny first made us, with our
sister nations on this hemisphere, joint heirs of European culture.
Fate seems now to compel us to assume the task of helping to
maintain in the western world a citadel wherein that civilization may be kept alive. The peace, the integrity, and the safety of
the Americas—these must be kept firm and serene."[51]

To maintain the peace, integrity, and safety of the hemisphere,
the State Department was, even as the president was addressing
Congress, putting the finishing touches on preparations for the
first gathering ever of the foreign ministers of the New World
republics—a gathering that would convene, in two days, at Panama.

8

"Fortunately, Our National Safety Is Not at Stake"

Shortly after the news of the German invasion of Poland reached Washington—news that could only mean one thing, a general European war—the Roosevelt policymakers began work on the problem of keeping the hemisphere isolated from the conflict. Thanks to the groundwork that had been laid at Buenos Aires and Lima, the administration could avail itself of a mechanism to fashion an inter-American response to the events in Europe. Accordingly, Under Secretary of State Sumner Welles busied himself that first day of September in drafting messages to leaders throughout Latin America, requesting that in compliance with commitments made at the 1936 and 1938 conferences the foreign ministers of republics in the hemisphere assemble at Panama in three weeks. This would be the first time that the White House would send a delegation to an important hemisphere meeting without Secretary of State Cordell Hull at its head. Ironically, it was not the U.S. "foreign minister" but Hull's subordinate (and nemesis) Welles who would be making this trip.[1]

This would also be the first time in recent years that American statesmen could attend a conference without having to worry about Argentina. Perhaps because they knew that Hull would not be at Panama, the Argentines speedily responded to Welles's cable notifying them of the consultative session. They would be at Panama, but in keeping with their desire never to be outdone by the United States at anything, they too would send a diplomatic subaltern along as head of their delegation. Representing Argentina would be Leopoldo Melo, who was instructed by his chief, Foreign Minister José María Cantilo, to uphold the nation's traditional policies of freedom of the seas and of no political or military commitments to anyone. Cantilo's decision to absent himself from Panama turned out to be a blessing for the Americans, since

146

Melo was, as one historian has written, "unwilling to play the traditional Argentine prima donna, . . . [and] worked hand in glove" with Welles in the formulation of a plan for the preservation of security in the hemisphere.[2]

That the two hemisphere rivals displayed an unusual ability to cooperate was not due to any angelic or otherwise placatory qualities of Melo. Rather, it was the rare coinciding of American and Argentine interests that made Sumner Welles's job infinitely easier than similar assignments had ever been for Hull. Unlike Cantilo at Lima, Melo was on this occasion acting in behalf of a nation that was, in the words of an American newsman, "thoroughly scared" by the prospect of Berlin carving out an empire at the expense of Latin republics like itself.[3] But *Time's* Charles Wertenbaker was not the only observer to notice the changed Argentine position on unity in the hemisphere. The German chargé d'affaires in Buenos Aires, Otto Meynen, also remarked the change, and blamed it on Washington's anti-Axis propaganda offensive of the past year. "One frequently encounters here," he wrote the Wilhelmstrasse on 28 September, "the foolish but accepted notion that expansionist ambitions would make Germany a territorial and general threat to South America after the victorious conclusion of the war." Only a handful of "intellectuals" really comprehended that the Reich had completely innocent aims, but fortunately, said Meynen, this small group was extremely influential in business and military circles.[4]

The American military attaché in Buenos Aires, Col. Lester Baker, reported in September that Argentine public opinion was solidly against the Axis. Movie audiences were hissing newsreel images of Hitler and Mussolini, cheering those of Roosevelt and King George. And one could even detect in Argentina an anti-Nazi pulse running through the "better class" of the German community itself.[5] Although some German diplomats in Latin America understood that Latin opinion was swinging against Germany, in Berlin policymakers had not yet realized that at the upcoming Panama conference they could no longer count on the usual Argentine opposition to the United States. On 17 September the Wilhelmstrasse vainly cabled its diplomats in South America, especially those in Argentina, Brazil, and Chile (the so-called ABC powers), to take action designed to stir up the latent anti-Americanism of Latin policymakers and opinion leaders.[6] Ber-

lin could not understand that tactics that had achieved some results the year before at Lima were not going to work at Panama.
In the first place, the spirit of harmony in Panama was, as Sumner Welles put it, "so strong as to be palpable." No fundamental
differences would arise to taint this spirit, which Welles argued
was bolstered by the realization on the part of all the delegates
that an Axis victory would signal "inevitable peril to the integrity of the hemisphere."[7] In the second place, Berlin misunder-
stood American intentions: the United States did not attempt,
as Germany feared it would, to align the republics of the hemisphere in a pro-Allied bloc. The central element in the package
that Welles brought to Panama was the unique proposal that the
American republics create a security zone of vast dimensions, gir-
dling almost the entire New World, within which *all* belligerent
acts would be proscribed.

The conception of a maritime security belt circling the nonbel-
ligerent states of the hemisphere (Canada had gone to war on 10
September) apparently resulted from a discussion that Roosevelt
had had with Adolf Berle, shortly before the Germans marched
into Poland. The president believed that by cordoning off the New
World (south of Canada), the United States could achieve two vital purposes: it could practically ensure the isolation of the hemisphere from acts of war; and it could accord assistance to the naval
powers, Britain and France, who would find themselves spared
the job of patrolling endless stretches of the western Atlantic.
Roosevelt anticipated that Germany would refuse to honor the
demarcation line, which he intended to draw somewhere in the
middle of the ocean, and which would be enforced by the United
States Navy, aided by such Latin nations as were capable of ren-
dering assistance. Berle liked the idea, not because of the incidental help that it would give to the Allies, who—it was wrongly
presumed—would respect the security zone, but because of its
insulating qualities. "It does really change the status of the New
World," the assistant secretary exulted, as he hailed the birth of
a "kind of Pax Americana."[8]

Roosevelt's plan was enthusiastically adopted at the foreign
ministers conference, under the impressive title, the Declaration
of Panama. In voting to erect an oceanic barrier to war, of an ap-
proximate average breadth of three hundred miles from hemispheric shorelines, the American republics were arrogating to

themselves a novel "right" of neutrals: the "inherent right . . . to have those waters adjacent to the American Continent, which they regard as of primary concern and direct utility in their relations, free from the commission of any hostile act by any non-American belligerent nation, whether such hostile act be attempted or made from land, sea, or air."[9]

A British scholar has remarked of the foreign ministers' action that it was "creating American international law with a vengeance."[10] Cordell Hull thought so, and did not hesitate to point out to Roosevelt that the American republics had no "inherent right" to do much of anything in their offshore waters, let alone forbidding warring nations to ply their arts hundreds of miles out to sea. The secretary, always a stickler for international law, objected to the precedent-shattering scheme for three reasons: the neutrality zone was unenforceable, because there was too much ocean and too little navy; it was likely to involve the United States in the war, through an incident at sea; and it had absolutely no legal standing.[11]

Hull had a further grievance against the security zone, although this one he kept to himself: it had been, if not the child, then at least the nephew of his bitter foe Welles, with whom the president had worked out the details of the proposal.[12] So upset was Hull with the Declaration of Panama that he was seriously considering airing his grievances in public. At least this is what he told Berle on 8 October, adding that he was prepared to accept the consequences, which as both men knew would probably entail his resignation. The secretary might have been sincere about his willingness to risk resignation, but he soon began to have second thoughts about the wisdom of breaching administration unity, so he let the matter drop quietly.[13]

Hull was not the only one to disapprove of the neutrality zone, which some had taken to calling the "Pan American chastity belt." In truth, the zone had no shortage of opponents. Conservative columnist John T. Flynn saw in it further evidence of the president's imperialistic pretensions—pretensions that had been growing since Roosevelt's tenure as assistant secretary of the navy during the World War, when he had campaigned for an enlarged fleet so that the United States might be able to extend its influence in a proper great-power manner.[14] To support his claim that the security belt notion had had a lengthy gestation period, Flynn cited

an article Roosevelt had written for *Scientific American* in early
1914, where the young navalist had commented that in time of
war the United States could not "be content like the turtle to
withdraw into our own shell and see an enemy supersede us in
every outlying part. . . ."[15]

Men who were charged with protecting those "outlying parts"
were stunned by the magnitude of the task conferred upon them
by the Declaration of Panama. To be sure, the Pacific side of the
zone could safely be left untended, but the Atlantic side was a
different matter altogether. To patrol watery realms that in some
places extended halfway to Africa, the navy had only the over-
worked Atlantic Squadron, consisting of four old battleships, four
heavy cruisers, one aircraft carrier, and a squadron of destroyers.
And while the average breadth of the zone was three hundred
miles, at places—for example, off the coast of Maryland—the
navy would have to patrol nearly a thousand miles out into
the Atlantic.[16]

The European belligerents had the same disdain for the zone
as did the United States Navy. Unable to agree on anything else,
the warring states were unanimous in refusing to respect the security belt, fearful that the other side would do likewise. Despite
the suggestion of its minister to Panama that Germany steal a
march on the Allies by announcing that it would obey the Panama resolution, the Wilhelmstrasse decided, after weeks of de-
liberation, that the "creation of a closed zone is unfavorable to
us on technical and naval grounds, but we do not wish to draw
upon ourselves the odium of lifting it. It is rather in our interest
to let England and France take the lead."[17]

This the Allies refused to do. As unwilling as Germany to accept the obloquy of ignoring such a solemn and unanimous edict
as the Declaration of Panama, they joined their foe in an Alphonse
and Gaston act of "after you." On 5 October the first lord of the
admiralty, Winston Churchill, cabled the president that, in principle, he "liked the idea" of outlawing war from seas that washed
American shores. Now, if only Roosevelt could get all the other
belligerents to agree to accept the security zone, His Majesty's
government would be delighted to follow suit, on the condition
that the United States make a strenuous effort to patrol for violations. "We should have great difficulty in accepting a zone which
was only policed by some weak neutral," said Churchill. "The

more American ships cruising along the South American coast the better. . . ."[18]

The ball was back where it had started in August, in the president's court, and as he was unable to persuade all the belligerents to abandon the principle of freedom of the seas that was so dear to the United States, the Pan-American security zone was left standing as an eloquent but empty tribute to the hemisphere republics' desire for isolation from war—and to the futility of lofty aspirations unsupported by power. For a short time, this latter point was masked by the reluctance of the warring powers, especially Germany, to allow themselves to be caught in the act of scoffing at the "law" of the hemisphere. But the mask fell off in December 1939, when the Battle of the Rio de la Plata brought into crisp focus the shortcomings of the Declaration of Panama.[19]

Welles would later remark that the declaration had been the last throe of a dying era. Not only was it the final, and perhaps the most forceful, American attempt to isolate the Western Hemisphere from war, but, said Welles, it was, "I trust, the last official expression of the belief in this modern world that the responsibility for the repression of war can be other than universal."[20] It would take the shock of the fall of France and the near defeat of Britain to drive this lesson home, not only to the American public and their elected representatives, but to the administration's top policymakers as well. For in the early months of the war, Welles himself was of a completely different mind on the subject of extrahemispheric collective security. On the afternoon of 25 September, at Panama, he sang a paean for the concept of hemispheric isolation, telling his fellow delegates that it was their duty to assert the "inalienable right of the American Republics to protect themselves, as far as conditions in this modern world make it possible, from the dangers and the repercussions of a war which has broken out thousands of miles from their shores and in which they are not involved."[21]

Despite the tenor of Welles's speech, which, as one scholar has rightly remarked, "smacked of pure isolationism,"[22] the Panama conference was not solely devoted to the search for a way to seal off the hemisphere from the shocks of European war. Also on the agenda was the nettlesome problem of how to ensure that the sorts of economic difficulties suffered by many Latin countries in the First World War would not recur in the Second. Welles promised that the United States would not disappoint its less fortunate neighbors, whose substantial trade ties with Europe rendered them vulnerable to the vicissitudes of war. Transportation bottlenecks, short-term exchange problems, even the chronic dilemma of competing hemisphere economies—all these tangles, asserted Welles, could be smoothed without resorting to measures that would subvert the structure of liberalized trade that had been the hallmark of American economic diplomacy since 1934.[23]

Within a half year or so, hardly anyone in the administration, apart from Cordell Hull, would be extolling the virtues of multilateral liberalized trade as an answer to the economic problems associated with the war. But at Panama it was still possible for Welles to preach the doctrine of reciprocal trade agreements as the best defense for the economy of the hemisphere. "To the extent," he said, "that we sustain bases of commercial policy that are universal in character and leave trade open to all countries on substantially the same terms, and to the extent that our commerce is not dictated by special agreements of an exclusive character, to that extent can we insure that our political independence cannot be subjugated to alien political systems operating through commercial channels."[24] Welles's homages to free trade, coming as they did at a time when Germany was making strides with its bilateral trading system, raised the hackles of Nicholas John Spykman, who termed them "either an irrelevant expression of admiration for a dead past or an inspired formula for a suicide pact."[25]

In the event, not much in the way of concrete results came from the Panama conference. The session did lead to the formation of the Inter-American Financial and Economic Advisory Committee, which commenced its duties in November.[26] It also demonstrated that the inter-American system was capable of displaying a higher degree of solidarity than most observers thought possible, given the rifts of the previous meetings. But few Americans were unaware of the real basis for this newfound solidarity; in Duncan Aikman's words, Panama revealed that "Uncle Sam was thus due for a good deal of affectionate, and not wholly insincere whisker-stroking if only because he had suddenly become the only banker and grocer on his street."[27]

Welles's categorization of the Panama conference as the last stand for the administration's policy of isolation was inaccurate.

More to the point, it was a prochronism; for the Roosevelt White House would need the jolt of a cataclysm in Europe, and an apprehended one in Latin America, to convince it of the logic of extending military aid to Great Britain—aid that might even involve the United States itself in the war. Insofar as public opinion was concerned, Panama came at a moment when most Americans were beginning to draw, after a brief period of anxiety following the outbreak of war in September, their second and final isolationist breath. Congress, too, was daily becoming more confident that this war need not concern the United States— although, it scarcely needs saying, the sympathies of the overwhelming majority of legislators were with the Allies. In a Senate debate over neutrality revision, on 10 October, Henry Cabot Lodge, Jr., of Massachusetts dismissed as "slim indeed" the chances of Great Britain and France losing to Hitler, adding that "even if Germany were victorious and desired to conquer the United States, she could never do so." On one point the Bay State Republican was firm: "No European power can occupy or vanquish the United States, and it is fanciful to suggest that it could. Fortunately, our national safety is not at stake."[28]

Lodge may have been amiss in this judgment, but at least his view of American security was significantly more realistic than one advanced by a supporter of revision, Sen. Matthew M. Neely of West Virginia, who actually declared that unless Hitler were halted in Europe by the Allies, he would transform Canada into an "armed camp of Hitlerites, with a Siegfried line on our northern border from ocean to ocean. . . ." Should this happen, said Neely, "listen for his warning that he intends to set up Sudeten areas for those of German blood in Milwaukee, and St. Louis, and San Francisco, and New York."[29] It is assumed, charitably, that the West Virginia Democrat was invoking senatorial license with his lurid prognosis. At any rate, it is obvious that no one close to the president, and certainly not Roosevelt himself, ever imagined that America's security could be menaced in quite this manner.[30] Instead, top policymakers were nervously looking south, where they knew the real danger lurked. At the end of the war's first month, the FBI reported the presence in Mexico of 250 Nazi pilots—pilots who, should the United States go to war against Germany, would have at their disposal twenty-five bombers with which to raid cities in the southern United States. Furthermore,

stated this same FBI report, the Mexican government was believed
to have made a secret agreement to supply Germany's petroleum
needs throughout the war, for which it would be awarded British
Honduras when the time came to divide the spoils of conquest.
The FBI, the true nervous Nelly of the American intelligence
network, also feared that eight Nazi submarines were operating
out of the port of Vera Cruz, on Mexico's east coast.[31]

The American people, public opinion polls reveal, were never
as confident as Henry Cabot Lodge, Jr., that America was totally
safe; neither were they as worried as J. Edgar Hoover that the enemy was indeed at the gates. In October 1939, a time when the
congressional debate on the arms embargo was raging and, by way
of contrast, the fighting in Europe was abating, leading barome-
ters of opinion showed that 90 percent of the nation believed in
the inevitability of a German defeat.[32] This percentage had remained essentially unchanged from the year before, and it revealed
nothing so much as the appalling ignorance of the American public in respect of changing strategic realities in Europe. For if Americans could have eavesdropped on a conversation that had recently
taken place in Paris, they would have been far from optimistic.
In early September the French finance minister, Paul Reynaud,
had learned to his horror, after meeting one of France's principal
aircraft manufacturers and touring his factory, that the nation's
aviation industry was tragically unprepared for wartime production. Reynaud conveyed this shattering discovery to the man he
would succeed as premier, telling an incredulous Edouard Dala-
dier to "get into your car and see for yourself. We're going to lose
the war."[33]

Paradoxically, at the very same time they were forecasting
Hitler's eventual downfall, Americans were believing nonetheless that should the unexpected transpire and Germay win in
Europe, it would soon turn against the United States and its
neighbors. Significantly, 72 percent of the public would support
the use of American force against any German incursion within
fifteen hundred miles of the Panama Canal; and over half (53
percent) would fight to repel an invasion of Brazil, Chile, or any
other major South American land. [34] It was clear from the polls
that Americans were not averse to the thought of fighting Germany; they were just not willing to fight for or in Europe. As that
continent settled into what Sen. William Borah dubbed the "Phony

War," public confidence in an Allied victory increased. So, however, did public reluctance to assist the Allies in any significant way. In October, *Fortune* had discovered that 36.7 percent would support Britain and France, through either material aid or outright American participation in the war. But by December, this figure had shrunk to 26.1 percent, while by the same month the percentage of those favoring a strict neutrality had risen from 54 in October to 67.4. Gallup, also in December, found that nearly half the nation (47 percent) considered "keeping out of war" to be the single most important problem confronting the United States.[35]

Germany could not fail to draw a logical inference from such figures as these: the United States must be reassured (again) that the Reich would continue to respect the Monroe Doctrine. Foreign Minister Joachim von Ribbentrop sought to supply some reassurance in late October, when he said at Danzig that "only a pathological imagination could imagine points of conflict or opposition between [Germany] and the United States."[36] Berlin was encouraged, but misled, by overly optimistic (that is, blatantly incorrect) observations of its military attaché in Washington, Gen. Friedrich Boetticher, who professed to detect widespread pro-German sentiment among the United States Army's high command. "The general staff," he cabled on 1 December, "still has understanding for Germany and her conduct of the war." Despite this, Boetticher warned, the United States would enter the war "if it considers that the Western Hemisphere is threatened."[37]

Neither Ribbentrop nor Boetticher really understood Americans. Notwithstanding German disclaimers of aggressive intentions, civilian and military decision makers in Washington persisted in brooding over an Axis threat to the hemisphere—even though it was generally conceded that, pending the outcome of the war, the menace to Latin America could be considered to be in a suspended state. Even so, Latin watchers in the United States had no reason to let themselves become too relaxed. On 7 December, two years to the day before the bombing of Pearl Harbor, the Standing Liaison Committee met to discuss a matter that Welles held to be of "considerable importance," a report that suspicious radio signals had been detected emanating from southern Mexico, not too distant from the Panama Canal.[38] And, in a suspended state or not, American security nerves were not soothed by a mem-

orandum from the army's War Plans Division warning that both
Germany and Japan had the capability to bomb targets in the
hemisphere—Germany from air bases across from Natal (in northeastern Brazil), and Japan from any of her eight aircraft carriers.[39]

But it was not the subterfuge of Axis minions in Latin America, or even Axis war potential there, that warranted headlines
throughout the hemisphere in December 1939; something far
more dramatic—if less damaging to American security—was taking place off the coast of Uruguay. The dragons of war were dar-
ing to belch their smoke and fumes into the pristine atmosphere
of the Pan-American security zone. During the early morning of
13 December, a trio of British cruisers spotted the German pocket
battleship *Graf Spee* some three hundred miles off Montevideo.
For more than an hour the four ships were locked in combat, the
smaller British vessels (the *Achilles,*, the *Ajax,* and the *Exeter)*
reeling under the salvoes of the German commerce raider, but
giving, withal, almost as good as they got. When the cruisers finally broke off the action, the badly damaged *Graf Spee* made for
the safety of Montevideo harbor, where it became bottled up by
British warships (including the *Achilles* and the *Ajax).* According to the terms of the Hague Convention of 1907, a belligerent
man-of-war was only entitled to stay in a neutral port for twenty-
four hours, unless it had sustained damage, in which event it
would be up to the neutral government—buffeted of course by
strong diplomatic pressure from both belligerents—to decide what
repairs were necessary and how long the ship could remain in port.
In this case, Uruguay gave Capt. Hans Langsdorff seventy-two
hours to leave Montevideo.

Langsdorff did not want to leave. He had been monitoring British radio messages that stated, quite falsely so as to deceive the
Germans, that the Royal Navy had no fewer than five ships lying
in wait at the mouth of the Rio de la Plata estuary: the carrier
Ark Royal, the battle cruiser *Renown,* and the cruisers *Exeter,*
Achilles, and *Ajax.* In reality, the British had only the latter two
cruisers and a third, the *Cumberland,* ready to intercept the
Graf Spee. Langsdorff, thinking himself to be hopelessly out-
numbered, and not prepared to squander the lives of his crew,
scuttled his ship on 17 December, upon the expiration of his port
stay. Following the scuttling, the crew members were taken to
Buenos Aires where, instead of receiving the heroes' welcome that

they expected for their valiant struggle, they were interned. The unfortunate Langsdorff was publicly ridiculed as a coward. Disconsolate, he wrote to his wife, parents, and the German ambassador in Buenos Aires, and then took his life with a bullet to the head.[40]

By the time the din of battle had subsided, it was apparent that more than just the *Graf Spee* had been eliminated. The Pan-American security zone was also a casualty of the fray. A Panamanian protest over the security zone's violation, made shortly after the fighting had ended, was categorically rejected by the belligerents, who insisted that they would not abandon freedom of the seas unless each could be certain that the enemy would do the same. Winston Churchill reminded Roosevelt that it was as much in the interests of the United States as of Great Britain that German commerce raiders be cleared from the high seas. "If we should break under the load," the admiralty lord cabled, sounding a theme to which the president was very responsive, "South American republics would soon have worse worries than the sound of one day's distant seaward cannonade. And you also, sir, in quite a short time, would have more direct cares."[41]

The demise of the feckless security zone did not cause Roosevelt much anguish. And it positively delighted some men in Washington. In the aftermath of the battle, Sen. Robert Taft of Ohio denounced the zone as a "joke," which, because it was likely to involve the United States in the war, was "perfectly indefensible and ridiculous."[42] A satisfied Cordell Hull suggested that the United States might yet salvage something from the wreckage by drastically restricting the scope of the Declaration of Panama. Instead of trying to guarantee that no fighting whatsoever would take place within the zone—a guarantee that Hull thought would take four fleets to uphold—why not simply proscribe only those belligerent actions that patently interfered with the rights of neutrals?[43]

Nothing ever came of Hull's suggestion, partly because he refused to press the issue with Roosevelt, but mainly because of the relative calm that prevailed in the Atlantic after the drama off Montevideo. The cessation of combat everywhere in Europe but Finland (which was invaded by the Soviet Union in December) seemed to bode a mediated settlement of the war. British, French, Americans—all were lulled into a mood of relative tranquility,

and the latter especially were growing hopeful that the great conflagration everyone had been dreading for well over two years
might never start. France was quite safe behind the Maginot Line,
Britain had the Channel, and the United States was protected by
an entire ocean. As 1939 gave way to 1940, it was becoming much
more difficult for the American public to imagine any real dangers to their security. The *New York Times* welcomed in the New
Year by affirming its belief in the possibility of a militarily isolated (and protected) United States. "If there were no other continents besides the two Americas," said a *Times* editorial, "we could
sleep quietly and work and play hopefully."[44] The popular mood
had indeed shifted in just one year.

In top government circles, on the other hand, optimism was
less in evidence. For the president especially, the frightening potential of a Russo-German tandem—however improbable such a
partnership might seem to others—caused no little concern. At
year's end, he had written his friend, the Kansas editor William
Allen White, that American defense strategy was contingent upon
a resolution of the puzzling Hitler-Stalin rapprochement. If, suggested Roosevelt, the Russo-German Pact had been concocted by
Hitler merely to keep Britain and France from going to the defense of Poland, and if Hitler himself was now worrying about
Russian advances into the Baltic states, then the United States
could breathe a little easier. But if, to the contrary, Germany and
Russia had compacted to split up between themselves Europe,
Asia Minor, and the imperial possessions of Britain and France,
"then the situation of your civilization and mine is indeed in peril.
Our world trade would be at the mercy of the combine, and our
increasingly better relations with our twenty neighbors to the
south would end—unless we were willing to go to war in their
behalf against a German-Russian dominated Europe."[45]

There is no question that the president did not agree with either public opinion or temporarily sanguine opinion shapers like
the *New York Times* on the possible consequences of the European war. Roosevelt had wanted for some time to bring into his
cabinet the Chicago publisher, Frank Knox, who had been the
Republican vice-presidential candidate in 1936. But as of late
December, the president was still unable to offer Knox a position,
because he was afraid that public opinion would be hostile to what
had the earmarks of an obvious political ploy, an attempt to engen-

der a feeling of crisis by forming a national government along clear bipartisan lines. "The country as a whole does not yet have any deep sense of world crisis," Roosevelt wrote Knox on 29 December, adding that things could quickly change "if there should develop a real crisis such as . . . a German-Russian victory."[46]

The president was an accurate reader of public sentiment. By the end of the winter of 1939–40 America had, in the words of Sumner Welles, "reached another climax of out-and-out isolationism."[47] Gallup discovered in February that only 32 percent of the public now believed that the United States would sooner or later go to war—a decline of fourteen points from October. In January, *Fortune* had reported a slippage in the willingness of Americans to rush to the defense even of some nations in the hemisphere: in the case of Brazil, more people would *not* go to war to protect it (40 percent) than would (37 percent). And over a quarter of the respondents said that they would not even fight for Mexico.[48] Edward Mead Earle of Princeton's Institute for Advanced Study reviewed two books that had been instrumental in alerting the nation, during the past two years, to the Nazi penetration of Latin America, and he concluded that "the evidence of these two volumes [Carleton Beal's *Coming Struggle for Latin America* and John Whitaker's *Americas to the South*] is that the outbreak of war in Europe has relieved the United States of an embarrassing and perhaps threatening situation in the Western Hemisphere."[49]

Earle was not the only observer to argue that the danger to the hemisphere had been reduced by Europe having gone to war. In January 1940 Adolf Berle, the most imaginative of the president's men when it came to making worst-case analyses, felt confident enough to tell a Washington audience that the biggest challenge to the New World was neither military nor political, but economic. "It so happens," said Berle, "that this hemisphere is not, up to now, directly threatened."[50] Two months later, Chief of Naval Operations Harold Stark presented the president a draft entitled "The Foreign Situation as It Exists Today," a paper predicting that the war would probably turn into a stalemate. This document concluded that a "successful attack by either belligerent on the fortified Western Front is . . . highly improbable," and suggested that if any side were to win, it would do so through control of trade and finance, and not through fighting.[51]

The "Phony War" was in its final calming month when Sumner Welles left for Europe to see if he could find some basis for a negotiated peace. More than the Panama conference, this mission constituted the "last official expression" (to use the phrase that Welles had applied to the foreign ministers meeting) of the administration's policy of isolationism. By offering to the warring nations of Europe the mediatory facilities of the United States, the under secretary was reiterating America's desire to remain aloof from the fighting, extending nothing but words to preserve interests that, it would soon become apparent, were vital to national and hemispheric security. The Welles mission was utopia's last stand, and not much of one at that. The under secretary returned to Washington, fortified in the belief that the war would continue—only in earnest this time—and surfeited with official German assurances that the Reich was pursuing no aims of power in the Western Hemisphere.

On 1 March, Ribbentrop, striving to impress Welles with the sincerest form of flattery, told his visitor that all Germany wished to do was to imitate the United States by erecting a Monroe Doctrine of her own in central Europe. No territory in Latin America would ever tempt the Reich, the foreign minister promised. This assurance was repeated three days later, at the north German estate of Hermann Goering, where the Luftwaffe baron personally stated to Welles that "it is needless for me to say to you that Germany has no ambitions of any other kind than those I have indicated to you [viz., certain gains in east central Europe, Austria, and the Sudetenland], and least of all any ambitions which could affect the Western Hemisphere."[52]

If Welles's hosts failed to convince him that the United States had nothing to worry about in the Western Hemisphere, it was not because they did not try hard enough. By March 1940, German leaders had become fixed upon the idea that if they repeated often enough the line, "You have no problems with us in Latin America," Washington officials would be bound to catch on sooner or later. When they did, the results would be wonderful. At least, this is the way that journalist Colin Ross explained it to Hitler on 12 March. In an interview with the Fuehrer, Ross (who published widely in German journals) predicted that once the Americans were brought around to the German point of view on the New World, they "automatically would take a position directed against England." Hitler remarked after his meeting with Ross that the latter was a "very intelligent man who certainly had many good ideas."[53]

Another very intelligent man with interesting thoughts was Assistant Secretary of State Berle. While his friend Welles was still overseas, Berle began revising his own roseate forecasts about the security of the hemisphere. Russian successes in the Finnish campaign had aroused in the assistant secretary the old specter of a Russo-German Europe bringing all its weight to bear upon the New World; on 3 March he noted in his diary that this was becoming "more of a reality than I like to think about." The best hope for the United States would be if Germany and Russia so exhausted themselves that even in victory they became incapable of raising up sufficient power to hurl against the Western Hemisphere. Then, he stated, "our great test will be economic: can we maintain enough economic life for this hemisphere so that one after another country in South America will not be forced by trade relations to fall into the Berlin orbit?" Berle discussed this question with Cordell Hull, and the secretary agreed that unless the administration undertook to support the Latin economies, several South American lands would devolve into the status of German satellites—assuming, of course, a German triumph in Europe.[54]

Toward the end of March, Berle produced a policy memorandum for Hull that went far beyond the notion of a hemisphere menaced solely, or even primarily, in an economic manner. With a German offensive in the West now a certainty, Berle reverted to the conceptual perspective that had marked his strategic musings in the worrisome months following the Munich settlement. He informed the secretary that despite the existence of a "balance of chance" against an Allied defeat, the administration could not afford to assume that Hitler would be stopped in Europe: Germany and Russia had a "two and five" prospect of winning,[55] but "even if the chances of a German-Russian victory are only one to ten, . . . no American government is warranted in taking even a 10 percent chance on the national safety." American policy must be made on the hypothesis that Britain and France were doomed; and should the supposition become fact, the United States would have to realize that opposing it was a "strong imperialist alliance with access to the Atlantic, . . . actuated by a policy which apparently knows no limit."

Of one thing only was Berle certain: the conquerors of Europe would be starved for raw materials—raw materials that only the New World possessed in abundance. With Italy likely to sink its teeth into the carcass of European democracy before long, three predators would be casting sidelong glances at the wealth of Latin America. "It must therefore be assumed," Berle argued, "that an immediate result of the German victory permitting access to the Atlantic will be an attack politically, economically and, possibly, naval, on the hemispheric block *[sic]* which has been built up here within the line of the Monroe Doctrine." There could be, he warned, no blinking this challenge—a challenge made all the more serious by the vast skeleton network of subversive groups that Germany had created in Latin America during the 1930s.[56] Unless the United States could count on the unflinching cooperation of the Latin governments, "we should be, in a word, in no better relation to South America than Great Britain has proved to be in respect of Finland or Czechoslovakia."[57]

From this moment, a full two months before German armor made a shambles of the French army, the assistant secretary resumed his counterattack against the Axis in the Western Hemisphere. The first thing that needed to be done was to alert the American public to the danger. With this end in view, Berle persuaded Walter Winchell to include in his Easter Sunday broadcast (24 March), a "stiff editorial" decrying the lack of adequate defense preparations throughout the hemisphere. The cautious Hull felt that perhaps Berle was being rash, but the favorable public response to Winchell's program indicated to the assistant secretary that politicians like his chief were "far more timid than they need to be. . . ."[58]

Five days later, the battle of Latin America began to rage in earnest in the confines of Berle's imagination. For the first time since the German annexation of Czechoslovakia in the previous March, a top American policymaker discovered himself contemplating the distressing prospect that Britain would betray the United States and strike a bargain with Hitler. "This sounds fantastic" conceded Berle, who had always suspected the worst of any British action, "but there has always been a strong opinion in Great Britain for making peace with the Germans on the best terms, presumably granting them such spheres of influence as they need. It would be just like some bright Englishman to concede them a sphere of influence in South America, leaving it up to us to meet the ensuing situation."[59]

The midnight ride of Adolf Berle was ably assisted by the arrival in Washington, in this same month of March, of the flamboyant American ambassador to France, William Bullitt, who proceeded to tell anyone who would listen that the New World was in peril, in dire peril. Like his counterpart in London, Ambassador Joseph Kennedy, Bullitt suffered none of the illusions of the American public and its elected representatives about the "ability" of the Allies to halt Hitler. Bullitt hosted a dinner party in Washington on 8 March, where he informed his guests that France and Britain would crumble unless they were able to obtain substantial American support. The ambassador doubted whether such support would materialize, but he had no doubts whatsoever that Germany's next target would be South America, which would be used as a launching platform for a subsequent attack on the United States. At least one—and probably not the only one—of Bullitt's guests, Secretary of the Interior Harold Ickes, needed no persuading on this score; no scenario could be easier for the old Nazi-baiter to imagine, once the fighting in Europe resumed. "I am convinced," he wrote in his diary, "that this is absolutely what Hitler would attempt to do. After a war that would leave Europe exhausted and penniless, what more natural than that he should seek the gold that he will have to have in the country that possesses practically all of the world's gold?"[60]

Arguments that the Western Hemisphere was imperiled were almost always based, as was Bullitt's, on the assumption of a German victory in Europe; this was a necessary condition that had to be satisfied if the challenge to the hemisphere was to be taken seriously. Hitler was now about to fulfill that condition.

9

"Ominous Days" for the American Republics

The German invasion of Norway and Denmark on 9 April 1940 gave officials in Washington cause once again to be concerned about the Western Hemisphere. It had been easy enough, during the "Phony War," for Americans—in and out of Washington—to imagine that the war in Europe posed no problem for the nations of the New World. Had not the under secretary of state, Sumner Welles, himself said as much at Panama back in September? And was not isolation from war the announced goal of the administration, a goal that had summoned forth some of Franklin Roosevelt's finest oratory during seven years in the White House? The answer to both these questions was still yes, the president told the nation, a week after the start of hostilities in Scandinavia. In his annual Pan American Day address, Roosevelt declared that the United States and its Latin neighbors would remain on the "path of peace"—but never at the cost of appeasement. Peace *could* be maintained, but "only if we are prepared to meet force with force if challenge is ever made against us."[1]

Later that week, during another annual event, his press conference with the American Society of Newspaper Editors, the president addressed himself to what he termed the "silly, fool, old question of the pacifists: 'Who are you trying to protect us against?' " To answer this, he posed a counterquestion: "What is American defense?" He told the editors that, a few years earlier, he had raised this query at a cabinet meeting, and had discovered that his secretaries would readily protect every Latin state as far south as Brazil. When the cabinet hesitated, however, to recommend defending that giant but distant land, Roosevelt told them that a certain nation in Europe had five thousand bombers capable of reaching Brazil in about fourteen hours. Making this disclosure had, Roosevelt explained to the editors, changed the cabinet's

164

collective mind; for that body soon reached the consensus that "we will have to go whole hog on the Monroe Doctrine," or else the anonymous European power, once it had established a foothold in the hemisphere, would be within a few hours' striking time of Miami.

Returning to the current situation, the president reminded his auditors that Napoleon had never set out to conquer all of Europe, nor Alexander all of Persia. "The thing grows, as the French say," he remarked, adding that it was a matter of eminent common sense for Hitler to carry on his aggression once he had eliminated his opposition in Europe; anyone at the press conference, were he Hitler, would do the same. "Why leave an entire continent, North, Central, and South America, absolutely all alone?" He was having a bit of trouble this day putting his thoughts into coherent English, and at times he sounded more like Slip Mahoney, leader of the Bowery Boys, than Franklin Roosevelt, president of the United States. But amid the welter of words, one clear thought managed to surface: a victorious Germany, even if it did not try to invade the Western Hemisphere, would nevertheless be able to exert intolerable economic pressure. All Hitler would have to do, declared Roosevelt, would be to say to the Argentines, "Listen, sweetness, you people are dependent for your existence on selling cattle to Europe. The United States won't buy them." The president did not have to explain what everyone at the news conference well knew, that because of opposition from domestic cattle raisers the United States could not purchase Argentine livestock. The result, he concluded, would be that Hitler would capture the trade of much of the hemisphere, and he would reap its political allegiance in the bargain.[2]

If the German invasion of Scandinavia was a jolt to American policymakers, the invasion of the Low Countries and of France on 10 May came as a severe shock. The day after Nazi forces crossed the Dutch and Belgian frontiers, the Wilhelmstrasse received an important cable from Germany's chargé d'affaires and military attaché in Washington, reporting that the only way in which the United States would be brought into the fighting was if it became convinced that the Western Hemisphere was in jeopardy as a result of German successes on the western front.[3] Of course, this is exactly how Roosevelt had looked at the situation since well before Munich; but up to now, with the brief excep-

tion of the few months following Czechoslovakia's dismember-
ment in 1938, the threat to the hemisphere had always been
conditioned by the perceived ability (and willingness) of Great
Britain and France to resist Hitler, changing in intensity in in-
verse proportion to the fortunes of the European democracies. The
time was fast approaching for the president to decide how best to
defend the United States: by massive support for the front-line
nations, Britain and France, who might not even be able to make
effective use of American supplies; or by cutting off the Allies,
hardhearted as that might seem, and concentrating, as Berle and
others were advising, on building an impregnable defense position in the New World.

Roosevelt was receiving persuasive advice from advocates of
either course, and it would take a few months during which the
world was being turned upside down for him to decide finally
that he must gamble on the survival of Great Britain. Of great
importance in the president's choice to back Britain to the hilt
was his conviction that the nations of Latin America were utli-
mately incapable of being successfully defended against Hitler.
Having no doubts as to the Fuehrer's aspirations, which he assumed to be nothing less than global conquest, Roosevelt would
by August 1940 arrive at the realization that Germany's capabilities were now commensurate with its goals. It would take a dozen
weeks from the start of the German western offensive for the
White House to cross the geopolitical divide separating isolationism from interventionism; and to many observers at home and
in England, those weeks passed as slowly as years.

Some British onlookers had no difficulty in choosing the best
path for the administration to follow, and they eagerly composed
epitaphs, during the late spring of 1940, to what they assumed
was the dying policy of isolation. It will be recalled that as far
back as October 1938,[4] the *Economist* had ventured the premature speculation that the president would jettison isolation now
that he realized that, for the first time in more than a century,
American security was imperiled by extrahemispheric aggression.
Now, with French defenses buckling under the force of the pan-
zer onslaught, the British ambassador to the United States, Lord
Lothian, was certain that America would have to use its tremendous weight to redress the European equilibrium. To his friend,

the American-born Lady Astor, Lothian cheerily declared, in a letter of 20 May, that the "old isolationism is dead."[5]

In this postmortem, the ambassador explained that American policy with respect to the war in Europe was bound to change, simply because "the U.S.A. is at last profoundly moved and frightened. It had been dreaming on that it could keep out and that the Allies would keep the tiger away. And now the spectre has suddenly arisen that the British fleet may disappear. . . ." Should the Royal Navy cease to rule the Atlantic, Lothian foresaw that Roosevelt would have to make a hard choice: leave the bulk of the navy in the Pacific, or move it to the Atlantic. The United States could not protect both oceans by itself. "If it keeps [its navy] in the Pacific," predicted Lothian, "Germany and Italy will be able to take Brazil . . . and threaten the Canal. . . . If we went, could it protect Greenland, and Alaska, and Hawaii and South America and the Canal—obviously not. So there is very grave heart searching."[6]

What Lothian was overlooking in this analysis was the possibility that the United States would withdraw from the Far East (in which area, in any case, it has lesser interests than it had in the Western Hemisphere), and then refuse to aid Britain on the basis that it would need all the military hardware its factories and arsenals could produce to defend its own part of the world. This is exactly what many influential advisors were urging the president to do in the critical months of May and June, when Germany seemed on the verge of subjugating all of Europe. And this is what Roosevelt himself was prepared, albeit with great reluctance, to do. Although he may have personally detested his ambassador to England, the president could not ignore the reports that Joseph Kennedy was cabling during those last frenetic weeks of spring. For what the ambassador had to say were words that many people in Washington were now forming on their own trembling lips: "It seems to me that if we have to fight to protect our lives, we would do better fighting in our own backyard."[7]

At the War Department, resistance was mounting to the idea of squandering any more precious supplies on the Allied cause. This attitude was being touted not only by the flagrantly anti-interventionist secretary of war, Harry Woodring, but also by the assistant secretary and the chief of staff, Louis Johnson and George

C. Marshall. When the new British prime minister, Winston Churchill, wired Roosevelt on 15 May asking for the transfer of forty to fifty World War I destroyers, plus some other military equipment—including several hundred fighter planes—the War Department successfully interceded with the president, persuading him of the urgency of retaining the requested ships and aircraft for future use in defense of the hemisphere. On 17 May, Marshall explained his opposition to ship and fighter transfers to the secretary of the treasury, Henry Morgenthau, one of the administration's biggest supporters of the Allied cause. "We have got to weigh the hazards in this hemisphere of one thing and another," said the chief of staff. Whatever planes the United States could spare in its own moment of military nakedness would only amount to a "drop in the bucket on the other side, and it is a very vital necessity on this side and that is that. Tragic as it is, that is that." Marshall continued his campaign against aid to the Allies on the next day, 18 May, when he sent Morgenthau a memorandum citing the "uncertainties of the situation in . . . the Western Hemisphere and . . . the defense of the Panama Canal" to support his claim that the country had no aircraft to spare for Britain and France.[8]

The chief of staff's part in all this is worth a comment, for in later years the impression gained currency that he had been an early and strong advocate of all-out help to the Allies. One of Marshall's early biographers, William Frye, set the ball rolling in 1947 when he wrote that, after Dunkerque, "to Marshall, and to Admiral Harold R. Stark, the chief of naval operations, the one immediate imperative was to prevent the fall of Britain."[9] Two decades later Joseph Alsop, who had been an active interventionist in the summer of 1940. explained to a historian that at that time only a few Roosevelt cabinet members "and a very few farsighted officers like General Marshall grasped the necessity for immediate aid to Britain."[10]

Even the estimable Marshall biographer, Forrest C. Pogue, has presented an account of a chief of staff who, although vexed by the awesome problem of building an American army, was still willing to share what little he had with the valiant British. When, on 15 May, Churchill seemingly was asking Roosevelt for the moon—the destroyers; an American declaration of nonbelligerency; several hundred modern aircraft; a visit by the United

States Navy to Irish ports; action to "keep that Japanese dog quiet in the Pacific"; and antiaircraft guns, ammunition, and steel— Marshall would only consent to part with a relative trifle, albeit a potentially invaluable trifle to the Home Guard in England. Vetoing the sale of any of the fighter planes requested by Churchill, and expressing his disapproval of any ship transfer (gratuitously, since he had no jurisdiction over naval craft), the chief of staff would only agree to send to Britain supplies that were not critical to American defense: 500,000 World War I rifles; 900 field pieces; 80,000 machine guns; 300 mortars; 25,000 Browning automatic rifles; 20,000 revolvers; and a limited supply of ammunition for these weapons.[11] The British were undoubtedly appreciative of this assistance, but is it accurate to see in it evidence that Marshall was in agreement "with Roosevelt and his supporters that heroic efforts must be taken to sustain Britain . . ."?[12]

There is a different sense in which, by the middle of May, Roosevelt and his chief of staff were in agreement on the question of military aid to Britain. On 16 May, Roosevelt responded to Churchill's request for massive American aid, ruling out the destroyer transfer and offering only slight hope that a few of the other points might be resolved to the prime minister's satisfaction.[13] Even without the War Department's non possumus in the matter of the aircraft, the president would have hesitated to aid Britain, for in his mind there loomed, more frighteningly than ever, the awful prospect of Latin America in Hitler's grasp. If, as seemed likely, the British were soon to follow the French onto the list of Germany's apparent conquests, and if—again, as seemed likely— any American help to England would be too little and too late, why waste precious supplies, when the next battle would be taking place in the Western Hemisphere?

On 16 May, the same day he spurned Churchill's appeal for the destroyers, Roosevelt sent a message to Congress asking for a supplementary defense appropriation: nearly a billion dollars was demanded for the army and navy, and the legislators were informed that America's aircraft manufacturers must be assisted in bringing up their production capacity as rapidly as possible to fifty thousand planes a year. "These are ominous days," the president declared, "days whose swift and shocking developments force every neutral nation to look to its defenses in the light of new factors." Not only had the technology of warfare, as he had said on countless occasions, made American invulnerability a thing of the past ,but the "treacherous use of the 'Fifth Column' " had been shown to be a powerful weapon of aggression. "The clear fact is that the American people must recast their thinking about national protection."[14]

Although the president's invocation of the nefarious "Fifth Column" makes quaint reading today, it is important to remember that at the time he was delivering his message to Congress, many otherwise sober individuals were being swept up in the great fear that gripped the West during those cheerless days of May and June 1940. On 11 June Congress—by now thoroughly shaken out of its reverie—appropriated even more monies for defense than Roosevelt had requested, voting 1.3 billion dollars (though the president had asked for only 896 million dollars). The American public was quickly becoming convinced of the compelling need to rearm. Princeton University's Public Opinion Research Project discovered that the once-complacent public was now almost as pessimistic about American security as formerly it had been optimistic. After the battle of France ended in June, a full 77 percent of those polled by the Princeton team answered "No" to the question, "Do you think our country's army, navy, and air force are strong enough so that the United States is safe from attack by any foreign powers?"[15]

This figure should not be taken as evidence that the public was prepared to discard isolationism and to join Britain in the fighting; Gallup had found, on 29 May, that only 7 percent favored this option. However, one week later 84 percent said they would fight to prevent Germany from taking possession of any Allied territorial holdings in the New World.[16] The fear that Germany would absorb the New World colonies of its victims was as pervasive as the corollary apprehension that it had unleashed the dastardly fifth column below the Rio Grande. So widespread were these worries becoming in the United States that Chargé d'affaires Hans Thomsen wired the Wilhelmstrasse in the middle of May to suggest that Berlin issue a public declaration that it had no interest in colonies in the Western Hemisphere, and that it would always respect the sovereignty of the Latin American republics. In somewhat of an understatement, Thomsen reported that "many Americans are beginning to believe in the danger of a German attack on the Western Hemisphere, either direct or by infiltration through Latin America after a possible Anglo-French defeat."[17]

Thomsen's perception was not quite an accurate reflection of American concerns; far more Americans were worried about an indirect challenge to the United States through either the invasion or subversion of Latin America than were worried about a direct assault on United States territory itself. And among the indirect methods of menacing the United States, none was as dreaded as the fifth column. The phrase itself had slipped inadvertently into demotic usage as a by-product of the Spanish Civil War, when one of Franco's generals, Emilio Mola, had boasted that the fall of Madrid would be accomplished not only by the four nationalist columns descending upn the capital, but by a fifth inside the city itself. In 1938, as a result of German successes in Austria and in the Sudetenland, the conception began to assume the sinister dimensions that would traumatize the West within two years. Secretary of State Hull recollected that by late May 1940 Hitler's schemes for and in South America were being blatantly previewed in Europe: "We had before us the vivid examples of what Nazi 'fifth columns' had accomplished during the invasions of Scandinavia, the Low Countries, and France, the full details of which were only then coming to our attention."[18] And Roosevelt, in a fireside chat of 26 May, detailed the peril now facing the hemisphere: "The Trojan Horse. The fifth Column that betrays a nation unprepared for treachery. Spies, saboteurs and traitors. . . ."[19]

A marvelous glimpse of the prevailing paranoia is given in the diary of Assistant Secretary of State Berle. On 26 June, Berle related a "shattering experience" that he had just had: he had met with a Hearst Newsreels executive who had given him details of a Nazi plan to take New York after the capitulation of Britain. "His story of the way the Fifth Column was already in control of New York was so graphic that it frightened me completely," Berle wrote. "Only after I got the FBI, which had heard the story in detail, to check, did I begin to pull myself together."[20] Adolf Berle pulling himself together might have entailed a lessening concern for the subways and streets of Manhattan, but it in no way involved a diminished sense of worry about Latin America, where

two countries in particular during the late spring and early summer were giving American policymakers cause for alarm: Argentina and Uruguay.

Argentina, long an object of nervousness to American diplomats who had to deal with its celebrated reluctance to cooperate
at most inter-American conferences, was held to be especially
susceptible to Axis infuence, for two reasons: it had large Italian
and German communities within its boundaries; and it was almost totally dependent economically upon a Europe that was
being brought, link by link, into the chain of Nazi conquests. The
sixteenth of May, the day the Allied armies began their retreat
from the cul-de-sac that was Belgium, the day the world learned
of the enormity of the German breakthrough on the Meuse, was
also the day that Washington discovered from the American military attaché in Buenos Aires that "the Argentine army, navy, the
higher circles of society and the wealthy classes [are] definitely
pro-Nazi and pro-Fascist. . . ." Five days later, this same source
informed the War Department that even the administration of
the pro-Allied president, Roberto Ortiz, was "honeycombed with
Nazis," and that, in preparation for German landing operations,
"German nationals in South America have been ordered to buy
up ranches with frontage on the South Atlantic both in Argentina and Brazil."[21]

There was not much question in Washington of the loyalties
of both Ortiz and his foreign minister, José María Cantilo; it was
well known that the two men were staunch supporters of the Allied side, especially of France. For these two statesmen, and for
scores of thousands of their fellow Latin Americans, there was
much truth in what Benjamin Franklin had said a century and a
half before: "Every man has two countries, his own and France
besides."[22] Manuel Ugarte, an ideologist of Pan-Americanism sans
North Americanism, had written effusively of "the great fatherland" in 1925.[23] Six years later, another Latin writer observed that
"in no other place in the world has everything French such drawing power as in South America."[24] Even in lands off the beaten
path of general European influence, identification with France was
pandemic among the educated classes. An amateur historian and
grandee of Quito society told a visiting correspondent in the early
1940s that Ecuador's esteem for France was so lofty that "at one
time the natives and servants thought that outside Ecuador and

Peru there was only France, and the only other city besides Guayaquil and Quito was Paris."[25]

Thus it was that the rapid conquest of France came almost as a personal tragedy for many Latin Americans, who saw the terrible subjugation of their spiritual homeland as proof of the invincibility of Hitler's legions—and as an indication that the wisest thing Latin statesmen could do would be to cooperate with the new master of Europe.[26] An Argentine journalist, Juan Carulla, has written movingly of his own reaction to the news that German troops had entered Paris: he recalled encountering an old friend on a Buenos Aires street on 14 June, the day Georg von Küchler's Eighteenth Army marched in triumph along the Champs Élysées. Ordinarily, the friend was a fastidious dresser, but this day "he had a growth of beard and his clothing was rumpled. After a brief greeting, he sadly murmured, 'Paris has been taken. . . .' 'It is true,' I answered, and we spoke no more. Emotion was choking both of us."[27]

Another adage, this time from the Bible and not Benjamin Franklin, best conveyed American fears for Argentina during the weeks of France's agony: "The spirit indeed is willing, but the flesh is weak."[28] Argentina had to export the products of its farms and fields to live, so it was only logical that it be expected to try to cultivate ties with the power that was in the process of gaining physical control over its market. At the end of May, Military Attaché M. A. Devine cabled that Ortiz was taking no "positive action against [pro-Nazi] agitators, although they were well-known. I have confirmed that the troops are sleeping on their arms in barracks." Devine concluded that the government was unsure of itself, was waiting to see which way the political wind was blowing, and was undoubtedly afraid of offending Germany.[29] The caution of Argentina's leaders stemmed from more than a fear of jeopardizing the nation's standing in Hitler's new order; the Casa Rosada was also worried about the immediate danger of an armed insurrection, should it do anything that could be construed as anti-German. American Ambassador Norman Armour interpreted Cantilo's "somewhat defeatish mood" as a signal that he feared Argentina might become another Belgium or Denmark, overrun by German forces. As Cantilo himself pointed out to Armour, the United States was a long way from Argentina; how could it possibly protect it?[30]

Cantilo had cause to be nervous. On 24 May, word had been sent to Washington from the French foreign office that a Nazi coup impended in Argentina. The plot was said to involve top Argentine generals, Chilean leftists (who were allegedly allied with the Nacistas in Chile), and the thousands of Nazis who pullulated in southern Brazil. It would be set in motion immediately after the fall of France, simultaneous with the invasion of Britain. Washington was uncertain how much credibility to attach to the report, although Attaché Devine took the coup rumors seriously enough. So did the Argentine government.[31]

Armour tried to shed some light on the confusing situation when he cabled, on 5 June, that he had been confidentially informed by the pro-American head of the Argentine naval air corps that the French were misled; the danger of insurrection was, for the moment at least, low. However, said Capt. Marcos A. Zar, should Italy enter the war—a contingency that was developing all the earmarks of a certainty—the situation in Argentina would rapidly change for the worse. As Armour put it, the "three million Fascists in Argentina would be thrown into the Nazi camp, bringing the forces of totalitarianism in this country up to almost one-third of the total population." And to make matters still worse, the nation's communists were already in league with the Nazis, a fact Armour deduced from the remarkable similarity in the anti-American propaganda emanating from the printing presses of the two parties.[32]

As bad as things might look in Argentina, the picture reaching Washington from Uruguay was even more dismal. This small republic, tucked uncomfortably between the Latin "superpowers" Brazil and Argentina, was considered to be the soft underbelly of South America, the likeliest target of any nation seeking to invade the hemisphere. Not only did Uruguay contain a large proportion (10 percent) of Germans and Italians in its total population of slightly more than 2 million, but it was situated much too close, in American thinking, to the dangerous German enclaves in Brazil and Argentina. So vulnerable was the tiny republic perceived to be that the FBI estimated it would take only a few well-trained and well-led units to seize control of the mouth of the Rio de la Plata from the Uruguayan side, thus blocking all river movement to and from the Uruguay and Paraná basins.[33]

To the horror of officials in Washington, it appeared in the late spring of 1940 as if Uruguay was about to be overrun by the Nazis. Even before the German sweep through France startled the world, stories of an imminent fifth column insurrection had been circulating inside Uruguay. The stories were the product of the unremitting toil of that nation's leading countersubversive, radio personality Hugo Fernández Artucio, who for six lonely months had been waging, through his "Difusoras el Espectador" broadcasts, a frustrating (for himself, not for the Germans) war against the internal Nazi menace. It was not until early May that Fernández Artucio gained the vast audience that he had longed for. Ironically, the radio campaigner's breakthrough came not over the airwaves, but in the pages of two Buenos Aires newspapers that circulated in nearby Montevideo. A week before the start of the German offensive against France and the Low Countries, *La Prensa*, a very well-respected metropolitan daily, and *La Vanguardia*, the journal of the Argentine Socialist Party, published Fernández Artucio's sensationalist exposé of rampant subversion and treason in Uruguay. Montevideo, and indeed the whole nation, was scandalized. The allegations, in conjunction with the terrifying advances Germany was making on the western front, shocked the Uruguayan congress into appointing a special investigatory committee to explore the web of intrigue suddenly enveloping the land.[34]

Fernández Artucio, whose disclosures were quickly picked up by international press agencies, claimed that a conspiracy existed between local Nazis and a group of ultraconservative nationalists who had recently vowed to lead a "march of the countryside upon Montevideo" to oust the government of President Alfredo Baldomir.[35] The American minister to Uruguay, Edwin C. Wilson, gave a great deal of credence to the reports of incipient upheaval; from the middle of May his despatches began to assume a tone that worried observers in Washington. On 30 May, Wilson sent one of his most dramatic cables: "The situation is deteriorating here; the government is well-meaning but weak, undecided and confused; things are drifting; people are climbing on the Nazi bandwagon; and armed movement is a possibility."[36]

The investigating committee appointed by the Uruguayan congress kept headline writers around the hemisphere busy during the course of its hearings in late May and early June. In the United States, the *New York Times* was paying careful attention to what was going on in Uruguay, beginning on 29 May, when it published the news that Montevideo expected to be invaded at any moment by Germans based in southern Brazil. But editors at the *Times* and elsewhere saved their largest type for the high drama that took place in the second week of June, when the Brena Committee (as the special investigating body was called, after its chairman, Tomás Brena of the Catholic Party) raided a house in the hinterland city of Salto, turning up spectacular evidence of a monstrous Nazi plot to overthrow the government. The house in question belonged to a photographer named Gero Arnulf Fuhrmann, a member of the Uruguayan section of the Nazi Party. The evidence in question consisted of a collection of "suspicious" pictures of beaches, bridges, and highways, as well as the outline of a planned military coup. Fuhrmann, who with twelve other Germans was speedily arrested, admitted that he had drafted the plan, but sloughed it off as a practical joke. The Uruguayan government failed to see the humor, and declared the nation to be in a state of emergency, which meant inter alia that Uruguay's transportation system was placed under military control.[37]

It is highly unlikely that Berlin even knew of, much less approved, Fuhrmann's grandiose scheme to subvert Uruguay; the plot itself was, in the words of one scholar, nothing more than a "sign of the aggressive disposition of its slightly pathological author."[38] Indeed, probably the last thing that Berlin wanted to do at this juncture was to rile the United States. Unfortunately for policymakers in the Wilhelmstrasse, though, the jubilant Volksdeutsche of the Western Hemisphere did not comprehend German policy, and acted as if they had been mandated to bring about the creation of the new order in the New World. "There appears to be," reported the *New York Times* on 30 May, in a colossal understatement, "a decided lack of cooperation between the Nazis in Latin America and Germany."[39] Berlin, although not involved in the Fuhrmann plot, did feel some responsibility for the jailed Germans and sought to obtain their release. In the case of the ringleader, Fuhrmann, the Wilhelmstrasse calculated that chances of an acquittal were nonexistent, "unless we succeed in having him declared insane."[40] Berlin reasoned that not only was a finding of non compos mentis Fuhrmann's best hope, it was the simple truth. The Uruguayans, on the other hand, were fully convinced of both the rationality and seriousness of the plot.

Tomás Brena was certain that Fuhrmann had intended nothing less than to convert Uruguay into an agrarian colony of the Reich.[41]

In the United States, observers of Latin America took recent developments in Uruguay with great seriousness. Charles Wertenbaker, foreign news editor for *Time* magazine, wrote in the aftermath of the Fuhrmann business that "if the Nazis held Uruguay, they would soon claim their nationals in Brazil and Argentina, and from there might go on to conquer the continent."[42] The Roosevelt administration, it goes without saying, was convinced both of the earnestness of the plotters and of the necesity for quick action to protect the vulnerable Uruguayan glacis. Even before the bizarre Salto events had transpired, Roosevelt had sent the cruiser USS *Quincy* to the Rio de la Plata, in response to an urgent request from Minister Wilson, who wanted a show of American naval power that would allay the nervousness of Presidents Baldomir and Ortiz. A day later, 1 June, John White wrote in the *New York Times* that the Brena Committee was uncovering "an almost unbelievable Nazi political penetration into South America"—and this story was filed more than a week before the news of the Fuhrmann plot galvanized the little republic.

The *Times* supplied some electricity of its own the next morning, 2 June, greeting its readers with a banner headline announcing:

GERMANS BOMB RHONE VALLEY AND MARSEILLE:
DUNKERQUE HOLDS OUT: FIGHTING ALONG SOMME:
U.S. IS STUDYING NAZI THREAT IN SOUTH AMERICA.

Assistant Secretary of State Adolf Berle observed on the same day that "it is increasingly plain that the greatest [German] pressure would be brought to bear on Uruguay, Brazil and Argentina, in the order named, and the greatest chance of success is in Montevideo. I am not too happy about the situation."[43] Neither was Roosevelt, who promptly ordered a second cruiser, the *Wichita*, to South America, in hopes of somehow containing the volatile situation. American diplomats in Uruguay and Argentina had requested a dramatic demonstration of U.S. naval might, involving some forty or fifty ships, but the president, acting on the advice of the chief of naval operations, Admiral Harold Stark, decided to keep the bulk of the fleet in the Pacific for the time being.

Stark reasoned that a withdrawal from the Pacific would weaken
the American position in that ocean, without guaranteeing any
balancing gains in the Western Hemisphere; for it was not certain that the presence of numerous American vessels would have
a deterrent effect in Latin America, where the principal threat
seemed to be internal subversion rather than invasion. Indeed,
said Stark, a naval demonstration might very well prove coun-
terproductive, for it might give enemies of the United States the
opportunity to raise once again "the old cry of imperialism." Despite his conviction that the fleet belonged in the Pacific, Stark
concluded that "in the last analysis, our own hemisphere is of
course the vital consideration."[44]

Laurence Duggan, the chief of the State Department's Division
of American Republics, worried that the two cruisers the president did send south would not reach their destinations in time,
and he recommended ordering a flight of six army bombers to
the east coast of South America. To Under Secretary of State
Welles, Duggan wrote that "it is daily clearer that the situation
in Argentina, Uruguay and Brazil is deteriorating in the sense that
a successful revolution backed by the Nazis is becoming a more
likely possibility."[45] This comment indicates a fairly widespread
perception among top American policymakers at the beginning
of June. On 2 June the *New York Times* captured this prevailing
mood of fear and uncertainty when it related that in Washington
"the belief was general that, if they won the war, the Germans
would physically invade South America; their present activity
was described as boring from within in an attempt to set up totalitarian regimes."

Brazil, the last of the three east coast republics over which Washington fretted during the fifth column panic, seemed on the surface to be deceptively calm—at least in comparison with its
southern neighbors. To be sure, the White House assumed that
it knew of the danger in which the largest Latin republic lay, but
so far the danger was only potential; there was less, much less,
talk of revolt or invasion in Rio than in Buenos Aires or in Montevideo. Whatever mollifying effect this state of affairs may have
had on worried American policymakers was more than undone
by the behavior of President Getulio Vargas, who, sniffing the
changing political winds in Europe with the fine nose of a blood-
hound, started to make overtures toward the new master of that

continent. Since the start of the German offensive, at which time he had announced that Brazil would remain strictly neutral in the war,[46] Vargas had given Berlin absolutely no cause for complaint. Quite to the contrary, the Wilhelmstrasse was delighted with Rio's frank wait-and-see attitude—so delighted, in fact, that the German ambassador was instructed to award the Great Cross of the German Eagle to the minister of war, Eurico Gaspar Dutra, and the chief of staff, Pedro Aurelio de Góes Monteiro.

The awards were part of an intensive German effort to repair relations with Brazil, shattered in May 1938 by the nocturnal gunplay at the presidential palace. Germany made sure that its side of the European war was reaching Brazilian readers, making great use of its Transocean news service to provide newsrooms throughout Brazil and other Latin states with low-cost (and, in many instances, free) wire copy. In addition, the Reich enjoyed a cordial relationship with the director of the Department of Press and Propaganda, Lourival Fontes. All of this prompted a troubled military attaché in Rio, Maj. Lawrence C. Mitchell, to report to the War Department in late May that the regnant pro-Allied sentiment of September 1939 had dissipated. "It is obvious," Mitchell wrote, "that few Brazilians realize what a German victory would mean to their country. Stories recounting German plans to take over sections of Brazil in the event of victory are generally discounted." They certainly were not being discounted by the attaché, who noted that "the presence of a million Germans in Brazil along with numerous German sympathizers can leave no doubt as to the existence of a potential 'Fifth Column' undoubtedly already at work."[47]

American Ambassador Jefferson Caffery was not as dubious as Mitchell about the allegiance of Rio, if not to the Allied cause, then at least to Pan-American solidarity. Unlike the attaché, Caffery believed that pro-Nazi elements made up only a small minority of the ruling elite (and were concentrated in the War Ministry), while both the president and his foreign minister, Oswaldo Aranha, were firmly behind the United States. On 24 May, the ambassador informed the State Department that "the Government is aware of the fifth-column danger here and aware that German residents even in Rio de Janeiro are now talking openly in unguarded fashion of 'what will take place here later on.' " He also reported, erroneously, that in addition to the outspokenly pro-American Aranha, Chief of Staff Goés Monteiro was ready to give the United States full cooperation in the matter of securing base facilities for American forces in northeastern Brazil and on Fernando de Noronha.[48]

Military Attaché Mitchell persisted in seeing the situation in a much gloomier light, and while his despatches to Washington were more alarmist than those of Jefferson Caffery, they were in many ways more accurate indications of how Brazilian policymakers tended to assess the latest European developments. "These are troubled times for Brazil," wrote Mitchell on 30 May. "Confronted with the possibility of a German victory in Europe, Brazil is also faced with German domination of its own territory. A number of Brazilians appreciate this danger, but the Brazilian masses are apathetic." Worse, by far, than mass indifference was the boring from within that the Nazis had been performing in critical government departments. For example, the head of the gestapo in Rio, Robert Lehr, was considered to be a good friend of Góes and other top military figures. Mitchell was especially distressed that the chief of staff, who had heretofore been "ready to cooperate in every way possible" with the United States, was beginning to show a "decided enthusiasm for Germans and German military accomplishments."[49]

Impressed by Caffery's confident prediction (made six days before Mitchell filed the above report) that Vargas, Aranha, and Góes would all stand alongside the United States, and alarmed by news from London that six thousand German soldiers were on the way to Brazil, hidden aboard merchant vessels, Roosevelt ordered his military chiefs in late May to prepare to move an army of more than a hundred thousand to northeastern Brazil. Laboring feverishly thoughout the weekend of 25 to 27 May, army and navy planners pasted together the POT OF GOLD, an invasion scheme premised on two assumptions: that Britain and France would fall and that the United States had Rio's approval to occupy its territory. Fortunately for Washington, the first condition was never fulfilled, for the second assumption was erroneous, and had POT OF GOLD been implemented Roosevelt would surely have committed, as one Brazilian historian put it, "a politically irreparable error."[50] Nothing could have better played into the hands of German propagandists than the spectacle of the Colossus of the North once again invading a Latin American nation.[51]

To circumvent the obvious political difficulties that would attend any emergency military action that the United States might be forced to take, the administration began in late May to woo the Latin governments, with a view to securing bilateral defense pacts. The one-sided (for the most part) courtship would grow increasingly passionate during the summer of 1940, as emissaries from the War and Navy Departments attempted, in most cases successfully, to obtain the cooperation of Latins on a wide range of issues, the most important of which was base rights for American forces. Although the quasi-commitment to collective security undertaken in 1938 at Lima had represented to Washington a step in the right direction, it was nonetheless a small step, for it had been weakened by the provision that pledged each nation to look out solely for itself. Clearly, by the late spring of 1940, this modest gesture was inadequate for the purposes of defending the inter-American condominium. More than ever did American policymakers appreciate the truth of Mark Twain's epigram about another common shelter: "Almost any man worthy of his salt would fight to defend his home, but who ever heard of a man going to war for his boarding house?"

Of course, the White House never expected, nor even desired, that the defenseless Latin nations would actually try to fend off a foreign enemy by themselves; that was a job that was best left to the army and navy of the United States, the only power in the entire hemisphere with the ability to turn back an invader. What the administration did expect was that the Latin republics would take all due precautions against subversives operating within their borders; for the belief was general in Washington that the existence of the fifth column, and not the prospect of an immediate military invasion, constituted the supreme danger to the hemisphere, inasmuch as "the Nazi technique is to avoid frontal attack by a series of flanking maneuvers which render the prospective victim virtually impotent."[52]

Although Argentina, Uruguay, and possibly Brazil manifested symptoms of extreme fifth column infestation, they were far from being the only Latin American nations to cause concern in Washington. As Roosevelt expressed it on 22 May in a letter to his ambassador to Chile, Claude Bowers, "there is no doubt that in the event of a continued German victory in Europe, German agents in Latin American countries will immediately undertake activities with the view to overthrowing existing governments."[53] Bowers, who had become painfully familiar with the fifth column in his prior posting as ambassador to war-torn Spain, was certain that the first blow struck against South America would land in Chile, because that country had in abundance two ingredients that were guaranteed to result in trouble: large numbers of militant Nazis; and vast stores of raw materials. As the ambassador saw it, nothing could be clearer than that Hitler would use the former to acquire the latter.[54]

To Sumner Welles, Bowers related on 25 May that "I have heard that there are ten thousand Germans in Chile who have actually been trained and drilled for war purposes. . . . Let me reiterate with all possible emphasis my own conviction that these German agents count confidently on the assistance of the Fifth Column, so effectively used in Spain."[55] Everywhere Americans looked they were glimpsing the fifth column, and for the remainder of the summer, this specter would haunt the Roosevelt administration. Washington's fascination with subversion in Latin America quickly became annoying to most governments below the Rio Grande, who argued that the real menace was the "Sixth Column" of people who believed in the fifth column. In Brazil, the Department of Press and Propaganda even went so far as to prohibit the press from using the term *fifth column.*[56]

United States Army and Navy officers who ventured south to conduct bilateral defense talks that summer were deeply convinced of the ubiquity of subversion. One of them, Maj. Maxwell D. Taylor, reported to the War Department in late July that "it may be assumed that plans now exist for wide use of the Fifth Column in case the totalitarian powers try to support their economic penetration [of Latin America] by arms after peace in Europe. While it is improbable that military invasion will occur earlier than six months after the destruction or neutralization of British sea power, the American republics should be alive to the importance of controlling and breaking up now, the groups from which the wartime Fifth Columnists will find their support."[57]

Later that summer, a lengthy memo from military intelligence in Washington stated that the strictest caution should be used in the fight against the fifth column, which had by now attained colossal proportions in the American psyche. No one, declared G–2, was above suspicion; agents were everywhere in Latin

America, exploiting "all human frailties" in their diabolical workings. Even victims of Nazi oppression could not be trusted. Especially suspect were Jewish refugees from Germany, for "before the German invasion, Holland was full of German Jews, each a potential Fifth Columnist. . . . Many of the countries of Latin America have the same problem to face today, and it may be expected that the German government will take full advantage of the refugee situation to introduce German agents—Jews, or Aryans passing as Jews—and control by threat of reprisal the bona fide refugees."[58]

By the summer of 1940, the White House was expecting the worst in Europe, preparing for the worst in Latin America. Only if we keep well in mind the atmosphere of almost unbelievable shock that followed the Allied debacle in France can we begin to comprehend the tortuous course run by the administration in shaping American policy toward the war. It is now time to examine how, and why, Franklin Roosevelt decided to abandon isolation, and to analyze the part that Latin America had to play in that decision.

10

"Latin America, from Mexico Down, Is Loaded with Dynamite"

It is sometimes imagined, even today, that, in the wake of the German conquest of France, Franklin Roosevelt and a few other stalwart champions of England stood united against the "defeatist" counsel of such men as Ambassador Joseph Kennedy, and gallantly pledged the future of the United States to the survival of Great Britain. Although this makes flattering reading for certain of those erstwhile "champions," nothing could be farther from the truth; for in those dark days of late May and early June 1940, the consensus of the administration was that England—brave as it might be—*might* be finished and that the United States might shortly be fighting the battle of its life in Latin America. This was not a prospect that pleased him, yet Roosevelt accepted it as a probabilistic, if gloomy, scenario. He was thus confronted with the need to make an agonizing choice—a choice whose difficulty was compounded by his deep and genuine sympathy for the British cause. Should the United States shore up Britain, even to the point of getting into war against Germany, and, more importantly, even at the risk of squandering precious military hardware on what looked like a dying and beaten ally? Or should it keep for itself the matériel it would need to repulse the Nazi invaders, when they finally came to take possession of a continent weakened by years of incessant subversive activity?

To the British, logic seemed to compel one answer only. Prime Minister Churchill had resumed his quest for American destroyers and a declaration of nonbelligerency on 20 May, even as the British Expeditionary Force was making plans to abandon the battle in France. The current British government, declared Churchill in a cable to Roosevelt, would never capitulate to Hitler, but there was no guaranteeing what a future British government might accept in the way of peace terms. "You must not be blind to the fact," stated the prime minister, "that the sole remaining bargaining counter with Germany would be the fleet, and if this country was left by the United States to its fate, no one would have the right to blame those responsible if they made the best terms they could for the surviving inhabitants. Excuse me, Mr. President, putting this nightmare bluntly."[1] To underscore his argument, Churchill instructed his ambassador to the United States, Lord Lothian, to remind Roosevelt that if the British lost control of the seas, Germany would soon establish bases in Brazil, where it would be within easy bombing distance of the Panama Canal.[2]

If the prime minister wanted to instill fear in the heart of the president, his warning that the fleet might pass to Germany was made to order. Among all the security concerns of the United States, this "nightmare" was by far the greatest. If Roosevelt could have been convinced—by late May—that the chances of Britain carrying on the fight were sufficiently good to justify the gamble, he would have given Churchill the support he wanted. (Indeed, he would do just that later in the year, when it began to appear that the reports of Britain's death had been exaggerated.) But by late May history had not done Washington decision makers the honor of tipping its hand, and consequently, plans were being formulated in the American capital that commenced with the preconception of a British defeat.

On 22 May, two days after Churchill's latest entreaty had reached Washington, the army's War Plans Division presented Chief of Staff Marshall a memorandum on the "imminently probable complications of today's situation." The planners argued that the United States had no alternative to concentrating all its efforts on meeting the Latin American situation. There was only a slight chance that American interests in Europe and the Far East could be defended, and even if they could be, the understanding was that the protection of Latin America had the first claim upon the nation's military resources. After reading this memorandum, Marshall went to the White House for a strategy conference with the president, Sumner Welles, and Harold Stark. According to the chief of staff's minutes of this meeting, "all felt that we must not become involved with Japan, that we must not concern ourselves beyond the 180 meridian, and that we must concentrate on the South American situation."[3]

On 22 May, the day before the above meeting, Roosevelt had

received a letter that reflected the prevailing American mood of pessimism concerning Britain's ability to survive. An extremely excited Elmer Thomas, Democratic senator from Oklahoma, wanted the president to ensure that the British fleet would be kept out of German hands when (he did not write *if*) Great Britain capitulated. The senator also advised that Latin America be placed on alert against the "possible attack by Germany and perhaps joined by Italy and Japan, almost immediately following the fall of France and Great Britain. . . ." Roosevelt replied that the latter point was well taken care of, but that the moment was not "opportune" to press London on the disposition of the fleet.[4]

Well into the month of June, American policymakers labored under the heavy load of their assumption that France and England were a hair's-breadth from defeat. On the same day that he met with Marshall, Stark, and Welles, the president also met to discuss strategy with members of the Business Advisory Council, telling them that "we have to look ahead to certain possibilities." Foremost among these possibilities was the "domination of Europe . . . by Naziism—including also the domination of France and England. . . ." This would remove at one sweep the "buffer" of the British fleet and the French army, which had up to now permitted the United States to isolate itself from the Nazi contagion. Should this most somber of forecasts eventuate, said Roosevelt, "there is nothing between the Americas and the new forces in Europe. And so we have to think in terms of the Americas more and more and infinitely faster."[5]

While Roosevelt was speaking, German armored units were exploiting their breakthrough to the sea, isolating the Allied forces in Belgium from the bulk of the French army.[6] Three days later, with Belgium tottering and the Allies falling back on Dunkerque, Assistant Secretary of State Adolf Berle recorded in his diary the unpleasant observation that the United States had "just begun to wake up to the shuddering possibility that the Germans may win this war, including a seizure of the British fleet—and that then we shall have German interference all up and down the coast of South America, to say nothing of some incidental troubles here."[7]

Washington's overriding concern with Latin America at the moment of the Allies' greatest peril was not without an element of sublime irony: For the better part of two years, the willingness of the administration to countenance measures leading away from isolationism and toward support of the European democracies had grown in direct proportion to American perceptions of an increased threat to the security of the United States—a threat stemming mainly from the possible Axis domination of Latin America. The British and French had perceived this connection early, and had striven to highlight the manifold dangers that Nazi expansionism posed to the hemisphere. This strategy had worked exceedingly well up to now, and it had been of some importance in convincing the White House of the wisdom of removing the arms embargo (although, of course, self-generated security fears were strong enough by themselves to have caused the president to seek revision of the neutrality legislation). The argument was, really, unanswerable, and rested on the following quasi-syllogism: Hitler is out to dominate Latin America; Britain and France stand in his way in Europe; therefore American security interests demand that Britain and France be given aid. A fairly straightforward line of reasoning, this was one to which the administration had subscribed, while at the same time it had remained faithful to a coequal premise of American foreign policy, namely that the nation must not get involved in another European war.

But there was a near-fatal flaw in this process of deduction, a reductio that threatened not only to demolish the prospect of further aid to the Allies, but also to establish the probability of the United States finding itself in a war. This flaw, the product of a combination of seeming German omnipotency and Allied vulnerability, was also the result of a simple, ostensibly unanswerable syllogism: Hitler is out to dominate Latin America; Britain and France are beaten; therefore aid wasted in their behalf only serves further to weaken United States defenses against the coming battle for Latin America. At a press conference in late May, Secretary of Commerce Harry Hopkins, by now the president's closest adviser, intimated that it might be necessary for the United States to fight Germany after all, notwithstanding the administration's resolve to stay out of the European war. To a correspondent from the *American Banker*, Hopkins remarked that recent events in Europe were forcing the administration to consider some new, and increasingly probable, policy implications: "Hell, I mean the tough implications: Suppose that Germany wins the war in the next two months and does on the economic fronts what they have done on the military fronts. What will they do in South America, presuming they win, and then, what are we going to do about it?"[8]

Put into the perspective of Hopkins's question, Allied endeavors to depict the hazardous consequences that a German victory must portend for the hemisphere now became self-defeating. Thus, whether issuing from Paris or London, counsels for a greater American undertaking in the cause of stopping Hitler in Europe were bound to prove fruitless; indeed, to some American policymakers they even seemed insulting, as if the Allies were trying deliberately to drag the United States down with them to a defeat for which they had only themselves to blame in the first place. Churchill, at least, should have understood the administration's reluctance to come to the aid of the Allies, for Britain had been playing a similar kind of game with France in recent days. Despite numerous clamant telegrams from Premier Paul Reynaud, begging for more fighter support, the British War Cabinet decided on 15 May, over Churchill's strenuous objections, to send "no more planes to France." The decision was taken after a heated discussion, during which Air Chief Marshal Sir Hugh Dowding persuaded the cabinet that further air support of the French and British divisions in northeastern France could well cost Britain its life, once the Battle of France ended and the Battle of Britain began.[9]

When the American ambassador to France, William Bullitt, cabled Roosevelt on 28 May to ask that the Atlantic fleet be sent to the Mediterranean, he stressed the great peril to America itself, declaring emphatically that "I believe as strongly as I have ever believed anything that you will be unable to protect the United States from German attack unless you have the cooperation of the French and British fleets."[10] The ambassador, by now an impassioned interventionist, was temporarily out of step with—and ahead of—thinking in Washington. On 30 May, Secretary of State Cordell Hull tried to educate Bullitt on recent developments in national security by wiring that the fleet was staying where it was, because "what vessels we have in the Atlantic are required under present conditions either for patrol duty or for special service in South and Central American waters."[11]

Bullitt's latest advice was lost on the president as well as on Hull. Roosevelt was being very attentive to the kind of counsel that such men as Cornelius Vanderbilt Whitney, chairman of the board of Pan American Airways, were offering. On 27 May, Whitney wired the president that the United States must keep its war production from leaving the hemisphere, husbanding it for its own defense, because "as we are aware, the South and Central American republics have only a combined air strength of less than an estimated one thousand modern first-line fighting planes."[12] This cable reflected Roosevelt's own thinking at the end of May, except that the president was more aware than Whitney of the real air strength of the American republics and knew that combined air forces below the Rio Grande had closer to one hundred than one thousand "modern first-line fighting planes."

On the same day (30 May) that Hull informed Bullitt of the administration's decision not to send ships to the Mediterranean, Roosevelt was telling delegates from the Conference on National Defense that the Allies were on the brink of elimination. "It is extremely serious for England and France," the president announced, speaking (obviously) off the record. "We are not saying so out loud because we do not want to intimate in this country that England and France have gone." If, as Roosevelt and others expected, the Germans did win, there was no certainty that they would then launch an invasion of the Western Hemisphere; instead of using military force, they might try to achieve their ends by applying economic coercion against such nations as Argentina, which were dependent upon exports to Europe for their very lifeblood. That, the president suggested, was the "peaceful" scenario. On the other hand, Hitler might think, "'I have taken two-thirds of the world and I am armed and ready to go; why shouldn't I go the whole hog and control, in a military way, the last third of the world, the Americas?' And there is no one of us," continued Roosevelt, "can guess definitely as to what will be the decision on the part of Germany and Italy if they completely control all of Europe, including the British Isles. We don't know."[13]

One man who thought he knew was Adolf Berle, who recorded his latest impressions in his diary on the same evening that Roosevelt made the above remarks. "The military news is worse than ever," the assistant secretary of state wrote. "The German claque of triumph grows, and of course is having repercussions all up and down South America. Sumner seems unhappy about it, fearing that there might be a breakaway and that the hemisphere

would be split up. In that case there is not much question but
that we should be in for a chaotic period in South America."[14]

By the end of May, the belief that Britain and France would
lose the war was almost as prevalent in Washington as had been,
back in the heyday of the "Phony War," the contrary view that
they would win (or, at worst, draw). Even so staunch an admirer
of the Allies as Frank Knox, who would shortly move into the
cabinet as secretary of the navy, assumed that a Hitler victory
was a foregone conclusion. According to Interior Secretary Harold Ickes, Knox "believes that as soon as Germany has consoli-
dated its gains in Europe—all of this, of course, on the theory that
Germany will win—it will proceed to penetrate South America,
and then we will have our work cut out for us in this country."[15]

Other Allied partisans felt similarly. Journalists Joseph Alsop
and Robert Kintner, appending a 6 June postscript to the latest
edition of their study of Roosevelt's foreign policy, *American
White Paper*, wrote that the likely outcome of the war in Europe
would be either a smashing German victory and the destruction
of the Allied fleets, or the German victory with the *capture* of
the fleets. In the latter instance, the authors concluded that the
United States would have to retrench its defense commitments
in the hemisphere, effectively writing off to Nazi conquest most
of South America, and concentrating on the protection of North
America, the Panama Canal, and the Caribbean. With the southern part of the hemisphere about to be sucked into the vortex of
revolution—Argentina, Uruguay, Brazil, Chile, Mexico, "and
probably Colombia" were all seen to be prime targets of Nazi
insurrection—the United States would have its hands full just
safeguarding its own territory.[16]

Although it was not they who gave it the name *quarter-sphere
defense*, Alsop and Kinter were sketching the outlines of the strategic theory that came to bear that label. The thought of con-
stricting the defense perimeter of the United States to more
manageable proportions was appealing to many Americans, including men in the armed forces who saw themselves as primary
protectors of the nation. In early June, when the Allies' chances
seemed most hopeless, army and navy planners recommended
that the use of American land forces be restricted within the hemisphere to lands north of thirteen degrees south latitude (i.e., a
line transecting the northeastern Brazilian state, Bahia, just south

of the city of Salvador). If this was not exactly the concept of quarter-sphere defense, the planners were still proposing much less than the total defense of the hemisphere that the White House was publicly pledging itself to provide. On 13 June, Secretary of War Woodring and Secretary of the Navy Edison approved this proposal, which was embodied in the latest American war plan, RAINBOW 4. Originally, the new RAINBOW plan was to have been a blueprint for the total defense of the hemisphere, but it was scaled down in the wake of German successes on the battlefield. In its revised version, RAINBOW 4 incorporated the essentials of the POT OF GOLD idea, calling for an expeditionary force of fifteen thousand men to "occupy necessary land positions in northeastern Brazil to deny the use by the enemy or by enemy sympathizers of potential sea, land, or air bases in northeastern Brazil. . . ."[17]

The restricted defense policy embodied in the latest war plan was the creation of, and represented the thinking of, the War and Navy Departments; in no sense did it indicate a consensus within the administration, and it was resented especially by the State Department, as the American ambassador to Colombia, Spruille Braden, discovered to his chagrin. Upon returning to Bogotá on 11 June, after a lengthy stateside leave, Braden thought that he would bolster the sagging spirits of President Eduardo Santos, who was worried about a rumored retrenchment of the American commitment to hemispheric defense, by letting him know that it was only the region "around [the] corner of northeastern Brazil" that would not be defended by the United States Army. When Sumner Welles learned from Braden of this conversation, he was appalled and sent off a blistering cable lambasting the ambassador for his remarks. "I do not know," sputtered Welles, "where you obtained the idea which you expressed to the President, . . . that in the event of the contingencies you mention the United States would not undertake to give assistance to the other republics 'around the corner of northeastern Brazil.'" The under secretary asserted that if Braden's statement leaked out, "nothing could be more fatal" to American interests in southern South America—especially in Chile, where there already existed a "very disquieting defeatist psychology."[18]

In a return cable, Braden sought to assure Welles that Santos could be trusted to keep the conversation confidential. He also informed Welles of the origin of the controversial "around the corner" phrase: "that idea and expression I obtained from President Roosevelt May 28." The ambassador further reported that following his two months' absence from Colombia, he discovered that "German successes have in surprising measure altered opinions of many Colombians . . . to pro-Nazi attitude." He concluded that should Germany emerge, as it appeared likely to, as master of the situation in Europe, "Colombia could not overlook for spiritual reasons the material consequences."[19]

The Commerce Department joined with the State Department in opposing the idea of anything less than total defense of the hemisphere, calling espousals of a restricted military effort in Latin America "counsels of appeasement, . . . dangerous in the extreme." But by June the concept of quarter-sphere defense was catching on with many Americans, one of whom was General Motors executive Graeme K. Howard, who wanted the administration to adopt a policy of "cooperative regionalism," meaning that American forces would protect the Caribbean region only, while the more southernly Latin states would be left to make the best deal they could with the new Europe, their natural market. "The design," wrote Howard, "to promote an economic and political hegemony for the entire Western Hemisphere at the expense of the European nations should be condemned in the strongest terms."[20]

To Harry Hopkins and others at the Commerce Department, Howard's proposal was a recipe for suicide. A departmental paper on defense of the hemisphere, issued 11 June, urged in the strongest terms that the United States follow the "imperative of geography," and cautioned that "the danger of delay cannot be overdrawn. Latin America, from Mexico down, is loaded with dynamite." The only safe assumption for policy purposes, the report stated, was that Germany would complete her triumph in a few weeks, eliminate Russia in "another Polish campaign," and then direct her full energies against Latin America. Noting that German "preponderance over us is now at its maximum," the Commerce Department analysts recommended that the administration pursue a three-pronged plan of action: 1) secure the bases that the United States needed so vitally in Latin America; 2) oust Germany from her strongholds in the hemisphere; and 3) buy up, on a preemptive basis, the strategic exports of the Latin nations.

This memorandum frankly advocated worst-case analysis as the only intelligent manner by which the administration could prepare for the coming challenges. "The experience of Britain has shown," declared the report, "that where the national interest and security are at stake, we dare make only the most pessimistic assumption. To do otherwise is to be too late at every stage, to invite attack when it suits the aggressor, to face conflict half prepared." Concluded the Commerce Department analysts: "The danger is great; our action must be immediate."[21] Assistant Secretary of State Berle was one of the many policymakers in the nation's capital to agree with the call for a speedy response to the Nazi challenge. "I cannot but see," he wrote in his diary in early June, "that [the Germans] will be in such bad shape economically that they will then try to open *pourparlers* with the Western Hemisphere. . . . It looks to me as though we had about a year in which to get ready, and every day lost is an added day of danger."[22]

Although public opinion had nearly unanimously come around to the belief that, as the Commerce Department memo expressed it, Latin America was "loaded with dynamite," and although almost all of official Washington had, by early June 1940, conceded that Germany would conquer all of Europe, there existed a tiny but articulate group of Americans who refused to give up on Britain. The more numerous the obituaries for Britain became, the more active grew the beleaguered nation's partisans, who knew exceedingly well how to utilize the communications media to muster support for their cause. One of the most powerful arguments in their arsenal was the contention that the British fleet was the first line of American defense. On 10 June, Whitney Shepardson, acting for a small set of Washington-area interventionists, released to the press "A Summons to Speak Out," which called upon the president to ask Congress for a declaration of war against Germany. Apart from being the honorable thing to do, the declaration of war would make eminent sense, for "if the British navy is destroyed or taken over, if the French army is defeated in final action, we shall have to face our job alone. We shall have to aid South America single-handed, in the presence of triumphant and hungry aggressors operating across both oceans."[23]

The belief that Latin America represented Hitler's next target figured heavily in the calculation of those who wanted all-out

aid to England, just as it was influential in the cautious White
House judgment that American matériel would have to be kept
in this hemisphere against the pending attack. Barry Bingham,
publisher of the *Louisville Courier Journal,* saw no hope for Latin
America if the British succumbed: "It will be a difficult enough
problem under such circumstances for us to defend our own territorial borders. Obviously it would be madness for us to set out
alone to defend two whole continents."[24] Raymond Leslie Buell
concurred in the view that the hemisphere would be difficult to
defend. With 30 percent of the globe's land area, and more than
forty-four thousand miles of coastline, the New World presented
its defense planners with a staggering problem, one made well-
nigh insoluble by the hemisphere's enormous distances (e.g.,
Washington is closer to Prague than to Rio; and San Francisco is
closer to Yokohama than New York is to Cape Horn). Clearly,
reasoned Buell, "the task of policing Europe would be less bur-
densome than that of defending this hemisphere." Not only would
South America have to be left undefended, it would also present
a temptation that Hitler could not pass up, because it was "one
of the most unpopulated continents and one of the greatest undeveloped reservoirs of raw materials in the world."[25]

A second pro-Allied lobby, not connected with the Shepardson
group, also took to the newspapers on 10 June in a move to gar-
ner public support for maximum American aid—short of war—for
Britain and France. William Allen White's Committee to Defend
America by Aiding the Allies inserted a full-page advertisement
in leading dailies from coast to coast, calling upon the White
House to keep Britain and France in the fight, so that America
would not have to confront "another Flanders, closer to home."
The ad, written by playwright Robert Sherwood, focused on what
was by now anything but a novelty, the idea that a violation of
the Western Hemisphere would be a direct and immediate consequence of the fall of Britain. "It is obvious that there is no immediate danger of direct invasion of the United States," declared
Sherwood, adding that such was not Hitler's way of making war.
Instead the Fuehrer operated furtively, utilizing insidious sapping
techniques, employing Trojan Horses that were even now "grazing
in all the fertile fields of North and South America." In the southern continent this had been going on for some time, said Sherwood,
recounting the familiar Nazi record of "persuasion, bribery, and

intimidation" below the Rio Grande. "They have been fighting a trade war and a political war and what we have already seen in Norway and Holland and Belgium proves to us that these agents are ready to fight a military war when the orders come through from home." Sherwood concluded by observing that anyone who thought the Nazis would not attack the New World was "either an imbecile or a traitor."[26]

This last statement rankled White, who wrote Sherwood that "you are bringing my gray hairs in sorrow to the grave."[27] The Kansan was seeking above all to attain unity on the crucial question of aiding Britain, and he believed that the advertisement, because of its concluding comment, would prove divisive. He also disagreed with the playwright's openly interventionist convictions. White honestly thought that by supporting the Allies with all aid short of war the United States could stay out of the fighting. This cautious approach to the issue of intervention was based on a revulsion toward war, a not uncommon sentiment in the United States (and elsewhere) during the interwar years.[28] Moreover, White entertained serious doubts that, even with American help, Britain could win, but he argued nonetheless that the United States should assist a cause that might very well be hopeless. He explained his position in June, in an open letter to his committee: "If we have the good will of the Allies when they are defeated, which seems likely, we can make arrangements to get their fleets. If we have their fleets, we can defy Hitler. . . . If we do not help the Allies, if we turn our backs on them now, they will see no reason for helping us by giving us their fleets."[29] Perhaps some people were persuaded by White's naïve reasoning; many, on the other hand, were more fearful than ever that White's committee would strip American defenses and get nothing in return. Especially angered was Verne Marshall, arch-isolationist editor of the *Cedar Rapids Gazette,* who labeled the White committee "The Committee to Defend America by Destroying Itself."[30]

At a press conference held the morning after the Sherwood ad first appeared (it was published on successive days, 10 and 11 June), President Roosevelt was asked if he cared to comment on it. He replied that he had not looked at it until he had been informed that Bob Sherwood was the author; now, having read it, he felt compelled to praise it as a "great piece of work, extremely educational for the people of this country and, without going into a specific endorsement of every phase, it is a mighty good thing that Bill White and his Committee are getting things like this out for the education of this country."[31] By this time, the country had become so well "educated" that it was becoming more difficult to find an American who did *not* believe that Hitler had aggressive plans for Latin America. In July, Gallup reported that more Americans (35 percent) expected a German victory than foresaw a British victory (32 percent); and *Fortune's* Roper poll listed 40.1 percent as certain of an Axis triumph, against only 30.3 percent who believed the British would win.[32] Hadley Cantril's Public Opinion Research Project revealed that 70 percent of the American public thought that Germany would try to get control of South America; and almost the same percentage (67) said they would fight Germany because of this. Yet, at the same time, only 37 percent would support Britain at the risk of getting involved in the war.[33]

It was wise that Roosevelt, in his comment on the Sherwood piece, issued the caveat enjoining his "going into a specific endorsement of every phase," for the president would not have been able to ratify honestly the advertisement's conclusion that massive aid must be sent to England. He certainly agreed with the premise that Hitler was a menace to Latin America—had he not been talking himself hoarse on this point for more than two years? —but he simply could not afford to count too heavily on Britain escaping defeat, and he most definitely could not afford to deliver the kind of help the British wanted most—American destroyers that might have to be used very soon to protect the hemisphere from invasion. As mentioned in the previous chapter, Roosevelt could and did make available to the British some guns and ammunition in early June; all of this matériel had been declared surplus by the War Department, in conformity with the law. And the well-known cooperation between Secretary of the Treasury Henry Morgenthau and the British purchasing agent, Arthur Purvis, continued to ensure the delivery of airplanes from private American manufacturers to British flight crews.

But with destroyers the president drew a firm line. He was not in a position to gamble with the nation's security. As one English writer, Philip Goodhart, has explained, "Americans have traditionally been a naval-minded people. Historically the Navy was the nation's front line and now in fact it provided the country's only serious defence—apart from the British Commonwealth. Handing over part of the country's front line of defence was psychologically quite diffrent from shipping some aged cannon or grease-packed rifles."[34] Goodhart hints that Roosevelt might have let the ships be transferred to the Royal Navy if he could have been assured of public support. This is a restatement of the theme that Roosevelt, an avowed and lifelong "internationalist," constantly found himself constrained by public opinion from pursuing a more active policy toward Europe. The problem with such a claim is that by early June 1940 the president was still extremely wary of emptying the American weapons cupboard to nourish a falling warrior; only by mid-July would he begin to perceive that Britain might just survive and confound all the pessimists, and that American and Latin American security would be enhanced by supporting the British struggle against Germany. Hadley Cantril, commissioned by the White House to conduct confidential public opinion surveys during this period, has discounted the argument that Roosevelt was kept from going to Britain's side in early June by public sentiment against American involvement in the war: "As far as I am aware, Roosevelt never altered his goals because public opinion appeared against him or was uninformed."[35] Nothing that I have read causes me to dismiss Cantril's assertion.[36]

On the night of 10 June, Roosevelt addressed the graduating class at the University of Virginia, in Charlottesville. He was in a fighting mood over Mussolini's opportunistic declaration of war earlier in the day—an action that Italy had timed to perfection, for now it was too late to run much risk of defeat, but it was early enough so that some of the spoils could be claimed on the basis of services rendered to the common cause; as it had in the First World War, Italy was again rushing to the aid of the victor. Over the objections of the ever-cautious Cordell Hull, the president included some vigorous and undiplomatic language in his speech, condemning the Italian move with the memorable phrase, "the hand that held the dagger has struck it into the back of its neighbor." An indignant Roosevelt began to make some strong promises. "In our American unity," he pledged, "We will pursue two obvious and simultaneous courses; we will extend to the opponents of force the material resources of this nation; and, at the same time, we will harness and speed up the use of those resources in order that we ourselves in the Americas may have equipment and training equal to the task of any emergency and every defense."[37]

If taken at face value, Roosevelt's words would seem to justify the conclusion that Charlottesville marked the end of isolationism and the beginning of full-scale material support of the Allies.[38] It is certainly true that the president's remarks to the students tended in the direction of, at the very least, a pro-Allied nonbelligerency; and it is quite easy to argue, in a linear way, that the destroyers-for-bases deal, which really *did* denote the end of the administration's isolationism, was a natural sequel to the Charlottesville address. But to so argue is to overlook the critical determinant in Roosevelt's decision to proceed with massive aid to Britain: the ability of the British to convince him that they really could carry on the fight, and that any aid sent would not be wasted or later turned against the United States itself by the conqueror of Europe. It is premature to conclude that by 10 June this crucial prerequisite, the survivability of Britain, had been met to Roosevelt's satisfaction; for as the documents reveal, a great deal of controversy erupted in the administration over the president's announced pair of "obvious and simultaneous courses"—giving material aid to the Allies while at the same time rearming the hemisphere. Many voices were raised in protest against what was considered to be an impossible promise. Indeed, by the most elementary arithmetic, it seemed that every gun sent overseas meant one less gun with which to defend the New World, once the struggle for the hemisphere got under way in earnest.

It seemed obvious in Washington policymaking circles that the menace to the hemisphere was mounting daily during the first weeks of June. The day after Roosevelt's Charlottesville speech, Brazilian dictator Getulio Vargas did some speechmaking of his own. The eleventh of June was a holiday in Brazil—the anniversary of the 1865 Battle of Riachuelo, when the Brazilian navy had taken the measure of the Paraguayan squadron in the War of the Triple Alliance—and Vargas was using the opportunity to express some of his thoughts on the current war. His words had a chilling effect in Washington, as cold and gray as the armor plating on the battle cruiser *Minas Gerais*, from whose decks he declared that "we are heading into a future different from what has prevailed in matters of economic, social, and political organization;

and we feel that the old systems and antiquated formulas are in decline. . . . It is necessary, therefore, that we remove the debris of dead and sterile ideas." Vargas was referring to ideals like democracy and liberalism, and despite the hasty effort made by Rio to assure the United States that the speech was intended for domestic purposes only, in Washington it was interpreted as a harbinger of a Brazilian-German rapprochement.[39]

Chief of Staff Góes Monteiro later claimed that he had tried to dissuade Vargas from making his provocative speech, but the president had been adamant, saying that "it was necessary to give the tree a hard shake so the dead leaves would fall off."[40] To Góes's dismay, the dead leaves fluttered to the ground within full view of the pro-Allied press of the hemisphere, which relished the opportunity of running headlines like this one, from *Crítica* of Buenos Aires: "Vargas, with Fascist Language, Justifies the Aggression of the Barbarians."[41] Ambassador Jefferson Caffery was skeptical of the clumsy attempt made by Góes and Aranha to reassure him that the speech really was harmless; along with other American observers of Brazilian politics, he regarded the affair as evidence that Vargas, a brilliant political weathercock who expected an Axis victory, was attempting to insinuate himself into Hitler's good graces.[42]

Almost as unwelcome in Washington as Vargas's discourse was a new cable from Winston Churchill, once again beseeching the president to transfer some of the navy's old destroyers to Britain. Since Italy's decision for war had increased the strength of the navies opposing the Allies, Churchill felt that the only way to redress the imbalance would be "for us to have thirty or forty old destroyers you have already reconditioned. . . . Not a day should be lost."[43] As much as it troubled Roosevelt to say no once more to a man and a nation he deeply admired, he could not do otherwise. Latin American difficulties showed absolutely no sign of abating, despite yet another German denial of aggressive intentions in Latin America—a denial that took the form of a *New York Journal American* interview between Hitler and Hearst correspondent Karl von Wiegand, in which the Fuehrer disclosed that his policy was "Europe for the Europeans and America for the Americans." At a press conference later that day, Roosevelt remarked that only a gullible person would put much stock in what Hitler had been quoted as saying. Besides, the president told delegates from the National Conference of Business Paper Editors, there was more than one way for Hitler to achieve his ends. Even assuming that he was sincere when he told von Wiegand that he had no intention of invading the hemisphere, a dubious assumption to say the least, he could accomplish his goal through economic blackmail of dependent nations like Argentina. "In other words," Roosevelt explained, "you can gain domination over a large portion of this continent without sending troops over, and that is something we have to watch out for."[44]

It was not just the president and his top advisers who thought like this. As public opinion samplers discovered, most Americans concurred in the Commerce Department's assessment that Latin America was "loaded with dynamite." Unfortunately for the United States, German battlefield successes were having a tremendous demonstrative effect on Latin public opinion, as well as on Latin leaders. This troubled a young American living in Quito so much that he took the trouble to compose a lengthy appeal to the White House, requesting immediate American action. Addressing his appeal to Eleanor Roosevelt, who read it and passed it along to the president, Robert L. Swarts described the United States predicament in South America as "catastrophic," and predicted that Germany could reduce the Latin republics to vassalage within a year. "Fifty thousand planes, or treble that number, will not suffice to protect this hemisphere once Germany acquires political and economic control of Latin America, the next logical move in her bid for world domination."[45]

While Americans were directing their attention southward, France's weary premier, Paul Reynaud was sending westward a last call for help: enter the war now, he said to Roosevelt, or France would be beaten. The American rejection of this appeal came the next day, 15 June, leaving the French cabinet to debate not *whether* to continue fighting, but how best to broach the humiliating subject of surrender to the Germans. For the fourth time in a month, Winston Churchill asked for the destroyers, this time spicing his request with the insistence that the ships were of life-and-death importance, now that it appeared that France was leaving the war. The prime minister reminded Roosevelt that if Britain went the way of her ally, and if the fleet were surrendered, Hitler and his Axis partners would have "overwhelming sea power" at their disposal.[46] As had happened three times before, the White House rebuffed Churchill. On 17 June the French, having been them-selves denied by the United States, notified Germany (through Spanish intermediaries) that they wished an armistice.

The combination of the French collapse and the British clamor for assistance of a kind that would likely involve the United States in the war rekindled in Washington the smoldering debate over the wisdom of continuing to aid the British. On the same morn-ing that France asked Hitler's terms, Chief of Staff Marshall met with his top staff officers to draft a War Department memoran-dum for use in the struggle to keep American arms from going overseas. More than any other government department, the War Department was apprehensive that the failure to stanch what it considered to be a flood—but what the British felt was more like a trickle—of arms and ammunition to Britain would lay open the hemisphere to depredation. Working from an outline prepared by the War Plans Division, Marshall and his aides, Brig. Gen. George V. Strong and Brig. Gen. Frank M. Andrews, agreed on the follow-ing recommendations: that the United States should stay purely on the defensive in the Pacific; that it should conduct an imme-diate mobilization of national effort for the purpose of defending the hemisphere; and, most importantly, that it should make "no further commitments for furnishing matériel to the Allies." This last suggestion was justified as a "recognition of the early defeat of the Allies, an admission of our inability to furnish means in quantities sufficient to affect the situation, and an acknowledg-ment that we recognize the probability that we are next on the list of victims of the Axis powers and must devote every means to prepare to meet the threat."[47]

Later that day Marshall attended a meeting of the Standing Li-aison Committee, where he hoped to be able to persuade Chief of Naval Operations Stark and Under Secretary of State Welles of the necessity of hoarding military and naval supplies for the defense of the New World—*in* the New World. Of all the prob-lems requiring the attention of America's armed forces, said Marshall, "perhaps the most serious and delicate, . . . and one which is now staring us in the face," was the creation of a net-work of Nazi satellite regimes throughout Latin America. Such regimes could be brought into existence by revolution, or they could eventuate as a simple consequence of the conversion to Nazism of an existing government. In either case, a strong American reaction would be needed; and Marshall wanted nothing less than the "preventive occupation of the strategic areas in the Western Hemisphere wherein German or Italian bases might be established to menace the Panama Canal or the Continental U.S." He hoped it was apparent to all that the United States could not afford to continue squandering resources on Britain. "The essence of the problem," Marshall concluded, "is time. Consequently the definite suspension of French *or* British resistance should become the signal for the start of complete mobilization of all our national resources."[48]

Although one of the necessary conditions for an abandonment of the administration's policy of isolation—the perception that the security of the United States was menaced—had been amply fulfilled by the third week of June 1940, the same cannot be said for another necessary (perhaps sufficient) condition for American involvement in the European war: the assumption that the remaining ally, Britain, could survive long enough to justify American diversion of war supplies that were otherwise vitally needed (or so it was thought) for the defense of the Latin American republics. The fall of France by itself did not make U.S. entry into the fighting inevitable.[49] What *did* make it possible for Franklin Roosevelt to commit American power to the support of Britain was the ability of the British to convince him that they could withstand the Axis onslaught long enough to allow the United States to rearm fully; in this case, American supplies sent to Britain would be a wise investment indeed, for they would buy the time that the administration needed to get the United States in shape to confront Germany.

11

Tolling the Passing Bell for Isolationism

The withdrawal of France from the war did not signal the inevitability of American intervention in Europe.[1] Instead, it touched off within the administration a lively debate on the wisdom of continuing to furnish matériel to Great Britain. The Army was particularly reluctant to gamble with the national security. On 11 June, nearly a week before France stopped fighting, Maj. Walter B. Smith had sent a memo to Chief of Staff George C. Marshall, setting forth reasons why the War Department should veto the transfer of some five hundred 75-mm guns to England: "If we were required to mobilize after having released guns necessary for this mobilization and were found to be short in artillery matériel, . . . everyone who was a party to the deal might hope to be found hanging from a lamp post."[2]

Marshall needed little coaching on the need to keep American war supplies from crossing the Atlantic. On 17 June, the day France was asking armistice terms of the Germans, he took his case to his colleagues on the Standing Liaison Committee, Chief of Naval Operations Harold Stark and Under Secretary of State Sumner Welles. His testimony, cited above,[3] made a favorable impression on Stark, the official who would have to approve any waiving of destroyers from active service with the navy—assuming, in the first place, that a way could be found to circumvent a federal statute seemingly prohibiting such a release. Welles was chary of Marshall's ideas on "preventive occupation" of strategic parts of Latin America, but otherwise he was in agreement with the chief of staff's analysis of the threat facing the nation.

Also in agreement with Marshall was Secretary of War Harry Woodring, who was fighting hard to keep American military equipment from leaving the Western Hemisphere. Not only did Woodring fear an imminent invasion of the New World; he also had a longstanding antipathy toward American involvement with any of the European powers. On 20 June, he became the only cabinet secretary fired by Roosevelt during four terms in office. The sacking is usually interpreted as stemming from Woodring's refusal to approve the transfer of ten B–17 bombers to England, with it being assumed by those who adhere to this view that Roosevelt wanted the planes sent across the Atlantic.[4] In fact, by 20 June, as we shall presently see, the president himself was still undecided about whether to continue to assist England; he even wrote to Woodring, five days *after* the latter's departure from the cabinet, that he believed the bombers should stay in the United States. But that did not mean Roosevelt wanted Woodring to stay in the cabinet. Quite to the contrary. The president was fed up with the incredible situation in the War Department, where Woodring and Assistant Secretary Louis Johnson had not even talked to each other for months, and he was using the crisis in Europe as the occasion to sweep away the deadwood from both the War and Navy Departments. It was at this juncture that Roosevelt finally formed his "national" government by bringing into the cabinet two prominent Republicans, Henry Stimson (at the War Department) and Frank Knox (at the Navy Department).

Outside the War Department there were those who challenged the assumption that further aid to Great Britain would constitute a waste of valuable resources. One could still find many exponents of the position that the only sure safeguard of Latin American independence was the survival of England. From Berlin, Chargé d'affaires Alexander Kirk reported to the State Department that Hitler would seek gains in the New World when he had disposed of his opposition in Europe. Kirk did not think that Hitler would actually invade the Americas; he had no need to, for other methods of achieving dominance would be more practical. "He will strangle the United States economically and financially," Kirk predicted, "and even if he does not succeed in breaking the solidarity of the countries of the Western Hemisphere, which may be precarious at present, he will confront the United States within a brief measure of time with the impossible tasks of adjusting its system to an economy in which it will be excluded from access to all foreign markets." The only way to avoid this destiny, so far as Kirk was concerned, was for the United States to take whatever steps were necessary to keep Britain alive and fighting.[5]

Henry Morgenthau, who remained a champion of increased aid to Britain throughout the period when that nation's survival seemed to hang in the balance, tried to prod Roosevelt into action on 18 June, the day after Kirk's cable reached Washington, by telling him that "unless we do something to give the English additional destroyers, it seems to me that it is absolutely hopeless to expect them to keep going."[6] Had Morgenthau's been the only kind of advice reaching him, the president would probably have decided to do just what the Treasury Secretary wanted him to. Roosevelt himself was earnestly hoping that Britain could stay in the war, and were it only possible to know for certain that American assistance *would* prevent Britain's collapse, he would doubtless have done all within his power to furnish the help that Churchill was requesting. But more authoritative military experts than Morgenthau were informing the president that all *was* lost in Europe. On 24 June, Marshall and Stark handed Roosevelt a joint memorandum entitled "Basis for Immediate Decisions Concerning the National Defense." The message contained therein was unequivocal: "It is believed that to release to Great Britain additional war material now in the hands of our armed forces will seriously weaken our present state of defense and will not materially assist the British forces."[7]

Roosevelt was not willing to go as far as the service chiefs wanted him to. Unwilling to foreclose the prospect of any future military aid to England, the president suggested a compromise, to which Marshall and Stark gave their reluctant assent during a White House conference on 24 June: Make further aid to Britain contingent upon that nation showing clear signs that it could survive until the beginning of 1941 (by which date the United States would have had a chance to strengthen its defenses in the hemisphere.) Marshall reminded Roosevelt that the needs of the hemisphere must be the first priority, to which the latter responded that "Yes, in general," he was in agreement with the chief of staff, and that further aid would depend entirely on the situation. The president also brought up the question of military assistance to the Latin American nations, most of whom were clamoring for American supplies. "To keep them sweet," he said, "We will have to give them a few tiny driblets which will not amount to anything to us."[8]

Thus was struck a compromise in the emotional dispute that

was racking the administration: Marshall and Stark would agree not to rule out the possibility of further aid to Britain; Roosevelt would agree to exercise the utmost caution with the nation's military hardware. All agreed that, from now on, Britain's fate would be in its own hands.[9] In a way, there was something diabolically clever about this proposition that Britain justify its sanctification by first arranging the preconditions that would make the sanctification unnecessary. Britain would be "saved" by the United States if it showed that it could save itself, with the posterior proposition being taken as evidence that salvation was indeed deserved. Put plainly, the administration was applying to the question of continued aid to Britain the aphorism of Benjamin Franklin: "God helps them that help themselves."

This is not the place to recount in detail the events of July that led to the cabinet decision of 2 August to extend aid to Britain in the form of the fifty overage destroyers that Churchill had been trying to obtain since May.[10] This decision was probably the most important one a Roosevelt cabinet ever made, for as a volume in the army's official history of the war has said, it "marked a clear departure from the path of neutrality and a clear confirmation of intent to give all aid to Great Britain short of declaring war. The United States had, indeed, entered into a limited participation in the war. . . ."[11] Suffice it to note that in Washington the worst fears of May and June had begun to dissipate in the sunshine of July and that each day that passed without a German invasion of Britain made the latter's survival less and less of an improbability. For this fortuitous state of affairs, oddly enough, the British had no one to thank so much as Hitler.

To be sure, nobody really expected an immediate invasion of England after 22 June; it would have taken some weeks to put into operation an assault on the island kingdom, even assuming that preparations for such an assault had been made well in advance—which they certainly had not. Still, it was believed that the Luftwaffe would, immediately upon the fall of France, go after the weakened Royal Air Force with unremitting fury, so as to achieve the air supremacy over the Channel without which any invasion would be destined to fail. But Hitler hesitated, and his curious inaction—no doubt largely explained by his ill-founded conviction that Britain was prepared to give up the useless struggle—proved to be his undoing, ultimately. There is reason to think that Hitler might have been content to leave England unconquered and in possession of its empire while he wheeled about to settle, at long last, the old scores with the Soviet Union. At any rate, it is known that he had a grudging admiration of his fellow "Aryans" in Great Britain, and it was not until the middle of July that he decided to go ahead with serious planning for OPERATION SEA LION, the assault on England.[12]

In contrast to German inaction, there were some very visible demonstrations of British resolve, predisposing the White House to consider that the British might indeed prove more durable in combat than their late ally, France. On 3 July, units of the Royal Navy smashed the bulk of the French fleet while it lay at anchor in the North African port, Mers-el-Kebir. This bloody incident, launched because of British fears that French vessels would be turned over to Hitler, portended by its very savagery the kind of resistance that Britain was capable of mounting. To plumb the depths of this encouraging show of spirit, Roosevelt sent to London, on 14 July, an important emissary, William J. (Wild Bill) Donovan, a World War I hero and close friend of the new secretary of the navy, Frank Knox. Donovan was instructed to assess the prospects of Britain's ability to withstand a German attack. After a fortnight in England, he reported that his hosts had a better than even chance (he placed the odds at sixty to forty) of repulsing the Nazi blow.[13] The American military attaché in London, Col. Raymond E. Lee, gave the British even better odds: "I will say a little better, say two to one, barring some magical secret weapon."[14]

Hitler's hesitancy; the Royal Navy's ferocity; optimistic reports from London; and the indomitable spirit of the British people, personified in the oratorical majesty of their prime minister—all these made their impressions on a wavering Roosevelt, allowing him to follow his heart and take the irrevocable decision of underwriting the survival of Great Britain. The weeks since May had not been easy ones for the president; he had taken no pleasure in rejecting Churchill's repeated demands for destroyers and other aid. But the rejections, Roosevelt felt, had had to be made, for the coming battle of Latin America would require all the military resources at the nation's disposal. From a remove of nearly four decades, it is perhaps difficult for us to imagine the genuine sense of alarm that pervaded Washington during the late spring and early summer of 1940. That this perceptual difficulty should exist says nothing for the intensity of the fear experienced by Roosevelt and the men around him, but rather it speaks volumes about our own inability to overcome the blinding glare of hindsight. While we take very seriously the fears of the present, we are apt to dismiss those of the past once subsequent developments have taken away the sting of uncertainty and dread.[15]

By late June 1940 there had not yet appeared any anodyne—temporal or otherwise—to take away the sting. The best that Washington decision makers could hope for was a miraculous resistance, a stiff holding action, by the British; the worst that they might expect, an early arrival of the Nazi hordes in Latin America. Before July, sensible observers could only be pessimistic observers; and from all quarters there poured into Washington messages of warning and suggestions of how to foil the Axis designs on the hemisphere.

Typical of this influx was a note of 24 June from novelist John Steinbeck, who wished an appointment with the president so that the latter might discover from a first-hand witness the true dimensions of the menace to Latin America. Steinbeck, who had just returned from a filming expedition to Mexico, wrote to Roosevelt: "In the light of this experience and against the background of the international situation, I am forced to the conclusion that a crisis in the Western Hemisphere is imminent, and is to be met only by an immediate, controlled, considered, and directed method and policy." Roosevelt could not have agreed more with this assessment of advancing peril, and he set aside time from his crowded schedule to receive Steinbeck at the White House on 26 June.[16]

Roosevelt relied to a surprising extent on information from various official and unofficial emissaries to supplement the data reaching him from regular channels in Latin America (which were the State Department, army and navy intelligence, and the FBI). He had even attempted, back in December 1939, to have Steinbeck get himself attached to navy intelligence, but the head of that division, Adm. Walter S. Anderson, was not interested in the proposal.[17] Another informal channel of information was the president's Hyde Park neighbor, Cornelius Vanderbilt, Jr., who had embarked on a journey to Latin America in May, promising to keep the White House filled in on everything he saw. Vanderbilt kept his promise, reporting at the end of August that a German invasion of Brazil and Central America was imminent—to be followed by an attack, via Mexico, on Texas! "In Colombia, Costa Rica and Mexico," wrote Vanderbilt, "I saw advance preparations for the Nazi invasion—private Nazi airports—private Nazi bombers—German civilians training natives. . . . It is not impossible that the United States might be conquered in a few weeks after England falls."[18]

Vanderbilt's letter portrayed a kind of hysteria that neither Roosevelt nor most of his leading advisers felt. At the White House, it was widely held that a victorious Germany *would* challenge the United States in Latin America, but it was never the case that American policymakers assumed a Nazi conquest of North America—although, to be sure, they could well conceive of a Nazi *invasion.* The president and the men around him did expect the nation to face a stiff fight ahead, but a fight from which it would, with effort, surely emerge victorious. And it was further assumed, in late June, that to earn its victory the United States would have to use all means at its disposal, including (and especially) economic warfare.

Thus it was that on 15 June Roosevelt instructed Harry Hopkins, the secretary of commerce, to prepare for him within five days a plan for the economic defense of the Western Hemisphere. The short deadline was unavoidable, the president said apologetically, "inasmuch as the matter is of great urgency." Hopkins was told to pay close attention to the task of creating countermeasures that would be "competitively effective against totalitarian techniques."[19] This was a clear indication that Roosevelt was losing all patience with the economic diplomacy of Secretary of State Cordell Hull, for whom it was an article of the deepest faith that reciprocal tariff reductions on the most-favored-nation principle would inexorably lead to a diminution of international tension, while at the same time benefiting American trade. Even before the war began, Hull's economic program had been running into mounting opposition from critics who worried about the growing Nazi menace in the New World. Early in 1938 Carleton Beals had written of the trade agreements that they were "based at present on childish reverence for trade principles that no longer operate. . . . They have mostly had but negligible effect."[20] Sumner Welles was not saying so at the time, but he agreed with Beals.

Invoking the simile of a Civil War politico whose sesquipedalian oratory was likened to a train of twenty cars from which emerged but a single passenger, Welles remarked that "in Mr. Hull's trains, the passenger was always the same—the trade agreements program."[21] Max Lerner and E. H. Carr were busy dismissing international laissez-faire as an illusion in the world of the 1930s; according to Lerner, "the voyage of the liberal mind takes place, as in Coleridge's poem, in a painted ship upon a painted ocean."[22]

What was possible for Roosevelt to tolerate in 1938 and 1939 became impossible to support in the wake of Germany's rout of France. In his instructions to Hopkins of 15 June, Roosevelt insisted that some means be found to allow the United States to absorb the Latin agricultural and mineral surpluses that so worried the White House. In addition, Hopkins was to try to eliminate intrahemispheric tariffs and other barriers to trade, to devise methods of channeling American private and governmental investment to Latin America, and to resolve somehow the nagging Latin debt controversy.[23] It would have been a tall order for Hopkins to fill if he had had five years instead of five days, but with the help of the State and Agriculture Departments he was able to cobble a blueprint solution to at least the ranking problem on the Roosevelt checklist, the surpluses.

Roosevelt announced the plan to the nation on 21 June, from the parking lot of the train station in his hometown, Hyde Park, where he had gone to spend a working weekend away from the heat and humidity of the nation's capital. To reporters who greeted his arrival, the president read a statement outlining the proposed Inter-American Trading Corporation (which became known, to the great displeasure of Adolf Berle, as the Inter-American Cartel).[24] Acknowledging the efforts of Hull, Roosevelt promised that the United States would continue to advocate the multilateral reduction of tariffs and other trade barriers. But, he continued, the current emergency made it mandatory that more direct measures be utilized to protect the economy of the Western Hemisphere; accordingly, he was going to ask Congress for 2 billion dollars to finance a new trading corporation that would be charged with marketing the exports of the New World.[25]

The Inter-American Trading Corporation idea bore some of the hallmarks of another hasty preparation undertaken during the emergency atmosphere of the late spring and early summer of

1940, the POT OF GOLD plan for the invasion of northeastern Brazil. What the two projects most had in common was not the element of surprise; it was the element of grandiosity. Where the military men would swoop down upon an ostensible friend, dispossessing him of strategic territory with only the most cursory of "by-your-leaves," the civilian economic planners would presume to conduct the trade relations of the twenty Latin republics in the same manner that Washington regulated the commerce of the forty-eight states. At a White House meeting convoked by Roosevelt on 27 June to flesh out the cartel proposal, Milo Perkins, the Agriculture Department's director of marketing, suggested that the new corporation be turned into a giant clearinghouse for trade in the hemisphere. Both Perkins and Secretary of Agriculture Henry Wallace knew that American farmers would not stand for the United States importing commodities that were already being overproduced at home. The next best move would be for the United States to be in a position to control the marketing elsewhere of Latin surpluses; that way, reasoned Perkins, it would become impossible for Hitler to put undue pressure on weak Latin exporters.[26] As Assistant Secretary of State Berle summarized the notion: "A line in the Atlantic and a line in the Pacific, and notice to all hands that we are prepared to open economic relations, provided politics on this side of the water are barred."[27]

The cartel differed from POT OF GOLD in one significant respect: it was widely publicized, and the publicity, not surprisingly, drew the attention of a host of critics at home and abroad. Domestic opponents of the cartel focused their attacks, as Perkins and Wallace knew they would, on the reasonable likelihood that American producers would have to bear nearly all the costs incurred in absorbing competitive Latin commodities. Well before the president's 21 June announcement at the Hyde Park train station, certain circles within the United States were already vocalizing their fear that they would be asked—or forced—by the administration to make sacrifices for the sake of security in the hemisphere. Three months after Sumner Welles had promised at Panama that the United States would assist republics whose export trade became dislocated by war and blockade, the American Grange declared that, inasmuch as the farmers of the United States were already choking on their own overproduction, no massive importations of Latin commodities could be tolerated.[28]

A few of the cartel's opponents suggested that the administration encourage Latin America to produce those manufactured goods that the United States had until lately imported from Europe. By so doing, Washington would be lessening the neo-colonial economic dependence of Latin America on Europe, while at the same time it would be contributing to a regime of international trade that would satisfy even the most orthodox of laissez-faire economists. This would also serve to defuse the charge made against the cartel, viz., that it was a device for entangling the Latin nations in the web of North American commercial imperialism.[29] Although Berlin did stress this theme in its commentary on the Inter-American Trading Corporation, many Americans also made use of the argument; one editor in the United States condemned the cartel for being an "almost Hitlerian-sized venture in economic imperialism. . . ."[30] Without employing quite the same wording, the Wilhelmstrassse tried to convince Latins that in addition to making them pawns of American plutocratic imperialists, Roosevelt's proposal would prejudice Latin America's standing with Germany, once the soon-to-be victorious Reich again began to trade with the New World.[31]

Attacked from all directions even before it had been officially announced, the fledgling cartel plan proved to be extremely short-lived. On 2 July, almost three weeks before the Havana conference at which it was to have been unveiled to the world in finished form, Assistant Secretary Berle remarked of the plan ("and I am sorry for whoever christened it 'cartel' ") that it was being whittled down to the lesser proportions of a policy of credits extended to enable the Latin nations to "swing" their surplus problems until the world situation improved.[32] By the end of July, the surplus commodity drama would have a new deus ex machina, the Export-Import Bank of the United States.

Who killed the Inter-American Trading Corporation? William Langer and S. Everett Gleason insist that it was Cordell Hull, to whom the cartel represented a stinging rebuke, a repudiation of everything he had worked for over the past seven years.[33] Hull was certainly no proponent of the scheme, and the resistance he and his supporters mounted within the State Department did not improve its chances of success, but this is not the same as saying that they, and they alone, scuttled it. It would have taken a far more vigorous and influential figure than Cordell Hull to deflect the president from what had originally seemed to him, in mid-June, to be a highly desirable, even vitally necessary, course of action.[34] It is true that the cartel was unpopular on other fronts as well. Numerous domestic foes of the idea made their opinions known to the White House, although there is no evidence that those opinions carried as much weight as they generated noise. And Latin America was not exactly oozing exuberance at the prospect of being allowed to watch the big brother to the north assume total control over the economic life of the hemisphere. Even had the Latin states been amenable to the cartel, it would have been a monumental task to get them to assent to cutbacks in production, without which the thought of regulating surpluses would have been an illusion.

Despite its having had much to discommend it, the cartel perished fundamentally because of events in the Old World, not the New. The Inter-American Trading Corporation only made sense in the context of an isolated Western Hemisphere. Once the assumption of hemispheric isolation was abandoned, then so too was the trade arrangement that was intended to make such isolation economically and financially possible. As I argued earlier in this chapter, July was a watershed month in the annals of American foreign policy. Prior to July, Washington decision makers had been energetically working to quarantine the Western Hemisphere from the military, political, and economic contagions of Europe; after July, these same decision makers opted to cast America's lot, not with the sister republics of the hemisphere, but with Great Britain. In one month, the foreign policy of the United States had been radically altered, in large part because the administration became convinced that if it did not accept the consequences of assisting Britain—even though the consequences would probably entail American entry, sooner or later, into the war—it would eventually have to fight Hitler in Latin America, without any effective allies. After early July of 1940, policymakers in Washington no longer allowed themselves the luxury of choosing whether to enter or to abstain from war. They were instead confronted with the simpler job of selecting the best means of protecting the United States from the war that was, in any case, seen to be coming to the Western Hemisphere.

In this context, it is easier to make sense of the abandonment of the cartel plan. Roosevelt and his advisers had never imagined that the job of controlling the trade of an entire hemisphere was going to be an easy one. It was simply that, prior to the decision to extend all aid short of war to Britain, the cartel scheme seemed absolutely imperative for the defense of the hemisphere and of the United States itself. But once agreement had been reached on discarding isolationism, administration planners realized that the cartel had quickly become redundant, for a far more direct and effective method of safeguarding national *and* hemispheric security was at hand. In the same way that the survival of Britain spared Roosevelt the pain of having to proceed with the invasion of northeastern Brazil, it also enabled him to avoid what could easily have developed into a truly imperialistic policy of economic interventionism.

As complicated as the economic life of the hemisphere was by the middle of 1940, it was no less complicated than the political relations between the United States and the Latin republics. There were numerous stumbling blocks to the administration's overriding goal of achieving inter-American solidarity—a solidarity that was, to repeat, of transcendent importance to Washington so long as the defeat of Britain seemed likely. Indeed, the seemingly insoluble challenge posed by the apparition of swarms of fifth columnists all over Latin America became, once the British began in July to show signs of an ability to carry on the fight in Europe, a compelling reason for the administration to channel aid to England.

It will be recalled that, except for during the panic months of May and June 1940, Roosevelt's strategic calculations had usually rested on the premise that the steadfastness of Great Britain was a very good guarantee of keeping the hemisphere safe from the Axis. At the beginning of July, the president began to reason thusly once again. For him, the preservation of Britain and the maintenance of security in the hemisphere became two sides of the same coin. Even in the War Department cracks were beginning to appear in the wall of opposition to further aid to Britain. On 2 July, the Military Intelligence Division forwarded a memorandum to Marshall that argued the necessity of sustaining Britain as an active combatant against Germany, for the sake of American security. The MID—fearing at the minimum an economic penetration of the hemisphere, and at the maximum a German military occupation of Argentina, Uruguay, Chile, and parts of Brazil—concluded that "a victorious Axis will present an immediate threat to the peace and stability of the Western Hemisphere and to the legitimate and vital interests of the United States."[35]

This memorandum was written by Sherman Miles, the assistant chief of staff for the Military Intelligence Division. It is noteworthy precisely because Miles was advising more assistance for Britain at a time when Marshall was campaigning for less. The willingness of the chief of G–2 to support the British was a function of his pessimistic belief that, failing such support, the Latin American nations must eventually enter the Nazi orbit. To Marshall, Miles reported that "the regimes in all the Latin American republics are unstable and tend to be authoritarian. They have more in common with fascism than democracy. . . . All of them, but particularly Argentina and Uruguay, are susceptible to the kind of economic pressure that Germany can generate. All of them have traditions of revolution and in all of them there are factions which would welcome Axis aid to seize and, in some cases to retain, power."[36]

The bleak picture that army intelligence painted was being reproduced by other branches of the War Department, and by the Navy Department as well. On 10 July, the War Plans Division outlined for Chief of Naval Operations Stark the most probable modus operandi Hitler would follow in subjugating Latin America. Initially, and commencing with the defeat of Britain, German efforts would be directed toward the economic domination of the southern half of the hemisphere. Then would come "Phase II," to be inaugurated either by a fifth column uprising in a South American state, or by the voluntary adhesion to the Axis bloc of any of several unstable governments (most likely those of Argentina, Brazil, or Uruguay). In the wake of Phase II would come an airborne invasion of northeastern Brazil, and a sizable landing operation to consolidate footholds in southern Brazil, Uruguay, or Argentina. Finally, the United States could expect the totalitarian powers to try to seize the Panama Canal.[37]

The War Plans Division memorandum analyzed the political stability of the individual Latin republics, judging the weakest regimes to be those in Argentina, Brazil, Chile, Uruguay, Costa Rica, and Ecuador. On the other hand, Mexico, Honduras, Nicaragua, Cuba, El Salvador, Haiti, and the Dominican Republic were all seen to be prepared to give unswerving support to the United States in defense of the "democratic" way of life.[38] With American security thought to be at stake, perhaps it was natural to overlook the seamier side of this second group of nations, of whom all but Mexico were dictatorships. But surely the war planners were going beyond the call of duty in eulogizing the Dominican Republic's Rafael Trujillo, the hemisphere's tyrant par excellence of the twentieth century, as "intelligent, energetic, forceful and progressive. Because of these qualities the Dominican Republic is the best governed country in the West Indies."[39]

It was one thing for economic policymakers like Harry Hopkins and Milo Perkins to construct their elaborate castles in the air, within which would be contained all manner of amicable solutions to the economic difficulties besetting the Western Hemisphere; it was a different matter altogether to devise some practicable means of ensuring that the military and political subversion of Latin America could be averted. As we know, the president, at the most worrisome moment of the battle for France, had seriously considered invading Brazil, over the objections of the State Department, which was certain that Roosevelt's cure would be as fatal as the disease it was intended to check. Roosevelt believed that most Americans would have supported such a dramatic show of determination; for public opinion polls had shown him nothing if not the eagerness of his countrymen to fight for the Monroe Doctrine. And he assumed that Congress was in a like frame of mind, because in the middle of June the Senate (unanimously) and the House (by a vote of 380 to 8) had approved the Pittman-Bloom Resolution, which authorized the administration to take over any European possessions in the New World that looked to be in danger of changing colonial masters.[40]

The Pittman-Bloom Resolution stipulated that the United States obtain control of threatened European colonies by "peaceful means," but it was obvious that Congress did not intend this caveat to be binding. Around Washington, the atmosphere was filled with talk of a preemptive American assault on a target in the hemisphere. Such talk worried Dana Munro, a leading academic authority on Latin America, who feared that if the White House breached its policy of nonintervention, the United States would find itself acting as it had in the unfortunate (to Munro) era of Theodore Roosevelt. Such action would give rise to the "danger that the other republics may come to mistrust and resent our vastly superior military power more than they fear that of our political enemies abroad."[41]

Most Americans did not share Munro's apprehensions about intervention. On 21 July a Gallup poll revealed that 84 percent of the public would fight if Germany tried to take over British, French, or Dutch possessions near the Panama Canal. Almost the same percentage (76.5) would go to war over Mexico, while more than half the nation (54.7 percent), according to an August *Fortune* poll, would confront Germany militarily if Brazil became endangered.[42] Clearly, a writer in *Foreign Affairs* was expressing the view of a majority of Americans when he stated in July that "we in the Americas are faced, as we have not been faced since the days of the Holy Alliance, with the possibility that the devastation of war may be brought to our very door."[43] "Never in our history," wrote another scholar some years later, "had we been so directly, so gravely threatened."[44]

The White House could count on the approval of the public and the Congress if it were forced to launch a preemptive strike against imperiled European colonies in the New World. There remained, however, the urgent matter of obtaining the sanction of the Latin American nations, who had lived for years in the uncomfortable shadow of a power that had habitually resorted to unilateral interventions in the affairs of its neighbors. To this task the State Department now bent its efforts, as the hemisphere's foreign ministers gathered in late July at Havana for a second conference under the auspices of the Buenos Aires and Lima accords of 1936 and 1938. Secretary of State Hull, who led the American delegation to the Cuban capital, must have experienced a profound sensation of déjà vu when he found himself dealing with yet another fractious delegation from Argentina, so unlike the placatory lot with whom it had been Sumner Welles's luck to have worked the previous September at Panama. At Havana, Argentina focused its opposition on United States proposals aimed at resolving the problem of the menaced European colonies.

It was not so much the Dutch possessions that excited administration imaginations as it was the disposition of the territories ruled by France. Under Secretary of State Welles later wrote of the "sinister possibility" of Vichy's delivering its West Indies islands and French Guiana to Germany, in which case the

American republics would "suddenly awake to find themselves confronted with actual Nazi rule in South America or in the Caribbean."[45] Cordell Hull was not concerned that Germany would itself absorb any proffered territories, but that it would offer them as bait to certain Latin states in return for "political and economic vassalage."[46] To the extent that captured New World colonies figured at all in German plans, Hull was probably closer to the truth than Welles. In early August the Wilhelmstrasse informed Germany's diplomatic missions in Latin America that "we have no aspirations for American colonies of European powers."[47]

Whatever Germany's aspirations were, the Roosevelt administration could only assume the worst. To avert the unsavory possibility that Hitler might try to claim some New World prizes of war, the United States delegation to Havana proposed the creation of a Pan-American trusteeship over the colonies in question. But the Argentines, led by a less tractable Leopoldo Melo than the Americans had known at Panama, objected that this plan would likely involve the American republics in a war with Germany, should that nation come for its booty. It was all very well for the Caribbean states to run the risk of incurring Hitler's wrath; they knew tnat they could count on the protection of the United States Army and Navy. But what could distant Argentina count on? wondered Melo. The Argentine statesman was almost certainly not aware that the new RAINBOW 4 plan had limited American land operations to areas north of the Brazilian bulge; but he did remember some remarks that Chief of Naval Operations Stark had made earlier that year, in an appearance before the House Naval Affairs Committee. Cordell Hull paraphrased Melo's comments on Stark's testimony: "From what Stark said, we're convinced you can't defend yourselves, much less come down here 6,500 miles to defend us."[48] Quite apart from the unreliability of any United States guarantees, Argentina had another concern. Having a longstanding dispute with Britain over the Falkland Islands (Islas Malvinas), Argentina did not want European powers to have *any* possessions in the Western Hemisphere; so why should it wager its security in the defense of some other nation's ill-gotten colony?[49]

In hopes of mollifying Argentina and any other reluctant Latin nations, the White House announced on 22 July, the day the Havana conference opened, that it was raising the lending powers of the Export-Import Bank by an additional half-billion dollars (from a ceiling of 200 million dollars). An unhappy delegation like Argentina's would be likely to think twice before jeopardizing the prospect of significant American economic assistance. Assistant Secretary of State Berle, for one, was well aware of the soothing effect that such a vast sum of money could have, even on the most irritated delegations. A few days before the conference started, he had reminded Roosevelt of the importance of properly timing his announcement that he was going to Congress for the additional Export-Import Bank funding: "If your message is released at noon, it starts the thing off with a bang."[50]

Bang it was. Exactly on cue, Roosevelt sent Congress a message asking it to "give prompt consideration to increasing the capital and lending power of the Export-Import Bank of Washington by $500 million, and removing some of the restrictions on its operations, to the end that the Bank may be of greater assistance to our neighbors south of the Rio Grande, including financing and handling the orderly marketing of some part of their surpluses."[51] Berle was exuberant over the message, which he took to be solid evidence that "we meant business."[52]

With the carrot of financial aid dangling so tantalizingly before them, the Latin delegations at Havana closed ranks behind the American program. On 30 July the Convention on the Provisional Administration of European Colonies and Possessions in the Americas was signed. Upon ratification by two-thirds of the American republics, this measure would permit any New World possession of a subjugated European state to be placed under a provisional Pan-American trusteeship. In addition, the conference adopted a crucial supplementary measure, the Act of Havana. This empowered *any* American republic to occupy, in an emergency, any endangered European colony, so long as the Convention had not been ratified. Berle considered this latter enactment to be "little short of amazing," because it extended a "blanket authority to the United States to seize any of the islands if there is threatened change of sovereignty, or if there is some kind of indirect control amounting to the same thing, or if they become a menace to the continental peace."[53]

A week after the Havana conference concluded its precedent-shattering business, and four days after the historic cabinet meeting at which approval had been given to the transfer of destroyers to Britain, Roosevelt announced to the press at his Hyde Park home that "it could be fairly said that the unity of the Americas is more nearly a fact than ever before in history, without any question."[54] On the one hand, Roosevelt was speaking in a Pickwickian sense, for he knew that should Germany win the war, the United States could expect to witness the formation of a long line of eager Latin suitors at Hitler's front door. Cordell Hull, back only a few days from his public-relations victory at Havana, told his cabinet colleagues and the president at the momentous meeting of 2 August that the vaunted solidarity of the hemisphere would remain in doubt so long as the European war was unresolved. After hearing what Hull had to say, Secretary of the Interior Harold Ickes remarked that "apparently there is no pretense at all that certain important South American countries, including the Argentine, Brazil, Uruguay, and probably Chile, may not be prepared to rush eagerly into the arms of Hitler if Hitler wins over England."[55]

But on the other hand, Roosevelt's statement to the press, that the unity of the hemisphere was at flood tide, was accurate. Indeed, all the president was saying, although no one could have guessed his deeper meaning at the time, was that the United States had gone about as far as it could in the Western Hemisphere. There were precious few rabbits left in the hat; and if the battle of Latin America was going to be won at all, it would have to be won on the other side of the Atlantic, for a Hitler who triumphed in Europe would be a Hitler capable of triumphing in much of South America. It is hardly necessary to reiterate that this would have created indeed an intolerable challenge to American security.

The destroyer transfer, although a flagrant breach of neutrality,[56] was not an act of war; Roosevelt and most of his advisers sincerely hoped that the United States could limit its participation in the fight against Hitler to the provision of material support alone.[57] But if not an act of war, the transfer was an important step toward the day when America, willingly or not, would be forced into the battle. Having decided to abandon isolationism and to extend enormous aid to its new ally, the United States would find itself bound by logic and duty to ensure that the stream of supplies continued to reach England, despite that nation's inability to continue paying for it. Then, when the Royal Navy proved unable to maintain by itself the transatlantic communications link, the United States Navy would step into the breach, and in so doing involve itself in an undeclared war with Germany by the summer of 1941.[58]

Two statements, made during the one-month hiatus between the cabinet's decision to proceed with the destroyers-bases exchange and the public announcement of this fait accompli, attest to the profound significance of the embryo alliance. The first statement was made in Philadelphia on 18 August by Ambassador William C. Bullitt, who told the American Philosophical Society that it was "as clear as anything that the United States will not go to war, but it is equally clear that war is coming to the Americas." Bullitt urged the White House to stand by Britain in its hour of need, to ensure that its fleet remained in reliable hands; for "the truth is that the destruction of the British Navy would be the turning of our Atlantic Maginot Line. . . ."[59]

The second statement was made in London two days later, when Winston Churchill, with more than his usual eloquence, tolled the passing bell for American isolationism. Announcing to Parliament that final agreement was near concerning the leasing of British New World bases to the armed forces of the United States—but carefully omitting any reference to the destroyers quid pro quo—the prime minister acknowledged that "undoubtedly this process means that these two great organizations of the English-speaking democracies, the British Empire and the United States, will have to be somewhat mixed up together in some of their affairs for mutual and general advantage. For my own part, looking out upon the future, I do not view the process with any misgivings. I could not stop it if I wished; no one can stop it. Like the Mississippi, it just keeps rolling along. Let it roll. Let it roll—full flood, inexorable, irresistible, benignant, to broader lands and better days."[60]

Adolf Berle, who usually lacked Churchill's usual eloquence, also knew that the passing bell had tolled for a policy in which, until recently, he had so strongly believed. By early October 1940 he had come to the unhappy conclusion that, as far as the administration was concerned, "war or peace is now a matter of fate."

Although he did not, for a moment, think that Britain was defending the "principles" for which the United States stood, he was confident that now, unlike in 1917, "we are helping the English not as a matter of British sentiment, but because we realize that we ourselves will be in difficulties if they go under—quite a different thing."[61]

Notes

Abbreviations

Berle Diary	Unpublished diary of Adolf A. Berle, Jr., Berle Papers, Franklin D. Roosevelt Library, Hyde Park, N.Y.
DGFP-D	Germany, Auswärtiges Amt, *Documents on German Foreign Policy, 1918-1945*, Series D, 13 vols. (Washington: Department of State, 1949-64).
FRUS	*Department of State, Foreign Relations of the United States* (Washington: United States Government Printing Office, 1862-).
MID	Military Intelligence Division, War Department Files, Record Group 165, National Archives, Washington.
Morgenthau Diary	Unpublished diary of Henry Morgenthau, Jr., Morgenthau Papers, Franklin D. Roosevelt Libary, Hyde Park, N.Y.
Roosevelt Papers [OF; PPF; PSF]	Unpublished papers of Franklin D. Roosevelt [Official File; President's Personal File; President's Secretary's File], Franklin D. Roosevelt Library, Hyde Park, N.Y.
SDDF	State Department Decimal File, Record Group 59, National Archives, Washington.
WPD	War Plans Division, War Department Files, Record Group 165, National Archives, Washington.

Chapter 1

1. For insights into the dependency approach, see C. Richard Bath and Dilmus D. James, "Dependency Analysis of Latin America: Some Criticisms, Some Suggestions," *Latin American Research Review* 11 (1976): 3–54; Ronald H. Chilcote, "Dependency: A Critical Synthesis of the Literature," *Latin American Perspectives* 1 (1974): 4–29; Tony Smith, "The Underdevelopment of Development Literature: The Case of Dependency Theory," *World Politics* 31 (January 1979): 247–88; David Ray, "The Dependency Model of Latin American Underdevelopment: Three Basic Fallacies," *Journal of Interamerican Studies and World Affairs* 15 (February 1973): 4–21; and Gabriel Palma, "Dependency and Development: A Critical Overview," in *Dependency Theory*, ed. Dudley Seers (London: Frances Pinter, 1981), pp. 20–78.

2. The dependency approach originated in Latin American scholarly circles, but for a Latin scholar who is critical of its utility, see Claudio Véliz, "The Wilder Shores of Politics," *International Journal* 37 (Winter 1981–1982): 1–12.

3. *Public Opinion Quarterly* 5 (Winter 1941): 677.

4. F. S. Northedge, *The International Political System* (London: Faber & Faber, 1976), p. 160.

5. Hubert Herring, *Good Neighbors: Argentina, Brazil, Chile and Seventeen Other Countries* (New Haven: Yale University Press, 1941), p. 327. The policy of "cultural rapprochement" is discussed in J. Manuel Espinosa, *Inter-American Beginnings of U.S. Cultural Diplomacy, 1936–1948* (Washington, D.C.: Department of State, 1976).

6. *Public Opinion Quarterly* 5 (March 1941): 118.

7. Nicholas John Spykman, *America's Strategy in World Politics: The United States and the Balance of Power* (New York: Harcourt, Brace, 1942), pp. 246–55. For a critical assessment of Spykman's view of cultural diplomacy, see Andrew Gyorgy, *Geopolitics: The New German Science*, University of California Publications in International Relations, vol. 3, no. 3 (Berkeley: University of California Press, 1944), p. 254.

8. Percy W. Bidwell and Arthur R. Upgren, "A Trade Policy for National Defense," *Foreign Affairs* 19 (January 1941): 295–96.

9. Eugene Staley, "The Myth of the Continents," *Foreign Affairs* 19 (April 1941): 491–92.

10. Quoted in Brian Connell, *Knight Errant: A Biography of Douglas Fairbanks, Jr.* (Garden City, N.Y.: Doubleday, 1955), p. 122.

11. The geographical determinism of Pan-Americanism is discussed in Ladis K. D. Kristof, "The Origins and Evolution of Geopolitics," *Journal of Conflict Resolution* 4 (March 1960): 24. How one felt about the issue of intervention often determined how one felt about Latin America, and vice versa, as Adolf Berle, an assistant secretary of state *and* hemisphere defense enthusiast, found out at a Washington dinner party in May of 1940. Seated near him were Mr. and Mrs. Walter Lippmann, advocates of increased aid to England, to whom Berle remarked that "South America was a fascinating and interesting place. Both said, bluntly and swiftly, that they had no interest in it. The fun then began." Berle Diary, 7 May 1940, box 211.

12. Even such evidently value-free entities as maps can be, and frequently have been, used for either explicit or implicit didactic (some would say propagandistic) purposes. Hans Speier, "Magic Geography," *Social Research* 8 (September 1941): 310–30.

13. John W. Holmes, *The Better Part of Valour: Essays on Canadian Diplomacy* (Toronto: McClelland & Stewart, 1970), p. 11.

14. Adams to Pres. James Monroe, 19 September 1820, quoted in Cushing Strout, *The American Image of the Old World* (New York: Harper & Row, 1963), p. 48.

15. Arthur P. Whitaker, *The Western Hemisphere Idea: Its Rise and Decline* (Ithaca: Cornell University Press, 1954).

16. Ibid., p. 155.

17. Howard J. Wiarda, "Social Change, Political Development, and the Latin American Tradition," in *Politics and Social Change in Latin America: The Distinct Tradition*, ed. Howard J. Wiarda (Amherst: University of Massachusetts Press, 1974), p. 3. Also see Margaret Daly Hayes, "Security to the South: U.S. Interests in Latin America," *International Security* 5 (Summer 1980): 133, where it is claimed that "Latin America has played only a minor role in U.S. strategic planning to date. . . ."

18. *Manchester Guardian Weekly*, 31 July 1983. For a critical assessment of administration policy toward Central America, see Piero Gleijeses, *Tilting at Windmills: Reagan in Central America*, Occasional Papers in International Affairs (Washington: Johns Hopkins Foreign Policy Institute, April 1982).

19. Carlos Fuentes, "Listen Yankee: Mexico Is a Nation, Not an Oil Well," *Manchester Guardian Weekly*, 4 March 1979, p. 7.

20. Robert E. Osgood, *Ideals and Self-Interest in America's Foreign Relations: The Great Transformation of the Twentieth Century* (Chicago: University of Chicago Press, Phoenix Books, 1964). The Lippmann quote is from Lippmann's 1944 essay, *United States War Aims*, cited by John Morton Blum, *V Was for Victory: Politics and American Culture during World War II* (New York: Harcourt Brace Jovanovich, 1976), p. 302.

21. Wilson's reasons for declaring war in 1917 are analyzed in Donald E. Nuechterlein, *National Interests and Presidential Leadership: The Setting of Priorities*, Westview Special Studies in International Relations (Boulder: Westview Press, 1978), pp. 41–50.

22. Basil Rauch, *Roosevelt, from Munich to Pearl Harbor: A Study in the Creation of a Foreign Policy* (New York: Creative Age Press, 1950), p. 194.

23. Robert Sobel, *The Origins of Interventionism: The United States and the Russo-Finnish War* (New York: Bookman Associates, 1960).

24. Arnold A. Offner, *The Origins of the Second World War: American Foreign Policy and World Politics, 1917–1941* (New York: Praeger, 1975).

25. Robert W. Tucker, *The Radical Left and American Foreign Policy*, Studies in International Affairs, no. 15 (Baltimore: Johns Hopkins University Press, 1971), p. 121.

26. These were the color plans: RED for the British Empire, ORANGE for Japan; they formed the backdrop for the serious planning that the Joint Planning Committee would undertake in the changed atmosphere of the late 1930s. When the color plans were elaborated, there existed no conceivable menace to the security of the United States; in the words of one scholar, "from the standpoint of the military planners, the period from the Washington Conference to the late 1930s was one of absolute security for the Western Hemisphere." William Everett Kane, *Civil Strife in Latin America: A Legal History of U.S. Involvement* (Baltimore: Johns Hopkins University Press, 1972), pp. 107–8.

27. The three works that are basic to an understanding of the revisionist critique of United States foreign policy in general and Latin American policy in particular are: William Appleman Williams, *The Tragedy of American Diplomacy*, 2d ed., rev. and enl. (New York: Dell Publishing, Delta Books, 1972); Lloyd C. Gardner, *Economic Aspects of New Deal Diplomacy* (Madison: Uni-

versity of Wisconsin Press, 1965); and David Green, *The Containment of Latin America: A History of the Myths and Realities of the Good Neighbor Policy* (Chicago: Quadrangle Books, 1971).

28. See Williams, *Tragedy of American Diplomacy*, p. 161: "Men who began by thinking about the United States and the world in economic terms, and explaining its operations by the principles of capitalism and a frontier thesis of historical development, came finally to define the United States in military terms as an embattled outpost in a hostile world. When a majority of the leaders of America's corporate society reached that conclusion, the nation went to war—at first covertly, then overtly."

29. Wayne S. Cole, "American Entry into World War II: A Historiographical Appraisal," *Mississippi Valley Historical Review* 43 (March 1957): 606–7; Ernest R. May, *American Interventionism: 1917 and 1941* (Washington: Service Center for Teachers of History, 1960), pp. 12–14; Alton Frye, *Nazi Germany and the American Hemisphere, 1933–1941* (New Haven: Yale University Press, 1967), pp. 2–3.

30. That it may be neither wiser nor safer to assume this is argued in David A. Baldwin, "Power Analysis and World Politics: New Trends versus Old Tendencies," *World Politics* 31 (January 1979): 174.

31. William Henry Chamberlin, *America's Second Crusade* (Chicago: Henry Regnery, 1950), p. 50; Norman Rich, *Hitler's War Aims: The Establishment of the New Order* (New York: W. W. Norton, 1974), p. 416.

32. Bruce M. Russett, *No Clear and Present Danger: A Skeptical View of the United States Entry into World War II* (New York: Harper & Row, 1972). For the claim that not only was its physical security unthreatened prior to America's entry into World War II but also prior to the War of 1812, the Mexican War, the Spanish-American War, World War I, and the Korean War, see Melvin Small, *Was War Necessary? National Security and the U.S. Entry into War*, Sage Library of Social Research, vol. 105 (Beverly Hills: Sage, 1980).

33. Hermann Rauschning, *The Voice of Destruction* (New York: G. P. Putnam's Sons, 1940), pp. 61–72, supplies an account of the author's conversations with Hitler in which Latin American countries formed the topic of discussion.

34. A. J. P. Taylor, *The Origins of the Second World War* (London: Hamish Hamilton, 1965).

35. Meir Michaelis, "World Power Status or World Dominion? A Survey of the Literature on Hitler's 'Plan of World Dominion' (1939–1970)," *Historical Journal* 15 (1972): 350. Also on this question, see Milan Hauner, "Did Hitler Want a World Dominion?" *Journal of Contemporary History* 13 (January 1978): 15–32; and Andreas Hillgruber, *Germany and the Two World Wars*, trans. William C. Kirby (Cambridge: Harvard University Press, 1981), pp. 52–54.

36. Hedley Bull, *The Anarchical Society: A Study of Order in World Politics* (New York: Columbia University Press, 1977), p. 18. For an intriguing analysis of the security concept, see Barry Buzan, *People, States, and Fear: The National Security Problem in International Relations* (Brighton, Eng: Wheatsheaf Books, 1983).

37. Especially helpful on threat perception are Raymond Cohen, *Threat Perception in International Crisis* (Madison: University of Wisconsin Press, 1979), pp. 3–15; Klaus Knorr, "Threat Perception," in *Historical Dimensions of National Security Problems*, ed. Klaus Knorr (Lawrence: University Press of Kansas, 1976), pp. 78–119; and David A. Baldwin, "Thinking about Threats," *Journal of Conflict Resolution 15* (March 1971): 71–78.

38. Charles A. Beard, *American Foreign Policy in the Making, 1932–1940: A Study in Responsibilities* (New Haven: Yale University Press, 1946); idem, *President Roosevelt and the Coming of the War, 1941: A Study in Appearances and Realities* (New Haven: Yale University Press, 1948); Frederic R. Sanborn, *Design for War: A Study of Secret Power Politics, 1937–1941* (New York: Devin-Adair, 1951).

39. Charles Callan Tansill, *Back Door to War: The Roosevelt Foreign Policy, 1933–1941* (Chicago: Henry Regnery, 1952), p. 652.

40. Russett, *No Clear and Present Danger*, pp. 34–35.

41. Joseph Alsop and Robert Kintner, *American White Paper: The Story of American Diplomacy and the Second World War*, 6th ed. (New York: Simon & Schuster, 1940), p. 4. (Emphasis is included in the source.)

42. Essential to an understanding of this contention is Alexander L. George, *Presidential Decisionmaking in Foreign Policy: The Effective Use of Information and Advice* (Boulder: Westview Press, 1980), especially chap. 3, "The Importance of Beliefs and Images."

43. Isaiah Bowman, "Geography vs. Geopolitics," in *Compass of the World: A Symposium on Political Geography*, ed. Hans W. Weigert and Vilhjalmur Stefansson (New York: Macmillan, 1944), p. 45.

44. Robert Jervis, *Perception and Misperception in International Politics* (Princeton: Princeton University Press, 1976), pp. 415–16.

45. Albert K. Weinberg, "The Historical Meaning of the American Doctrine of Isolation," *American Political Science Review* 34 (June 1940): 539. Compare this with Max Ascoli's whimsical observation that an isolationist was someone interested in a continent other than the one under discussion. Cited by James Burnham, "The New Isolationism," *National Review*, 26 January 1965, p. 60.

46. My understanding of ideology owes much to Clifford Geertz's conception of ideologies as systems of interacting symbols whose function is to "bridge the emotional gap between things as they are and as one would have them be. . . ." Clifford Geertz, "Ideology as a Cultural System," in *Ideology and Discontent*, ed. David E. Apter (New York: Free Press, 1964), p. 55.

47. For the regional variable, see Ray Allen Billington, "The Origins of Middle Western Isolationism," *Political Science Quarterly* 60 (March 1945): 44–64; Richard W. Leopold, "The Mississippi Valley and American Foreign Policy, 1890–1941: An Assessment and an Appeal," *Mississippi Valley Historical Review* 37 (March 1951): 625–42; Ralph H. Smuckler, "The Region of Isolationism," *American Political Science Review* 47 (June 1953): 386–401; and Marian D. Irish, "Foreign Policy and the South," *Journal of Politics* 10 (May 1948): 306–26. For ethnicity, see Samuel Lubell, *The Future of American Pol-*

itics (New York: Harper & Bros., 1952), pp. 132–36. For conservatism, see Selig Adler, *The Isolationist Impulse: Its Twentieth Century Reaction* (New York: Collier Books, 1961), p. 272; and Rauch, *Roosevelt*, p. 10. For progressivism, see Eric F. Goldman, *Rendezvous with Destiny: A History of Modern American Reform*, rev. ed. (New York: Vintage Books, 1955), pp. 181–87, 291; John C. Donovan, "Congressional Isolationists and the Roosevelt Foreign Policy," in *Causes and Consequences of World War II*, ed. Robert A. Divine (Chicago: Quadrangle Books, 1967), p. 77; Frederick L. Schuman, *Design for Power: The Struggle for the World* (New York: Alfred A. Knopf, 1942), p. 236; and Wayne S. Cole, *Senator Gerald P. Nye and American Foreign Relations* (Minneapolis: University of Minnesota Press, 1962), pp. 41, 230–34. For the variable of personality and intellect, see Bernard Fensterwald, Jr., "The Anatomy of American 'Isolationism' and Expansionism: II," *Journal of Conflict Resolution* 2 (December 1958): 280–309; Leroy N. Rieselbach, *The Roots of Isolationism: Congressional Voting and Presidential Leadership in Foreign Policy* (Indianapolis: Bobbs-Merrill, 1966), pp. 28–29; and Thomas A. Bailey, *The Man in the Street: The Impact of Public Opinion on Foreign Policy* (New York: Macmillan, 1948), pp. 134–37.

48. Williams, *Tragedy of American Diplomacy*, pp. 110–11.

49. William Appleman Williams, "The Legend of Isolationism in the 1920s," *Science & Society* 18 (Winter 1954): 1–20.

50. Gardner, *Economic Aspects of New Deal Diplomacy*, p. 26.

51. Bernard Fensterwald, Jr., "The Anatomy of American 'Isolationism' and Expansionism: Part I," *Journal of Conflict Resolution* 2 (June 1958): 111–12.

52. Nevertheless, some writers persist in trying to classify certain eras as isolationist from an economic standpoint. For example, see John A. Logan Jr., *No Transfer: An American Security Principle* (New Haven: Yale University Press, 1961), p. 278: "America retreated into political isolation and, with the towering tariff walls and the Johnson Act of the interwar years, economic isolation as well."

53. Felix Gilbert, *To the Farewell Address: Ideas of Early American Foreign Policy* (Princeton: Princeton University Press, 1961), p. 43.

54. Quoted in ibid., p. 145. (Emphasis is included in the source.)

55. Beard, *American Foreign Policy in the Making*, p. 17.

56. Adler, *Isolationist Impulse*, p. 24; and Fensterwald, "Anatomy of 'Isolationism': I," pp. 115, 118.

57. Livingston Hartley, *Is America Afraid? A New Foreign Policy for the United States* (New York: Prentice-Hall, 1937), pp. 118–19.

58. Rauch, *Roosevelt*, p. 131.

59. Adolf A. Berle, Jr., *Navigating the Rapids, 1918–1971: From the Papers of Adolf A. Berle*, ed. Beatrice Bishop Berle and Travis Beal Jacobs (New York: Harcourt Brace Jovanovich, 1973), pp. 231–33.

60. For the America First Committee's position on a possible Asiatic war, see two books by Wayne S. Cole: *America First: The Battle against Intervention, 1940–1941* (Madison: University of Wisconsin Press, 1953), pp. 189–90; and *Charles A. Lindbergh and the Battle against American Intervention in World War II* (New York: Harcourt Brace Jovanovich, 1974), p. 208.

61. Manfred Jonas, *Isolationism in America, 1935–1941* (Ithaca: Cornell University Press, 1966), passim.

62. Warren F. Kimball, *The Most Unsordid Act: Lend-Lease, 1939–1941* (Baltimore: Johns Hopkins University Press, 1969), p. 1.

63. Kalman H. Silvert, "The Kitsch in Hemispheric Realpolitik," in *Latin America: The Search for a New International Role*, ed. Ronald G. Hellman and H. Jon Rosenbaum (New York: John Wiley & Sons, 1975), p. 31.

64. Robert W. Tucker, *A New Isolationism: Threat or Promise?* (New York: Universe Books, A Potomac Associates Book, 1972), p. 12.

65. Ibid., p. 28.

66. Berle Diary, 29 November 1937, box 210, FDRL. (Emphasis added.)

67. But cf. Henry Steele Commager and Richard B. Morris, "Editors' Introduction" to William E. Leuchtenburg, *Franklin D. Roosevelt and the New Deal, 1932–1940*, New American Nation Series (New York: Harper & Row, Harper Torchbooks, 1963), p. x, for the comment that Roosevelt, like Wilson before him, was "almost instinctively isolationist."

68. Robert Strausz-Hupé, *In My Time* (New York: W. W. Norton, 1965), p. 176.

69. Quoted in Strout, *American Image of the Old World*, p. 205.

70. Hubert Herring, *And So to War* (New Haven: Yale University Press, 1938), p. 122.

71. For an excellent assessment of the role played by the interwar revisionists in the formulation of isolationist precepts, see Warren I. Cohen, *The American Revisionists: The Lessons of Intervention in World War I* (Chicago: University of Chicago Press, 1967).

72. William Allen White, *The Autobiography of William Allen White* (New York: Macmillan, 1946), p. 640.

73. Walter Johnson, *The Battle against Isolation* (Chicago: University of Chicago Press, 1944). For Vandenberg's position, see Arthur Hendrick Vandenberg, *The Trail of a Tradition* (New York: G. P. Putnam's Sons, 1926).

74. Quoted in John E. Wiltz, *In Search of Peace: The Senate Munitions Inquiry, 1934–1936* (Baton Rouge: Louisiana State University Press, 1963), pp. 148–51.

75. Cited by Charles G. Fenwick, *American Neutrality: Trial and Failure* (New York: New York University Press, 1940), p. 123.

76. Robert E. Sherwood, *Roosevelt and Hopkins: An Intimate History* (New York: Harper & Bros., 1948), p. 123. The best study of the neutrality policies of the Roosevelt administration is Robert A. Divine, *The Illusion of Neutrality: Franklin D. Roosevelt and the Struggle over the Arms Embargo* (Chicago: Quadrangle Books, 1968).

77. *Public Opinion Quarterly* 4 (March 1940): 102.

78. *Peace and War: United States Foreign Policy, 1931–1941* (Washington: Department of State, 1943). Beard, in *American Foreign Policy in the Making*, pp. 33–35, considered many of the claims made in this "pièce justificative" to be outright lies.

79. Willard Range, *Franklin D. Roosevelt's World Order* (Athens: University of Georgia Press, 1959), p. xi. For similar opinions, see James MacGregor

Burns, *Roosevelt: The Lion and the Fox* (New York: Harcourt, Brace & World, 1956); and Frank Freidel, *Franklin D. Roosevelt: Launching the New Deal* (Boston: Little, Brown, 1973).

80. Robert Dallek, *Franklin D. Roosevelt and American Foreign Policy, 1932–1945* (New York: Oxford University Press, 1979), p. 3.

81. Another scholar sharing this view is Irwin Gellman, who maintains that Roosevelt's Latin American policies, far from being a function of isolationism, actually constituted a faute de mieux internationalism. "[Roosevelt] realized his Latin American opportunity. Shut out of European deliberations by its governments and domestic opposition, and frustrated by Japanese ambitions in the Far East, the president moved toward internationalism through the only available opening." Irwin F. Gellman, *Good Neighbor Diplomacy: United States Policies in Latin America, 1933–1945* (Baltimore: Johns Hopkins University Press, 1979), p. 17. Also see, for this perspective, Wayne S. Cole, *Roosevelt and the Isolationists, 1932–45* (Lincoln: University of Nebraska Press, 1983), chap. 25, "Latin America—Side Door to Internationalism."

82. Frank Freidel, *Franklin D. Roosevelt: The Apprenticeship* (Boston: Little, Brown, 1952), pp. 250, 359–61.

83. Robert A. Divine, *Roosevelt and World War II* (Baltimore: Penguin Books, 1970), p. 56.

84. Taylor, *Origins of the Second World War*, p. 61.

85. Raymond Moley, *The First New Deal* (New York: Harcourt, Brace & World, 1966), pp. 31–35.

86. Arthur Krock, *Memoirs: Sixty Years on the Firing Line* (New York: Funk & Wagnalls, 1968), p. 199. For the isolationism of the early years of Roosevelt's presidency, see Victor L. Albjerg, "Isolationism and the Early New Deal, 1932–1937," *Current History* 35 (October 1958): 204–10; and Elliot A. Rosen, "Intranationalism vs. Internationalism: The Interregnum Struggle for the Sanctity of the New Deal," *Political Science Quarterly* 81 (June 1966): 274–97.

87. Quoted in Freidel, *Launching the New Deal*, p. 498.

88. Although it marked the first downward movement of tariff rates since the Underwood Act of 1913, the Reciprocal Trade Agreements Act was by no means a free-trade measure; perhaps it was best characterized as "adjusted protectionism." William Diebold, Jr., *New Directions in Our Trade Policy*, Studies in American Foreign Relations, no. 2, ed. Percy W. Bidwell (New York: Council on Foreign Relations, 1941), p. 23. For a study of the Trade Agreements Program, see Dick Steward, *Trade and Hemisphere: The Good Neighbor Policy and Reciprocal Trade* (Columbia: University of Missouri Press, 1975).

89. Arnold A. Offner, *American Appeasement: United States Foreign Policy and Germany, 1933–1938* (Cambridge: Harvard University Press, Belknap Press, 1969), pp. 35–36.

90. Samuel I. Rosenman, comp., *The Public Papers and Addresses of Franklin D. Roosevelt*, 13 vols. (New York: Random House, 1938; Macmillan, 1941–50), 3:239–40 (hereafter cited as *Public Papers*).

91. Cited by Wiltz, *In Search of Peace*, pp. 175–76. Eventually the job of drafting neutrality legislation was taken over by the Foreign Relations Committee.

92. Quoted in Freidel, *Apprenticeship*, p. 250. Cohen, *American Revisionists*, p. 161, notes that although Roosevelt did not accept the more "conspiratorial" theses on American intervention in the World War, he was clearly impressed by the less sensationalist revisionist writing, and had "concluded that intervention . . . had been a mistake."

93. Burns, *Lion and Fox*, p. 256.

94. *Public Papers*, 8:xxxii.

95. Quoted in Wiltz, *In Search of Peace*, p. 177.

96. Roosevelt to Dodd, 2 December 1935, *F.D.R.: His Personal Letters, 1928–1945*, ed. Elliott Roosevelt, 2 vols. (New York: Duell, Sloan & Pearce, 1950), 1:530–31 (hereafter cited as *Personal Letters*).

97. Hans L. Trefousse, *Germany and American Neutrality, 1939–1941* (New York: Bookman Associates, 1951), p. 213n.

98. Geoffrey S. Smith, *To Save a Nation: American Countersubversives, the New Deal, and the Coming of World War II* (New York: Basic Books, 1973), pp. 30–31. Ironically, the jingoistic Coughlin was himself an immigrant, having come to the United States from Hamilton, Ontario. For an account of his political influence during the 1930s, see Sheldon Marcus, *Father Coughlin: The Tumultuous Life of the Priest of the Little Flower* (Boston: Little, Brown, 1973).

99. Quoted in Julius W. Pratt, *Cordell Hull, 1933–44*, 2 vols., American Secretaries of State and Their Diplomacy, ed. Robert H. Ferrell and Samuel Flagg Bemis (New York: Cooper Square Publishers, 1964), 1:272–73.

100. Sherwood, *Roosevelt and Hopkins*, p. 79; Robert A. Divine, *The Reluctant Belligerent: American Entry into World War II*, America in Crisis Series (New York: John Wiley & Sons, 1965), p. 22; idem, *Roosevelt and World War II*, p. 13.

101. William E. Kinsella, Jr., *Leadership in Isolation: FDR and the Origins of the Second World War* (Boston: G. K. Hall, 1978), p. 72. Herbert Feis, *Seen From E. A.: Three International Episodes* (New York: Alfred A. Knopf, 1947), p. 229, recalls the efforts of State Department lawyers, desperately trying to fashion a public declaration of policy that would neither encourage League members to proceed with sanctions against Italy nor provide them with a pretext for not doing so; after much hard work, the legal experts succeeded in coming up with a "garment of formulas within which we could shrink."

102. *Public Papers*, 5:287–91. It is striking to note the similarity between Roosevelt's conception of isolationism ("We are not isolationists except in so far as we seek to isolate ourselves completely from war") and that of Sen. Robert Taft: "If isolation means isolation from war, I am an isolationist." Quoted in Ronald Radosh, *Prophets on the Right: Profiles of Conservative Critics of American Globalism* (New York: Simon & Schuster, 1975), p. 130.

Chapter 2

1. Roosevelt to Patterson, 9 November 1936, *Personal Letters*, 1:625.

2. Roosevelt to William E. Dodd, 9 November 1936, ibid.

3. Quoted in Sergio Bagú, *Argentina en el mundo* (Buenos Aires: Fondo de Cultura Economica, 1961), pp. 87–88.

4. Cited in Samuel Guy Inman, *Inter-American Conferences, 1826–1954* (Washington: University Press of Washington and Community College Press, 1965), p. 164.

5. In his postwar memoirs, Hull recalled that the State Department had been receiving ominous reports from Latin American posts for several months prior to the Buenos Aires conference. These reports, detailing German and Italian propaganda and espionage exploits, "created a picture of threatening colors." Cordell Hull, *The Memoirs of Cordell Hull*, 2 vols. (New York: Macmillan, 1948), 1:495–96.

6. Although the three-year war that Bolivia and Paraguay had waged over the long-disputed Chaco Boreal ended in a cease-fire in June 1935, a peace treaty was not concluded until July 1938. See David H. Zook, Jr., *The Conduct of the Chaco War* (New York: Bookman Associates, 1960); and Bryce Wood, *The United States and Latin American Wars, 1932–1942* (New York: Columbia University Press, 1966). For the peace conference itself, the best source is Leslie B. Rout, Jr., *Politics of the Chaco Peace Conference, 1935–1939* (Austin: University of Texas Press, 1970).

7. *Personal Letters*, 1:541–42.

8. Quoted in João Frederico Normano, *The Struggle for South America: Economy and Ideology* (London: George Allen & Unwin, 1931), pp. 121–22. For Argentine opposition to inter-American cooperation, see Inman, *Inter-American Conferences*, passim. For the roots of Argentine foreign policy, see two books by Arthur P. Whitaker: *The United States and Argentina*, The American Foreign Policy Library, ed. Donald C. McKay (Cambridge: Harvard University Press, 1954); and *Argentina*, The Modern Nations in Historical Perspective (Englewood Cliffs, N.J.: Prentice-Hall, 1964). Harold F. Peterson, *Argentina and the United States, 1810–1960* ([Albany]: State University of New York, 1964), pp. 323–24, contains an analysis of Argentine neutrality in World War I. Argentine neutralism in World War II is explored in Randall Bennett Woods, *The Roosevelt Foreign-Policy Establishment and the "Good Neighbor": The United States and Argentina, 1941–1945* (Lawrence: Regents Press of Kansas, 1979).

9. Spruille Braden, *Diplomats and Demagogues: The Memoirs of Spruille Braden* (New Rochelle, N.Y.: Arlington House, 1971), pp. 151–52. Braden wrote that Saavedra Lamas's scorn, like charity, began at home: "He sneered at his cabinet colleagues, and I have heard him refer repeatedly to [Argentine] President Justo as 'the little fatty upstairs.'"

10. Quoted in Wood, *United States and Latin American Wars*, p. 43.

11. Sumner Welles, *Seven Decisions that Shaped History* (New York: Harper & Bros., 1950), pp. 103–5. Not surprisingly, Welles, whose contempt for Hull eclipsed any like sentiment the latter felt for Saavedra Lamas, considered the Nobel laureate a "brilliant and enlightened statesman."

12. Berle Diary, 2 April 1939, box 210, FDRL.

13. Hubert Herring, *Good Neighbors: Argentina, Brazil, Chile and Seventeen Other Countries* (New Haven: Yale University Press, 1941), p. 99.

14. Ernesto Giudici, *Hitler conquista América* (Buenos Aires: Editorial Acento, 1938), p. 205.

15. Alberto Conil Paz and Gustavo Ferrari, *Argentina's Foreign Policy, 1930–*

1962, trans. John J. Kennedy (Notre Dame, Ind.: University of Notre Dame Press, 1966), p. 38.

16. Although he addressed the opening session of the conference on 1 December, President Roosevelt was not a member of the American delegation. The official delegates were Hull; Welles; Berle, then chamberlain of New York City; Alexander W. Weddell, ambassador to Argentina; Alexander F. Whitney, president of the Brotherhood of Railway Trainmen; Charles G. Fenwick, professor of international relations at Bryn Mawr; Michael F. Doyle, lawyer; and Elise F. Musser, Democratic national committee-woman and Utah state senator.

17. Cordell Hull, "The Results and Significance of the Buenos Aires Conference," *Foreign Affairs* 15 (April 1937): ii–x.

18. Inman, *Inter-American Conferences*, pp. 169–70. Jesús M. Yepes, like Inman a fervent advocate of Pan-Americanism, shared this impression; only Yepes insisted that it was yet another measure adopted at Buenos Aires, the Additional Protocol Relative to Non-Intervention, that "continentalized" the Monroe Doctrine. Under this protocol, the United States reaffirmed the commitment it had made at Montevideo in 1933 to abandon the practice of unilateral intervention. Jesús M. Yepes, *Philosophie du Panaméricanisme et organisation de la paix* (Neuchâtel: Éditions de la Baconnière, 1945), pp. 11–14.

19. Saul Friedländer, *Prelude to Downfall: Hitler and the United States, 1939–1941*, trans. Aline B. Werth and Alexander Werth (London: Chatto & Windus, 1967), p. 28.

20. William Everett Kane, *Civil Strife in Latin America: A Legal History of U.S. Involvement* (Baltimore: Johns Hopkins University Press, 1972), p. 133.

21. See the analysis written by one of the American delegates, Charles G. Fenwick, "The Buenos Aires Conference: 1936," *Foreign Policy Reports* 13 (1 July 1937): 90–100.

22. Quoted in Inman, *Inter-American Conferences*, p. 165.

23. Cited by Conil Paz and Ferrari, *Argentina's Foreign Policy*, p. 38.

24. American historians have accorded Saavedra Lamas a posthumous vote of thanks. Peterson, *Argentina and the United States*, p. 393, considered the foreign minister's performance at Buenos Aires "masterly." Whitaker, *United States and Argentina*, p. 107, agreed, adding that the neutrality legislation the American delegation sought to "multilateralize" was a totally negative "expression of the isolationism then rampant in the United States."

25. Hull, *Memoirs*, 1:211.

26. Sumner Welles, *The Time for Decision* (Cleveland: World Publishing, 1945), p. 206. That Welles could have forgotten all about the neutrality proposal in not quite a decade is highly improbable, for Buenos Aires was very special to him. Beatrice Bishop Berle, who accompanied her husband Adolf to the conference, noted in her diary on the evening of the opening session: "S. W. [Sumner Welles] très emotionné as this is the culmination and fruition of many years of work." Quoted in Adolf A. Berle, Jr., *Navigating the Rapids, 1918–1971: From the Papers of Adolf A. Berle*, ed. Beatrice Bishop Berle and Travis Beal Jacobs (New York: Harcourt Brace Jovanovich, 1973), pp. 119–20.

27. For a good treatment of the neutrality legislation of the 1930s, see Robert A. Divine, *The Illusion of Neutrality: Franklin D. Roosevelt and the Strug-*

gle over the Arms Embargo (Chicago: Quadrangle Books, 1968). The act passed on 24 August 1935 called for a mandatory arms embargo on an impartial basis, with presidential discretion in defining arms, munitions, and matériel. Also, American ships could not carry arms to belligerents; and American citizens, if the president so proclaimed, could only travel on belligerents' vessels at their own risk. The act would come into force whenever the president proclaimed the existence of a state of war. Legislation passed in 1936 extended the life of the 1935 act, and added a prohibition on loans to belligerents.

28. Nicholas John Spykman, *America's Strategy in World Politics: The United States and the Balance of Power* (New York: Harcourt Brace, 1942), pp. 373–74.

29. Arthur P. Whitaker, *The United States and South America: The Northern Republics*, The American Foreign Policy Library, ed. Sumner Welles (Cambridge: Harvard University Press, 1948), p. 115.

30. Hull, *Memoirs*, 1:499.

31. Braden, *Diplomats and Demagogues*, p. 175.

32. Hull, *Memoirs*, 1:500–502.

33. For the pedigree of this theme, see Loren Baritz, *City on a Hill: A History of Ideas and Myths in America* (New York: John Wiley & Sons, 1964), chap. 1. Also see Philip S. Haffenden, *New England in the English Nation, 1689–1713* (Oxford University Press, Clarendon Press, 1974), p. xii; and Daniel J. Boorstin, *America and the Image of Europe: Reflections on American Thought* (New York: Meridian Books, p. 1960), pp. 11–13.

34. Roosevelt to Joseph M. Patterson, 9 November 1936, *Personal Letters*, 1:625. Also see Samuel I. Rosenman, *Working with Roosevelt* (New York: Harper & Bros., 1952), p. 140.

35. Raúl Díez de Medina [Gaston Nerval], *Washington Star*, 15 November 1936.

36. Maj. Lawrence C. Mitchell, M/A Brazil, 30 November 1936, 2657–K–114/1, MID.

37. Braden, *Diplomats and Demagogues*, p. 175.

38. Edgar B. Nixon, ed., *Franklin D. Roosevelt and Foreign Affairs*, 3 vols. (Cambridge: Harvard University Press, Belknap Press, 1969), 3:516–21.

39. Quoted in Inman, *Inter-American Conferences*, p. 166.

40. *La Nación* (Buenos Aires), 20 January 1937.

41. *Crítica* (Buenos Aires), 21 January 1937. (Author's translation.)

42. *La Razón* (Buenos Aires), 20 January 1937. (Author's translation.)

43. Welles, *Seven Decisions*, pp. 97–98.

44. Manuel Ugarte, *The Destiny of a Continent*, ed J. Fred Rippy, trans. Catherine A. Phillips (New York: Alfred A. Knopf, 1925; reprint, New York: AMS Press, 1970). For a study of Latin American impressions of the United States during the 1920s, see Clarence H. Haring, *South America Looks at the United States* (New York: Macmillan, 1929). For the same general topic (with the exception of the omission of Brazil) over a much longer period of time, see John T. Reid, *Spanish American Images of the United States, 1790–1960* (Gainesville: University Presses of Florida, 1977).

45. Laurence Duggan, *The Americas: The Search for Hemisphere Security* (New York: Henry Holt, 1949), p. 54.

46. Ibid., p. 52. The four states supporting Hughes were Nicaragua, Peru, Panama, and Cuba. The Haitian intervention, although the longest, was not the only instance of United States military involvement in Latin America, particularly in the Caribbean area, where intervention was the rule rather than the exception. Samuel Flagg Bemis, *The Latin American Policy of the United States: An Historical Interpretation* (New York: Harcourt, Brace, 1943), chap. 14; Albert K. Weinberg, *Manifest Destiny: A Study of Nationalist Expansionism in American History* (Baltimore: Johns Hopkins Press, 1935; reprint, Chicago: Quadrangle Books, 1963), pp. 442–43; and D. A. Graber, *Crisis Diplomacy: A History of U.S. Intervention Policies and Practices* (Washington, D.C.: Public Affairs Press, 1959), chap. 8. For a good analysis of Hughes's Latin diplomacy, see Joseph S. Tulchin, *The Aftermath of War: World War I and U.S. Policy toward Latin America* (New York: New York University Press, 1971), pp. 245–53. Also see Betty Glad, *Charles Evans Hughes and the Illusions of Innocence: A Study in American Diplomacy* (Urbana: University of Illinois Press, 1966), chap. 16.

47. Quoted in Alexander De Conde, *Herbert Hoover's Latin-American Policy* (Stanford: Stanford University Press, 1951; reprint, New York: Octagon Books, 1970), pp. 61–65. There has been much debate in the past few decades over whether Hoover, not Roosevelt, should be considered the real father of the Good Neighbor Policy. For the pro-Hoover literature, see Arthur P. Whitaker, *The Western Hemisphere Idea: Its Rise and Decline* (Ithaca: Cornell University Press, 1954), pp. 135–36; William E. Leuchtenburg, *Franklin D. Roosevelt and the New Deal, 1932–1940*, New American Nation Series, ed. Henry Steele Commager and Richard B. Morris (New York: Harper & Row, Harper Torchbooks, 1963), p. 207; L. Ethan Ellis, *Republican Foreign Policy, 1921–1933* (New Brunswick, N.J.: Rutgers University Press, 1968), p. 278; William Appleman Williams, *The Tragedy of American Diplomacy*, 2d ed., rev. and enl. (New York: Dell Publishing, Delta Books, 1972), p. 157; and Lloyd C. Gardner, *Economic Aspects of New Deal Diplomacy* (Madison: University of Wisconsin Press, 1964), p. 51. For pro-Roosevelt arguments, see Bryce Wood, *The Making of the Good Neighbor Policy* (New York: Columbia University Press, 1961), pp. 124–28; Sumner Welles, *Time for Decision*, p. 191; and Irwin F. Gellman, *Good Neighbor Diplomacy: United States Policies in Latin America, 1933–1945* (Baltimore: Johns Hopkins University Press, 1979), pp. 8–9. Interesting light is shed on the infatuation of revisionists for Hoover, in Arthur Schlesinger, Jr., "Hoover Makes a Comeback," *New York Review of Books*, 8 March 1979, pp. 10–16.

48. Cited by Carleton Beals, *The Coming Struggle for Latin America* (Philadelphia: J. B. Lippincott, 1938), p. 245.

49. Luis E. Aguilar, *Cuba 1933: Prologue to Revolution* (Ithaca: Cornell University Press, 1972), chap. 17; Irwin F. Gellman, *Roosevelt and Batista: Good Neighbor Diplomacy in Cuba, 1933–1945* (Albuquerque: University of New Mexico Press, 1973), chaps. 2–4.

50. Wood, *Making of the Good Neighbor Policy*, pp. 118–19; Edward O. Guerrant, *Roosevelt's Good Neighbor Policy* (Albuquerque: University of New Mexico Press, 1950), p. 8.

51. Hull, *Memoirs*, 1:323–27.

52. Beals, *Coming Struggle for Latin America,* p. 246; David Green, *The Containment of Latin America: A History of the Myths and Realities of the Good Neighbor Policy* (Chicago: Quadrangle Books, 1971), p. 19.

53. Green, *Containment of Latin America,* p. 296.

54. Hull, *Memoirs,* 1:319.

55. Ibid., p. 486.

56. Roosevelt to Dodd, 9 January 1937, *Personal Letters,* 1:649.

57. Alberto Ciria, *Parties and Power in Modern Argentina, 1930–1946,* trans. Carlos A. Astiz and Mary F. McCarthy (Albany: State University of New York Press, 1974), p. 51.

58. Roosevelt to Cox, 9 December 1936, *Personal Letters,* 1:638.

59. Roosevelt to Viscount Cecil, 6 April 1937, ibid., p. 672.

60. Ibid., p. 649.

61. *Public Papers,* 6:158.

62. Roosevelt to Viscount Cecil 6 April 1937, *Personal Letters,* 1:672.

63. *Public Papers,* 6:229.

Chapter 3

1. See, for instance, the writings of Peruvian leftist Víctor Raúl Haya de la Torre on this subject: "The politics of the Good Neighbor, the anti-fascist front, the democratic alliance of North and Indoamerica to defend ourselves against International Fascism, are guarantees of immediate security, laudable, necessary and worthy of support." *Aprismo: The Ideas and Doctrines of Víctor Raúl Haya de la Torre,* ed. and trans. Robert J. Alexander (Kent, Ohio: Kent State University Press, 1973), p. 248.

2. Col. Lester Baker, M/A Argentina, 26 January 1937, 2657–L–122/1–2, MID.

3. Enrique Dickmann, *Recuerdos de un militante socialista* (Buenos Aires: La Vanguardia, 1949), p. 330: "The honor and glory of being the first to denounce the Nazi infiltration of Argentina fell to the Socialist Party, who gave timely warning to both the public and the government of the imminent peril of that infiltration." (Author's translation.)

4. Two accounts of Stephenson have been written: H. Montgomery Hyde, *The Quiet Canadian: The Secret Service Story of Sir William Stephenson* (London: Hamish Hamilton, 1962); and William Stevenson, *A Man Called Intrepid: The Secret War* (New York: Harcourt Brace Jovanovich, 1976).

5. Wallace to Roosevelt, 5 June 1936; Roosevelt to Hull, 8 June 1936; both in Roosevelt Papers, OF 198A, box 3.

6. "Outline Study of a Challenge to the Monroe Doctrine in Eastern South America by a European Dictatorship (Germany or Italy, or both)," undated (but either May or June 1936), OF 637, FDRL.

7. Roper to Roosevelt, 11 December 1936, OF 637, FDRL.

8. Carleton Beals, *The Coming Struggle for Latin America* (Philadelphia: J. B. Lippincott, 1938), pp. 18–20.

9. Sumner Welles, *The Time for Decision* (Cleveland: World Publishing, 1945), pp. 209–10.

10. Louis de Jong, *The German Fifth Column in the Second World War,* trans.

C. M. Geyl (Chicago: University of Chicago Press, 1956; reprint, New York: Howard Fertig, 1973), pp. 277–79; Alton Frye, *Nazi Germany and the American Hemisphere, 1933–1941* (New Haven: Yale University Press, 1967), pp. 65–68.

11. Cordell Hull, *The Memoirs of Cordell Hull*, 2 vols. (New York: Macmillan, 1948), 1:495–96.

12. Karl Loewenstein, *Brazil under Vargas* (New York: Macmillan, 1942), pp. 158–69.

13. The FBI figures come from the Bureau's report, "United States Dependency on South America," March 1942, Hopkins Papers, Group 24, container 144, FDRL. For other estimates of Axis populations in Latin America, see João Frederico Normano and Antonello Gerbi, *The Japanese in South America: An Introductory Survey with Special Reference to Peru* (New York: John Day, 1943); Frank D. McCann, Jr., *The Brazilian-American Alliance, 1937–1945* (Princeton: Princeton University Press, 1973), pp. 78–79; Ronald C. Newton, *German Buenos Aires, 1900–1933: Social Change and Cultural Crisis* (Austin: University of Texas Press, 1977), chap. 8; and Carl Solberg, "Germans and Italians in Latin America: Recent Immigration Research," *Latin American Research Review* 3 (1976):133–37. Also see Jean Roche, *La colonisation allemande et le Rio Grande do Sul* (Paris: Institut des Hautes Études de l'Amérique Latine, 1959); and Jean-Pierre Blancpain, *Les Allemands au Chili, 1816–1945* (Cologne: Böhlau Verlag, 1974).

14. Enrique Dickmann, *La infiltración nazi-fascista en la Argentina* (Buenos Aires: Ediciones Sociales Argentinas, 1939), pp. 11–12.

15. See, for example, João Frederico Normano, *The Struggle for South America: Economy and Ideology* (London: George Allen & Unwin, 1931), p. 76: "The Italian is a poor subject for the melting-pot; he is difficult to assimilate, and long continues to feel his attachment for his native country."

16. "Report of the Army Chief of Staff Secretariat on Fascist Propaganda in Latin America," 15 February 1938, contained in Standing Liaison Committee Minutes, 1938–40 vol., box 912, National Archives, Record Group 165; Maj. Lawrence C. Mitchell, M/A Brazil, 18 August 1936, 2657–K–111/1, MID.

17. Frye, *Nazi Germany and the American Hemisphere*, pp. 20–23; Z.A.B. Zeman, *Nazi Propaganda* (London: Oxford University Press, 1964), pp. 111–14; Edwin Muller, "Waging War with Words," *Current History 59* (August 1939): 26.

18. Richard F. Behrendt, "Foreign Influences in Latin America," *Annals of the American Academy of Political and Social Science* 204 (July 1939): 1; Pedro Motta Lima and José Barboza Mello, *El Nazismo en el Brasil: Proceso del Estado Corporativo* (Buenos Aires: Editorial Claridad, 1938), p. 86; Mordecai Ezekiel, "Economic Relations between the Americas," *International Conciliation*, no. 367 (February 1941), pp. 123–24; Cleona Lewis, *Nazi Europe and World Trade* (Washington: Brookings Institution, 1941), pp. 142–43; Herbert Feis, *The Changing Pattern of International Economic Affairs* (New York: Harper & Bros., 1940; reprint, Port Washington, N.Y.: Kennikat Press, 1971), pp. 58–62; Howard J. Trueblood, "Trade Rivalries in Latin America," *Foreign Policy Reports* 13 (15 September 1937): 157.

19. Berle Diary, 20 February 1937, box 210, FDRL.

20. M/A Argentina, 18 March 1937, 2657–L–123/1, MID.

21. McClintock to Roosevelt, 20 April 1937, OF 87, 1933–38 container, FDRL.

22. Quoted in Charles C. Colby, "Geographic Aspects of International Relations," unpublished transcript, Norman Wait Harris Memorial Foundation Round Table, University of Chicago, 21–28 June 1937, p. 192.

23. Roosevelt to Maphis, 29 June 1937, *Public Papers*, 6:284–85.

24. Livingston Hartley, *Is America Afraid? A New Foreign Policy for the United States* (New York: Prentice-Hall, 1937), pp. 4–5, 74–75, 114–17, 122, 129–30, 283–84, 289.

25. Raúl Díez de Medina [Gaston Nerval], "Europe versus the United States in Latin America," *Foreign Affairs* 15 (July 1937):642–45.

26. See Frederick B. Pike, *Hispanismo, 1898–1936: Spanish Conservatives and Liberals and Their Relations with Spanish America* (Notre Dame, Ind.: University of Notre Dame Press, 1971).

27. Actually, the label "Latin America" was anathema to Spanish imperialists. In 1921, the Second Congress of Sevilla ruled that inasmuch as Latin America was a name created by France to further its imperialistic interests, and "Ibero-America" was ungainly, the proper nomenclature for the former Spanish Empire, as well as for Brazil, would be "Hispanic America." Normano, *Struggle for South America*, pp. 81–82.

28. Quoted in H. Rutledge Southworth, "The Spanish Phalanx and Latin America," *Foreign Affairs* 18 (October 1939): 150–51.

29. Eleuthère N. Dzélépy, *Franco, Hitler et les Alliés* (Brussels: Éditions Politiques, 1961), p. 21. For the rise of Hispanism as a political force, see Clarence H. Haring, *South America Looks at the United States* (New York: Macmillan, 1929), pp. 139–40, 168–72.

30. Enrique Gil, "Repercussions of the Spanish Crisis in Latin America," *Foreign Affairs* 15 (April 1937): 547–53.

31. Beals, *Coming Struggle for Latin America*, pp. 159–60.

32. Since the Neutrality Act of 1936 had made no provision for the statutory embargo of arms and munitions to parties engaged in a civil war, Congress speedily enacted, in early January 1937, an embargo measure applying specifically to the fighting in Spain. Robert A. Divine, *The Illusion of Neutrality: Franklin D. Roosevelt and the Struggle over the Arms Embargo* (Chicago: Quadrangle Books, 1968), pp. 168–72, 223–28; F. Jay Taylor, *The United States and the Spanish Civil War* (New York: Bookman Associates, 1956), chap. 8. Concern for inter-American unity played a major role in the administration's Spanish policy; the administration feared that American partiality toward the elected Spanish government would have been poorly received by the Latin nations, which were, with the exception of Mexico and Colombia, Franco partisans. One scholar has concluded that "United States aid to the Spanish government could have destroyed the Good Neighbor structure which was so laboriously erected." Richard P. Traina, *American Diplomacy and the Spanish Civil War*, Indiana University International Studies (Bloomington: Indiana University Press, 1968), p. 147.

33. William L. Langer and S. Everett Gleason, *The Challenge to Isolation, 1937–1940* (New York: Harper & Bros., 1952), p. 19.

34. Charles A. Beard, *American Foreign Policy in the Making, 1932–1940: A Study in Responsibilities* (New Haven: Yale University Press, 1946), pp. 190–91; Basil Rauch, *Roosevelt, from Munich to Pearl Harbor: A Study in the Creation of a Foreign Policy* (New York: Creative Age Press, 1950), pp. 47–48. For similar interpretatons, see James MacGregor Burns, *Roosevelt: The Lion and the Fox* (New York: Harcourt, Brace & World, 1956), pp. 318–19; and Samuel I. Rosenman, *Working with Roosevelt* (New York: Harper & Bros., 1952), pp. 166–67.

35. *Public Papers*, 6:406–13.

36. Berle Diary, 30 September 1937, box 210, FDRL.

37. Sumner Welles, *Seven Decisions that Shaped History* (New York: Harper & Bros., 1950), pp. 8, 21.

38. *Public Papers*, 6:423–24.

39. Dorothy Borg, "Notes on Roosevelt's 'Quarantine' Speech," in *Causes and Consequences of World War II*, ed. Robert A. Divine (Chicago: Quadrangle Books, 1967), p. 48; William E. Leuchtenberg, *Franklin D. Roosevelt and the New Deal, 1932–1940*, New American Nation Series, ed. Henry Steele Commager and Richard B. Morris (New York: Harper & Row, Harper Torchbooks, 1963), pp. 226–27. Also see Robert Dallek, *Franklin D. Roosevelt and American Foreign Policy, 1932–1945* (New York: Oxford University Press, 1979), pp. 148–51.

40. Berle Diary, 17 September 1937, box 210, FDRL.

41. Dieckhoff to Foreign Ministry, 9 October 1937, *DGFP*-D, 1:634–35. (Emphasis is included in the source.)

42. Quoted in Rosenman, *Working with Roosevelt*, p. 166. For French reaction to the speech, see John McVickar Haight, Jr., "France and the Aftermath of Roosevelt's 'Quarantine' Speech," *World Politics* 14 (January 1962): 283–306.

43. Cited by Robert A. Divine, *Second Chance: The Triumph of Internationalism in America during World War II* (New York: Atheneum, 1971), p. 27.

44. Jay Pierrepont Moffat, *The Moffat Papers: Selections from the Diplomatic Journals of Jay Pierrepont Moffat, 1919–1943*, ed. Nancy Harvison Hooker (Cambridge: Harvard University Press, 1956), p. 157; Welles, *Seven Decisions*, pp. 74–76.

45. John Morton Blum, *From the Morgenthau Diaries*, vol. 1: *Years of Crisis, 1928–1938*; vol. 2: *Years of Urgency, 1938–1941*; vol. 3: *Years of War, 1941–1945*; 3 vols. (Boston: Houghton Mifflin, 1959–67), 1:393.

46. *New York Times*, 11–12 November 1937.

47. Summary of press coverage, Ambassador to Italy William Phillips to Hull, 13 November 1937, 832.00/1090, SDDF. Also see Hugo Fernández Artucio, *The Nazi Underground in South America* (New York: Farrar & Rinehart, 1942), pp. 74–75; and Samuel Guy Inman, *Inter-American Conferences, 1826–1954* (Washington: University Press of Washington and Community College Press, 1965), p. 180.

48. Dodd to Hull, 12 November 1937, 832.00/1086, SDDF; Norman P. Mac-

donald, *Hitler over Latin America* (London: Jarrolds, 1940), p. 89.

49. Bullitt to Hull, 12 November 1937, 832.00/1088, SDDF; Herschel V. Johnson to Hull, 18 November 1937, 835.51/1221, SDDF. "Pertinax" was André Géraud, a columnist for the daily, *L'Echo de Paris,* and the weekly, *L'Europe Nouvelle.*

50. *DGFP–D,* 5:815–16.

51. *New York Times,* 14 November 1937; Press report from Robert M. Scotten, counselor of the embassy in Rio, to Hull, 19 November 1937, 832.00/1110, SDDF.

52. Welles to Caffery, 12 November 1937, 832.00/1089A, SDDF; Caffery to Welles, 13 November 1937, 832.00/1092, SDDF; *New York Times,* 7 December 1937.

53. Louis Morton, "Germany First: The Basic Concept of Allied Strategy in World War II," in *Command Decisions,* ed. Kent Roberts Greenfield (Washington: Office of the Chief of Military History, Department of the Army, 1960), pp. 12–22. Also see Michael K. Doyle, "The U.S. Navy and War Plan ORANGE, 1933–1940: Making Necessity a Virtue," *Naval War College Review* (May–June 1980): 49–63.

54. Morgenthau Diary, 11 December 1937, 101:266.

55. Zeman, *Nazi Propaganda,* pp. 58–59.

56. Inman to Presidential Secretary Marvin McIntyre, 18 December 1937, OF 87, 1933–38 container, FDRL.

57. Stephen Naft, "Fascism and Communism in South America," *Foreign Policy Reports* 13 (15 December 1937): 226–36.

58. Dieckhoff to Weizsäcker, 20 December 1937, *DGFP–D,* 1:658–61.

59. James V. Compton, *The Swastika and the Eagle: Hitler, the United States, and the Origins of World War II* (Boston: Houghton Mifflin, 1967), pp. 65–67, 105, 123; Arnold A. Offner, *Amercan Appeasement: United States Foreign Policy and Germany* (Cambridge: Harvard University Press, Belknap Press, 1969), p. 235; Joachim Remak, "Two German Views of the United States: Hitler and His Diplomats," *World Affairs Quarterly* 28 (April 1957): 25–35.

Chapter 4

1. For a contemporary treatment of the minerals/power equation, see T. S. Lovering, *Minerals in World Affairs* (New York: Prentice-Hall, 1943).

2. C. W. Wright, "Germany's Capacity to Produce and Consume Metals," *Mineral Trade Notes,* Special Supplement no. 4 (Washington: U.S. Bureau of Mines, 20 November 1936): 34.

3. Moritz J. Bonn, *The Crumbling of Empire: The Disintegration of World Economy* (London: George Allen & Unwin, 1938), p. 209; Brooks Emeny, *The Strategy of Raw Materials: A Study of America in Peace and War* (New York: Macmillan, 1934), pp. 23–24; David L. Gordon and Royden Dangerfield, *The Hidden Weapon: The Story of Economic Warfare* (New York: Harper & Bros., 1947), p. 8; J. Hurstfield, "The Control of British Raw Material Supplies, 1919–1939," *Economic History Review* 14 (1944): 26–27.

4. Robert Strausz-Hupé, *Geopolitics: The Struggle for Space and Power* (New York: G. P. Putnam's Sons, 1942), pp. 99–100.

5. C. K. Leith, J. W. Furness, and Cleona Lewis, *World Minerals and World*

Peace (Washington: Brookings Institution, 1943), p. 172. By 1940, 25 percent of Germany's gasoline consumption was supplied by a synthetic, coal-based product.

6. Strausz-Hupé, *Geopolitics,* pp. 91–93. For the relationship between Axis "have-not" status and expansionary foreign policy, see Alfred E. Eckes, Jr., *The United States and the Global Struggle for Minerals* (Austin: University of Texas Press, 1979), chap. 3, "Minerals and the Origins of World War II."

7. Humboldt quote in Felipe Barreda Laos, *¡Hispano América en guerra!* (Buenos Aires: Linari, 1941), p. 243.

8. Hermann Rauschning, *The Voice of Destruction* (New York: G. P. Putnam's Sons, 1940), pp. 65–66.

9. John B. Glenn, "The Future of Pan Americanism Based on Financial Relations," unpublished transcript, 8 December 1937, OF 87, 1933–38 container, FDRL.

10. Juan T. Trippe, "The Business Future—Southward," *Survey Graphic* 30 (March 1941): 139.

11. Hubert Herring, *Good Neighbors: Argentina, Brazil, Chile and Seventeen Other Countries* (New Haven: Yale University Press, 1941), p. 329.

12. Manuel Seoane, *Nuestra América y la guerra* (Santiago de Chile: Ediciones Ercilla, 1940), pp. 47–59.

13. Hugo Fernández Artucio, *The Nazi Underground in South America* (New York: Farrar & Rinehart, 1942), p. 287.

14. Quoted in Bryce Wood, *The Making of the Good Neighbor Policy* (New York: Columbia University Press, 1961), p. 181.

15. The fifteen minerals were: chromite; coal and lignite; copper ore, matte, and concentrates; smelter copper (including refined); iron ore; lead ore and concentrates; refined lead; manganese ore; nickel; crude petroleum; refined petroleum—liquid; tin ore and concentrates; refined tin; zinc ore and concentrates; and refined zinc.

16. Leith, Furness, and Lewis, *World Minerals and World Peace,* pp. 236–46.

17. Charles A. Thomson, "Mexico's Challenge to Foreign Capital," *Foreign Policy Reports* 13 (15 August 1937): 136.

18. For Morgenthau's rivalry with Hull and the State Department, see Irwin F. Gellman, *Good Neighbor Diplomacy: United States Policies in Latin America, 1933–1945* (Baltimore: Johns Hopkins University Press, 1979), pp. 43–44, 117–18; and Randall Bennett Woods, *The Roosevelt Foreign-Policy Establishment and the "Good Neighbor": The United States and Argentina, 1941–1945* (Lawrence: Regents Press of Kansas, 1979), pp. 61–72. An interesting treatment of the broader context of U.S. decision making concerning Latin America is Ernest R. May, "The 'Bureaucratic Politics' Approach: U.S.-Argentine Relations, 1942–47," in *Latin America and the United States: The Changing Political Realities,* ed. Julio Cotler and Richard R. Fagen (Stanford: Stanford University Press, 1974), pp. 129–63.

19. Morgenthau Diary, 16 December 1937, 102:178–80, FDRL.

20. John Morton Blum, *From the Morgenthau Diaries,* vol. 1: *Years of Crisis, 1928–1938;* vol. 2: *Years of Urgency, 1938–1941;* vol. 3: *Years of War, 1941–1945;* 3 vols. (Boston: Houghton Mifflin, 1959–67), 1:495; Charles A. Thomson, "The Mexican Oil Dispute," *Foreign Policy Reports* 14 (15 August 1938): 127;

Cole Blasier, *The Hovering Giant: U.S. Responses to Revolutionary Change in Latin America* (Pittsburgh: University of Pittsburgh Press, 1976), pp. 123–24.

21. Morgenthau Diary, 31 December 1937, 104:285–86, FDRL.

22. Maj. William F. Freehoff, M/A Mexico, 20 December 1937, 9944–126/1, MID.

23. O'Connell's remarks were reported in *La Nación* (Buenos Aires); see Hugo Fernández Artucio, *Nazis en el Uruguay* (Montevideo: Talleres Gráficos Sur, 1940), p. 113.

24. Ernesto Giudici, *Hitler conquista América* (Buenos Aires: Editorial Acento, 1938), p. 54; Enrique Dickmann, *La infiltración nazi-fascista en la Argentina* (Buenos Aires: Ediciones Sociales Argentinas, 1939), p. 16.

25. *Public Papers*, 7:71.

26. Dudley W. Knox, "The United States Navy between World Wars," introduction to Samuel Eliot Morison, *The Battle of the Atlantic: September 1939–May 1943* (Boston: Little, Brown, 1947), pp. 1–li; William Everett Kane, *Civil Strife in Latin America: A Legal History of U.S. Involvement* (Baltimore: Johns Hopkins University Press, 1972), p. 110. The Hitler quote is from Ernst Hanfstaengl, *Unheard Witness* (Philadelphia: J. B. Lippincott, 1957), p. 141.

27. Quoted in Seoane, *Nuestra América y la guerra*, p. 79.

28. Quoted in Hubert Herring, *And So to War* (New Haven: Yale University Press, 1938), p. 51.

29. Cited by A. A. Hoehling, *America's Road to War, 1939–1941* (New York: Abelard-Schuman, 1970), p. 83.

30. Messersmith to Hull, 18 February 1938, *FRUS*, 1938, 1:20–21.

31. Précis of State Department memorandum on Axis infiltration of Latin America, 1 March 1938, Army Chief of Staff Secretariat, Standing Liaison Committee Minutes, 1938–40 vol., box 912, National Archives, Record Group 165. At this same time, the War Department learned from military intelligence in Buenos Aires that a fascist organization with more than ten thousand members was conducting an effective propaganda offensive in Argentina. Moreover, a fascist secret police was operating under the aegis of the Italian consulate. M/A Argentina, 3 March 1938, 2657–L–127/1, MID.

32. Press report, M/A Argentina, 24 March 1938, 2657–L–72/17, MID. For an account of the anti-German campaign mounted by the Brazilian government in 1938, see Frank D. McCann, Jr., "Vargas and the Destruction of the Brazilian Integralista and Nazi Parties," *Americas* 26 (July 1969): 15–34.

33. Giudici, *Hitler conquista América*, foreword.

34. Kennedy's reputation as an appeaser stemmed principally from an ill-advised public statement he made in the aftermath of the Munich settlement. See Michael R. Beschloss, *Kennedy and Roosevelt: The Uneasy Alliance* (New York: W. W. Norton, 1980), pp. 177–80. For Kennedy's relationship with the British, see David E. Koskoff, *Joseph P. Kennedy: A Life and Times* (Englewood Cliffs, N.J.: Prentice-Hall, 1974), pp. 210–95.

35. Kennedy to Roosevelt, 14 April 1938, OF 3093, FDRL.

36. Cultural Policy Department memorandum, 29 April 1938, *DGFP–D*, 5:832–34.

37. *Public Papers*, 7:255–58.

38. Cited by William E. Leuchtenburg, *Franklin D. Roosevelt and the New Deal, 1932–1940*, New American Nation Series, ed. Henry Steel Commager and Richard B. Morris (New York: Harper & Row, Harper Torchbooks, 1963), p. 283. Also see Philip La Follette, *Adventure in Politics: The Memoirs of Philip La Follette*, ed. Donald Young (New York: Holt, Rinehart & Winston, 1970), pp. 252–56.

39. For an account of the German absorption of Czechoslovakia, see Keith Robbins, *Munich 1938* (London: Cassell, 1968).

40. *Washington Post*, 18 May 1938; Inman to Marvin McIntyre, 26 May 1938, OF 87, 1933–38 container, FDRL; McIntyre to Roosevelt, 28 May 1938, ibid.

41. Circular despatch from Bohle to Latin American diplomatic missions, 18 May 1938, *DGFP*–D, 5:843.

42. Robert M. Levine, *The Vargas Regime: The Critical Years, 1934–1938* (New York: Columbia University Press, 1970), chapter 4, gives a good account of the Integralistas, whose strength Levine estimates at between 100,000 and 200,000 members, drawn largely from the ranks of white-collar workers, professionals, and the armed forces (especially the navy).

43. See the exchange of cables between the State Department and Ambassador Jefferson Caffery in Brazil from 16 May to 23 May 1938. 832.00 Revolutions; /603A, /605, /607, /608, /612; SDDF.

44. Karl Loewenstein, *Brazil under Vargas* (New York: Macmillan, 1942), p. 34.

45. Office of Strategic Services, Research and Analysis Branch, "Anti-Semitism as a Weapon of Axis Political Warfare in Latin America," 15 August 1944, Henry A. Wallace Papers, box 117, Franklin D. Roosevelt Library. Also see Bailey W. Diffie, "Some Foreign Influences in Contemporary Brazilian Politics," *Hispanic American Historical Review* 20 (August 1940): 421–24; and Adolfo Tejera, *Penetración nazi en América Latina* (Montevideo: Editorial Nueva América, 1938), pp. 128–29.

46. Ritter to von Ribbentrop, 18 May 1938, *DGFP*–D, 5:842–43.

47. Stanley E. Hilton, "Ação Integralista Brasileira: Fascism in Brazil, 1932–1938," *Luso-Brazilian Review* 9 (December 1972): 3–29; Alton Frye, *Nazi Germany and the American Hemisphere, 1933–1941* (New Haven: Yale University Press, 1967), pp. 104–5.

48. Adolf A. Berle, Jr., *New Directions in the New World*, 2d ed. (New York: Harper & Bros., 1940), p. 29.

49. Helio Lobo, *O Pan-Americanismo e o Brasil* (São Paulo: Companhia Editôra Nacional, 1939), p. 124.

50. Carleton Beals, *The Coming Struggle for Latin America* (Philadelphia: J. B. Lippincott, 1938), pp. 69–71, 83–85, 156, 380.

51. Ambassador to Argentina Edmund von Thermann to Foreign Ministry, 2 August 1938, *DGFP*–D, 5:863–67.

52. Circular despatch from Bohle to Latin American diplomatic missions, 18 May 1938, ibid., 5:843.

53. Auslandsorganisation memorandum, 8 August 1938, ibid., 5:869–72.

54. Chargé d'affaires Hans Thomsen to Foreign Ministry, 12 September 1938, *DGFP*–D, 1:731. For the Stuttgart congresses, see Giudici, *Hitler conquista América*, pp. 28–29; and José Bernal de León, *La Quinta Columna en el Conti-*

nente Americano (México, D.F.: Ediciones Culturales Mexicanas, 1939), p. 87.

55. *Public Papers,* 7:492.

56. Charles Callan Tansill, *Back Door to War: The Roosevelt Foreign Policy, 1933–1941* (Chicago: Henry Regnery, 1952), p. 410.

57. Berle Diary, 1 September 1938, box 210, FDRL.

58. Jorge González von Marées, *El Mal de Chile: Sus causas y sus remedios* (Santiago de Chile: Talleres Gráficos Portales, 1940), pp. 52–54. (Author's translation.)

59. Frederick M. Nunn, *The Military in Chilean History: Essays on Civil-Military Relations, 1810–1973* (Albuquerque: University of New Mexico Press, 1976), p. 234. Also see, for the putsch and its aftermath, Paul W. Drake, *Socialism and Populism in Chile, 1932–52* (Urbana: University of Illinois Press, 1978), p. 203; Brian Loveman, *Chile: The Legacy of Hispanic Capitalism* (New York: Oxford University Press, 1979), pp. 275–76; and John Reese Stevenson, *The Chilean Popular Front* (Philadelphia: University of Pennsylvania Press, 1942), pp. 85–88.

60. Th. Thetens and Ludwig Lore, "Chile as a Nazi Outpost," *Nation,* 24 September 1938, pp. 296–98.

61. John T. Whitaker, *Americas to the South* (New York: Macmillan, 1939), p. 75.

62. Frederick B. Pike, *Chile and the United States, 1880–1962: The Emergence of Chile's Social Crisis and the Challenge to United States Diplomacy* (Notre Dame, Ind.: University of Notre Dame Press, 1963), pp. 204–7.

63. Vera Micheles Dean, *Latin America and the War* (New York: Oxford University Press, 1942), p. 36.

64. Armour to Secretary of State Cordell Hull, 1 March 1939, 825.00N/12, SDDF.

65. Although the Nacistas were not as blatantly anti-Semitic as other Latin fascists (particularly those of Argentina), this was primarily due not to any attitude of forbearance on their part, but rather to the fact that in Chile, where Jews made up only one-half of one percent of the population, there were far bigger fish to fry, namely the communists. Nevertheless, the Nacistas did publish a Chilean edition of that staple item of anti-Semitic literature, "The Protocols of the Elders of Zion." See Office of Strategic Services, "Anti-Semitism as a Weapon."

66. Memorandum of conversation between Kirchway and von Marées, 23 December 1938, 825.00N/11, SDDF.

67. Carleton Beals, "Totalitarian Inroads in Latin America," *Foreign Affairs* 17 (October 1938): 86. For Nacista ideology, see Paul W. Drake, "Corporatism and Functionalism in Modern Chilean Politics," *Journal of Latin American Studies* 10 (May 1978): 97.

Chapter 5

1. George Fielding Eliot, *The Ramparts We Watch: A Study of the Problems of American National Defense* (New York: Reynal & Hitchcock, 1938), pp. 52, 74–75, 82.

2. Adolfo Tejera, *Penetración nazi en América Latina* (Montevideo: Editorial Nueva América, 1938), p. 65.

3. *Complete Presidential Press Conferences of Franklin D. Roosevelt,* 24 vols. (New York: Da Capo Press, 1972), 12:83–84 (hereafter cited as *Press Conferences*).

4. Bullitt to Roosevelt, 20 September 1938, in Orville H. Bullitt, ed., *For the President, Personal and Secret: Correspondence between Franklin D. Roosevelt and William C. Bullitt* (Boston: Houghton Mifflin, 1972), pp. 287–88.

5. Harold L. Ickes, *The Secret Diary of Harold L. Ickes,* vol. 1: *The First Thousand Days, 1933–1936;* vol. 2: *The Inside Struggle, 1936–1939;* vol. 3: *The Lowering Clouds, 1939–1941;* 3 vols. (New York: Simon & Schuster, 1953–54), 2:481.

6. Arnold A. Offner, *American Appeasement: United States Foreign Policy and Germany* (Cambridge: Harvard University Press, Belknap Press, 1969), p. 269.

7. Roosevelt to King, 11 October 1938, *Personal Letters,* 2:816.

8. Berle Diary, 26 September 1938, box 210, FDRL.

9. Ibid., 22 September 1938.

10. For the oil expropriation, see Luis G. Zorrilla, *Historia de las relaciones entre México y los Estados Unidos de América, 1800–1958,* 2 vols. (México, D.F.: Editorial Porrua, 1966), 2:467–73; Lorenzo Meyer, *Mexico and the United States in the Oil Controversy, 1917–1942,* trans. Muriel Vasconcellos (Austin: University of Texas Press, 1977); Jorge Basurto, *El conflicto internacional en torno al petróleo de México,* 2d ed. (México, D.F.: Siglo Veintiuno, 1980); Merrill Rippy, *Oil and the Mexican Revolution* (Leiden, Neth.: E. J. Brill, 1972); and Robert Freeman Smith, *The United States and Revolutionary Nationalism in Mexico, 1916–1932* (Chicago: University of Chicago Press, 1972).

11. Charles A. Thomson, "The Mexican Oil Dispute," *Foreign Policy Reports* 14 (15 August 1938): 132.

12. E. David Cronon, *Josephus Daniels in Mexico* (Madison: University of Wisconsin Press, 1960), pp. 192–93, 197.

13. Daniels to Hull, 22 August 1938, quoted in ibid., pp. 234–35.

14. Von Rüdt to Foreign Ministry, 21 March 1938, *DGFP-D,* 5:829n.

15. Von Rüdt to Foreign Ministry, 8 April 1938, ibid., 5:827–29.

16. Dillon to Office of Naval Intelligence, 25 October 1938, contained in 812.00N/31, SDDF.

17. Memorandum of the Standing Liaison Committee Secretariat, 26 September 1938, Standing Liaison Committee Minutes, 1938–40 vol., National Archives, Record Group 165.

18. Berle Diary, 19 September 1938, box 210, FDRL.

19. Daniels to Hull, 27 September 1938, quoted in Cronon, *Josephus Daniels,* pp. 227–28.

20. Cordell Hull, *The Memoirs of Cordell Hull,* 2 vols. (New York: Macmillan, 1948), 1:610.

21. *Public Papers,* 7:546.

22. *New York Times Magazine,* 16 October 1938.

23. Morgenthau to Roosevelt, 17 October 1938, in John Morton Blum, *From the Morgenthau Diaries*, vol. 1: *Years of Crisis, 1928–1938;* vol. 2: *Years of Urgency, 1938–1941;* vol. 3: *Years of War, 1941–1945;* 3 vols. (Boston: Houghton Mifflin, 1959–67), 1:526.

24. Ibid., 2:46.

25. "Nazidom and the Americas," *Economist*, 22 October 1938, p. 164.

26. Quoted in Stetson Conn and Byron Fairchild, *The Framework of Hemisphere Defense*, United States Army in World War II: The Western Hemisphere, gen. ed. Kent Roberts Greenfield (Washington: Office of the Chief of Military History, Department of the Army, 1960), p. 5. For a comparison with aircraft production of the European powers, see Robert Dallek, *Franklin D. Roosevelt and American Foreign Policy, 1932–1945* (New York: Oxford University Press, 1979), p. 566 n 3: "In 1938, Germany produced only 3,350 combat planes, and her total aircraft production in 1939 was only a few hundred greater than Britain's. At the outbreak of the war in Sept. 1939 the British and the French had approximately the same number of war planes as Germany."

27. *Public Papers*, 7:598–601.

28. Carleton Beals, "Totalitarian Inroads in Latin America," *Foreign Affairs* 17 (October 1938): 78–89.

29. Frederic R. Sanborn, *Design for War: A Study of Secret Power Politics, 1937–1941* (New York: Devin-Adair, 1951), pp. 42–43.

30. Robert A. Divine, *The Illusion of Neutrality: Franklin D. Roosevelt and the Struggle over the Arms Embargo* (Chicago: Quadrangle Books, 1968), p. 231.

31. Sabath to Roosevelt, 26 October 1938, OF 87, 1933–38 container, FDRL.

32. Sack to Roosevelt, 7 November 1938, PPF 1664, FDRL.

33. Roosevelt to Herbert C. Pell, 12 November 1938, *Personal Letters*, 2:826.

34. Military Intelligence Division memorandum, 19 November 1938, précis of Standing Liaison Committee meeting of 14 November 1938, Standing Liaison Committee Minutes, 1938–1940 vol., National Archives, Record Group 165.

35. Ickes, *Secret Diary*, 2:528.

36. Long to Roosevelt, 3 November 1938, PSF South America and Central America, box 69, FDRL.

37. Clarence H. Haring, *Argentina and the United States* (Boston: World Peace Foundation, 1941), p. 73.

38. Long to Roosevelt, 3 November 1938, op. cit.

39. MacLeish to Presidential Secretary Missy LeHand, 14 November 1938, OF 87, 1933–38 container, FDRL.

40. For the relationship between diplomatic goals in Latin America and American policy toward the civil war in Spain, see Richard P. Traina, *American Diplomacy and the Spanish Civil War*, Indiana University International Studies (Bloomington: Indiana University Press, 1968), chap. 7.

41. *New York Times*, 9 November 1938.

42. Cited by Evarts Seelye Scudder, *The Monroe Doctrine and World Peace* (London: Nelson, 1939; reprint, Port Washington, N.Y.: Kennikat Press, 1972), p. 164.

43. The American minister to Venezuela, Antonio González, informed Wash-

ington that the pro-American foreign minister of Venezuela had told him German and Italian agents were trying to pressure Latin delegates into opposing the United States on matters relating to hemisphere defense. González to Sumner Welles, 8 December 1938, *FRUS: 1938*, 5:50–51.

44. Hull, *Memoirs*, 1:601–2.

45. Laurence Duggan, *The Americas: The Search for Hemisphere Security* (New York: Henry Holt, 1949), p. 73.

46. González to Roosevelt, 21 November 1938, OF 535, FDRL.

47. Hull, *Memoirs*, 1:602.

48. Dearing to Roosevelt, 24 February 1937, PSF Diplomatic, box 64, FDRL. For a more sympathetic assessment of Benavides, see David P. Werlich, *Peru: A Short History* (Carbondale: Southern Illinois University Press, 1978), pp. 213–20.

49. "South America II: Peru," *Fortune*, January 1938, p. 128; James C. Carey, *Peru and the United States, 1900–1962* (Notre Dame, Ind.: University of Notre Dame Press, 1964), p. 104.

50. Carleton Beals, *The Coming Struggle for Latin America* (Philadelphia: J. B. Lippincott, 1938), pp. 101–2.

51. "Peru," *Fortune*, p. 138.

52. Ernesto Giudici, *Hitler conquista América* (Buenos Aires: Editorial Acento, 1938), pp. 48–49; David Efron, "Latin America and the Fascist 'Holy Alliance,' " *Annals of the American Academy of Political and Social Science* 204 (July 1939): 21.

53. Schmitt to Foreign Ministry, 26 March 1938, *DGFP–D*, 5:822.

54. Berle Diary, 10 January 1939, box 210, FDRL. Steinhardt, as it developed, would serve a tour of duty in Moscow.

55. In addition to Hull, the American delegates were Berle; Harry Norweb, minister to the Dominican Republic; Charles G. Fenwick, professor of international relations at Bryn Mawr; Green Hackworth, State Department adviser on international law; Alf Landon, Republican candidate for president in 1936; and Kathryn Lewis, daughter of labor chieftain John L. Lewis, and labor spokeswoman in her own right.

56. S. Pinkney Tuck, chargé d'affaires at Buenos Aires, to Hull, 3 November 1938, *FRUS: 1938*, 5:36–37; Robert M. Scotten, chargé d'affaires at Rio de Janeiro to Welles, 1 December 1938, ibid., p. 47.

57. M/A Argentina, 2 December 1938, 2657–L–72/22, MID.

58. Cited by Samuel Guy Inman, *Inter-American Conferences, 1826–1954: History and Problems* (Washington: University Press of Washington and Community College Press, 1965), pp. 183–84; and Alberto Conil Paz and Gustavo Ferrari, *Argentina's Foreign Policy, 1930–1962*, trans. John J. Kennedy (Notre Dame, Ind.: University of Notre Dame Press, 1966), p. 46.

59. *Il Mattino d'Italia* (Buenos Aires), 12 December 1938.

60. Hull, *Memoirs*, 1:605.

61. Ibid.

62. John T. Whitaker, *Americas to the South* (New York: Macmillan, 1939), p. 136.

63. Samuel Guy Inman, "Lima Conference and the Totalitarian Issue," *Annals of the American Academy of Political and Social Science* 204 (July 1939): 10.

64. Harold F. Peterson, *Argentina and the United States, 1810–1960* ([Albany]: State University of New York, 1964), p. 395.

65. Hull to American delegation to Lima, undated, *FRUS:* 1938, 5:54–55.

66. Berle Diary, 10 January 1939, box 210, FDRL. For an assessment of Welles's influence on U.S. policy toward Latin America, see Irwin F. Gellman, *Good Neighbor Diplomacy: United States Policies in Latin America, 1933–1945* (Baltimore: Johns Hopkins University Press, 1979), p. 81: "Of the State Department personalities concerned with hemispheric affairs, none held center stage like Welles. More than anyone else, he provided the guidance."

67. Welles to Scotten, 2 December 1938, *FRUS:* 1938, 5:48.

68. Welles to Hull, 16 December 1938, ibid., 5:81–82.

69. *New York Times*, 21 December 1938; Jay Pierrepont Moffat, *The Moffat Papers: Selections from the Diplomatic Journals of Jay Pierrepont Moffat, 1919–1943*, ed. Nancy Harvison Hooker (Cambridge: Harvard University Press, 1956), pp. 222–23.

70. *Peace and War: United States Foreign Policy, 1931–1941* (Washington: Department of State, 1943), pp. 439–40.

71. *Press Conferences*, 12:323–24.

72. Hull, *Memoirs*, 1:608–9.

73. Inman, *Inter-American Conferences*, pp. 193–94.

74. Alton Frye, *Nazi Germany and the American Hemisphere, 1933–1941* (New Haven: Yale University Press, 1967), p. 114.

75. *Peace and War*, p. 440. For a critical assessment of the Declaration of Lima, see J. Lloyd Mecham, *The United States and Inter-American Security, 1889–1960* (Austin: University of Texas Press, 1961), pp. 144–48.

76. Nicholas John Spykman, *America's Strategy in World Politics: The United States and the Balance of Power* (New York: Harcourt, Brace, 1942), pp. 380–81.

77. Hubert Herring, *Good Neighbors: Argentina, Brazil, Chile and Seventeen Other Countries* (New Haven: Yale University Press, 1941), p. 100.

78. Duncan Aikman, *The All-American Front* (Garden City, N.Y.: Doubleday, Doran, 1942), p. 7.

79. Ibid.

Chapter 6

1. Quoted in Werner Rheinbaben, *La Conferencia Panamericana de Lima*, contained in 821.00N/11, SDDF. For the German view of both the conference and the declaration, see Irwin F. Gellman, *Good Neighbor Diplomacy: United States Policies in Latin America, 1933–1945* (Baltimore: Johns Hopkins University Press, 1979), p. 78.

2. Rheinbaben, *Conferencia Panamericana de Lima*.

3. Wilhelm Faupel, "Estados Unidos de América, Ibero-América y nosotros," *Revista Alemana*, no. 29 (May 1939), pp. 18–19. For details of Faupel's career, see Allen Chase, *Falange: The Axis Secret Army in the Americas* (New York: G. P. Putnam's Sons, 1943), pp. 3–6.

4. *Public Papers*, 8:1–12. Also see William L. Langer and S. Everett Gleason, *The Challenge to Isolation, 1937–1940* (New York: Harper & Bros., 1952), p. 47.

5. Carroll Kilpatrick, ed., *Roosevelt and Daniels: A Friendship in Politics* (Chapel Hill: University of North Carolina Press, 1952), pp. 181–83.

6. Ibid.

7. *Public Papers*, 8:111–14.

8. For the relationship between the administration and France after Munich, see John McVickar Haight, Jr., *American Aid to France, 1938–1940* (New York: Atheneum, 1970), especially, chap. 4.

9. Quincy Howe, *Blood Is Cheaper than Water: The Prudent American's Guide to Peace and War* (New York: Simon & Schuster, 1939), pp. 69–71, 171–72. The Howe book that received German funding was *England Expects Every American to Do His Duty*. For details, see Saul Friedländer, *Prelude to Downfall: Hitler and the United States, 1939–1941*, trans. Aline B. Werth and Alexander Werth (London: Chatto & Windus, 1967), p. 300.

10. Howe, *Blood Is Cheaper*, pp. 121–22, 202–3.

11. Philip E. Jacob, "Influences of World Events on U.S. 'Neutrality' Opinion," *Public Opinion Quarterly* 4 (March 1940): 58–60.

12. Both ambassadors' statements cited by Hans L. Trefousse, *Germany and American Neutrality, 1939–1941* (New York: Bookman Associates, 1951), pp. 20–21.

13. *New York Times*, 7 March, 1939.

14. Berle Diary, 16 March 1939, box 210, FDRL.

15. Ibid., 17 March 1939.

16. M/A Argentina, 7 February 1939, 2657–L–131/1, MID.

17. Chargé d'affaires S. Pinkney Tuck to Cordell Hull, 1 April 1939, 835.00N/13, SDDF.

18. Enrique Dickmann, *La infiltración nazi-fascista en la Argentina* (Buenos Aires: Ediciones Sociales Argentinas, 1939), pp. 40–47, contains an account of the Patagonian affair, including the disavowals made by the German chargé d'affaires.

19. Beaulac to Hull, 12 April 1939, 835.00N/15, SDDF.

20. Tuck to Hull, 1 April 1939, 835.00N/13, SDDF.

21. State Department memorandum of early April 1939, 835.00N/19, SDDF.

22. Tuck to Hull, 11 April 1939, 835:00N/16, SDDF.

23. M/A Argentina, 22 April 1939, 2657–L–131/3, MID.

24. I lack the necessary documentary evidence to prove British complicity. However, circumstantial evidence suggests British agents were at work. In the first place, as I will demonstrate presently, Britain had a powerful *motive* for stimulating U.S. fears about Latin American security. Secondly, Britain did have—as subsequent documented undercover activities in Latin America revealed—the *means* to create an incident such as the Patagonian affair. For the role of British intelligence in Latin America, especially after 1940, see H. Montgomery Hyde, *The Quiet Canadian: The Secret Service Story of Sir William Stephenson* (London: Hamish Hamilton, 1962), pp. 144–50; William Stevenson, *A Man Called Intrepid: The Secret War* (New York: Harcourt Brace Jovanovich, 1976), pp. 268–69; Paul Kramer, "Nelson Rockefeller and British Security

Coordination," *Journal of Contemporary History* 16 (January 1981): 73–88; and David G. Haglund, "The Battle of Latin America: Franklin D. Roosevelt and the End of Isolation, 1936–1941" (Ph.D. dissertation, Johns Hopkins University, 1978), pp. 612–30.

25. For a study of World War I atrocities, see James Morgan Read, *Atrocity Propaganda, 1914–1919* (New Haven: Yale University Press, 1941).

26. Quoted in Arthur Ponsonby, *Falsehood in War-Time: Containing an Assortment of Lies Circulated throughout the Nations during the Great War* (New York: E. P. Dutton, 1928; reprint, New York: Garland Publishing, 1971), p. 113.

27. Harold Lavine and James Wechsler, *War Propaganda and the United States* (New Haven: Yale University Press, Institute for Propaganda Analysis, 1940; reprint, New York: Garland Publishing, 1972), pp. 89–92.

28. Sidney Rogerson, *Propaganda in the Next War*, Next War Series, ed. B. H. Liddell Hart (London: Geoffrey Bles, 1938), p. 148.

29. Berle Diary, 2 April 1939, box 210, FDRL.

30. Roosevelt's speech is in *Public Papers*, 8:201–5. Hitler's response is quoted in Langer and Gleason, *Challenge to Isolation*, p. 89.

31. Robert A. Divine, *The Illusion of Neutrality: Franklin D. Roosevelt and the Struggle over the Arms Embargo* (Chicago: Quadrangle Books, 1968), pp. 242–43; Elton Atwater, *American Regulation of Arms Exports*, Carnegie Endowment for International Peace, Division of International Law, no. 4 (Washington: Carnegie Endowment for International Peace, 1941), chap. 5.

32. *New York Times*, 6 April 1939.

33. "Washington Merry-Go-Round," 10 April 1939, included in documentary items published in "Neutrality, Peace Legislation, and Our Foreign Policy," *Hearings before the Committee on Foreign Relations, United States Senate*, 76th Cong., 1st sess. (Washington: United States Government Printing Office, 1939), pp. 458–59 (hereafter cited as "Neutrality," Senate *Hearings*).

34. Ibid., pp. 236–49.

35. *Press Conferences*, 20 April 1939, 13:304–20.

36. Ibid.

37. Glen Barclay, *Struggle for a Continent: The Diplomatic History of South America, 1917–1945* (London: Sidgwick & Jackson, 1971), p. 65.

38. For background information on the Joint Planning Committee, see Ray S. Cline, *Washington Command Post: The Operations Division*, United States Army in World War II: The War Department, gen. ed. Kent Roberts Greenfield (Washington: Office of the Chief of Military History, Department of the Army, 1951), pp. 44–46.

39. For contemporary treatments of American reaction to the Axis presence in Latin civil aviation, see Melvin Hall and Walter Peck, "Wings for the Trojan Horse," *Foreign Affairs* 19 (January 1941): 347–69; and William A. M. Burden, *The Struggle for Airways in Latin America* (New York: Council on Foreign Relations, 1943). For more recent analyses of U.S. aviation diplomacy in strategic (because of its proximity to the Panama Canal) Colombia see Stephen J. Randall, "Colombia, the United States, and Inter-American Aviation Rivalry, 1927–1940," *Journal of Inter-American Studies and World Affairs* 14 (August 1972): 297–324; idem, *The Diplomacy of Modernization: Colombian-American*

Relations, 1920–1940 (Toronto: University of Toronto Press, 1977), chap. 7; and David G. Haglund, " 'De-lousing' Scadta: The Role of Pan American Airways in U.S. Aviation Diplomacy in Colombia, 1939–1940," *Aerospace Historian* 30 (Fall 1983): 177–90.

40. Joint Planning Committee exploratory study, 21 April 1939, War Department Files, JB 325, Ser. 634, National Archives, Record Group 165.

41. Ibid.

42. Army War College, "Special Study—Brazil," 29 March 1939, WPD 4115–7, p. 25.

43. Ibid., p. 55, Appendix 5. For an insight into Brazilian military life in this period, see Frank D. McCann, Jr., "The Brazilian Army and the Problem of Mission, 1939–1964," *Journal of Latin American Studies* 12 (May 1980): 108–17.

44. "Special Study—Brazil," pp. 59, 67–68.

45. Ibid., p. 32.

46. M/A Argentina, 29 January 1938, 2657–L–126/1, MID.

47. Hanson W. Baldwin, "Our New Long Shadow," *Foreign Affairs* 17 (April 1939): 475.

48. "Neutrality," Senate *Hearings,* pp. 561–62.

49. John Crosby Brown, "American Isolation: Propaganda Pro and Con," *Foreign Affairs* 18 (October 1939): 42–43.

50. "Neutrality," Senate *Hearings,* pp. 452–61. Efron, an Argentine leftist who knew what it felt like to wear the label "subversive," is a case in point of the way in which the Latin American left, with the obvious exception of the Soviet-line Communists from August 1939 to June 1941 (the duration of the Russo-German Pact), became the most ardent countersubversives in the hemisphere and, consequently, champions of the diplomacy of Franklin Roosevelt. One of the members of the Foreign Relations Committee, Robert "Our Bob" Reynolds of North Carolina, was highly suspicious of Efron's leanings, clearly feeling that here was a much greater threat to the American way of life than that ostensibly posed by Axis activities in Latin America. (Reynolds's political reactionism was not the only factor predisposing him against the witness; the North Carolinian was one of those rare birds, a Southern isolationist.) For a leftist argument in favor of Pan-American solidarity, see the work by the Peruvian Aprista, Manuel Seoane, *Nuestra América y la guerra* (Santiago de Chile: Ediciones Ercilla, 1940). Before the shift in Soviet foreign policy, even the Communists sounded like the best of Good Neighbors. In the summer of 1939, the secretary general of the Peruvian Communist Party, Eudocio Ravines, denounced the Rome-Berlin-Tokyo Axis as well as the reactionary appeasers in Britain and France, and called for a "new and powerful Monroeism, a Monroeism of an emphatically democratic type, clearly anti-fascist." Quoted in ibid., p. 150.

51. "Neutrality," Senate *Hearings,* pp. 489–500. Johnson was referring to Busch's elimination of the trappings of Bolivian democracy (such as they were) during the previous week. Actually, Busch's move, which Herbert Klein has labelled a "great puritanical morality drive," had little in common with European totalitarianism, nor had it been brought about with Axis help. Nevertheless, there was some basis for concern in the United States, for Berlin's *Volkischer Beobachter* had applauded the change, congratulating Bolivia on becoming the

first truly totalitarian state in Latin America. Herbert S. Klein, *Parties and Political Change in Bolivia, 1880–1952,* Cambridge Latin American Studies, ed. David Joslin and John Street, vol. 5 (Cambridge: Cambridge University Press, 1969), pp. 308–11.

Chapter 7

1. Roosevelt's comments were recorded in a memorandum made by the State Department's Carleton Savage, who attended the White House meeting, and are quoted in William L. Langer and S. Everett Gleason, *The Challenge to Isolation, 1937–1940* (New York: Harper & Bros., 1952), pp. 138–39.

2. For congressional resistance to White House pressure, see Joseph Alsop and Robert Kintner, *American White Paper: The Story of American Diplomacy and the Second World War,* 6th ed. (New York: Simon & Schuster, 1940), pp. 40–41.

3. This is not to maintain that isolationists in Congress were politically impotent. What I am arguing is that the president was not so much out of step with prevailing trends in Congress as is sometimes asserted. For a good analysis of the changing mood in Congress during 1939 and 1940, see David L. Porter, *The Seventy-Sixth Congress and World War II, 1939–1940* (Columbia: University of Missouri Press, 1979).

4. Langer and Gleason, *Challenge to Isolation,* p. 232.

5. Outside White House circles there was still a healthy skepticism about the European democracies' resolve; some critics even thought that Britain and France might seek to deflect Hitler from expanding into their own spheres by offering him a "free hand" in Latin America. In August, a correspondent for the *Chicago Daily News,* John Whitaker, published a book on contemporary Latin politics, and concluded that the "ability of the United States to defend South America and ourselves against Germany, Italy, and Japan—should Britain and France be 'neutral' against us, as they were 'neutral' against Republican Spain—would be questionable in the extreme." Perhaps, observed this blunt newsman, the likelihood of such Anglo-German collusion was slim, but "the Chamberlain of Munich is not above it." John T. Whitaker, *Americas to the South* (New York: Macmillan, 1939), pp. 289–90.

6. Berle Diary, 25 May 1939, box 210, FDRL.

7. Ibid., 28 June 1939.

8. Willy Feuerlein and Elizabeth Hannan, *Dollars in Latin America: An Old Problem in a New Setting,* Studies in American Foreign Relations, no. 1, ed. Percy W. Bidwell (New York: Council on Foreign Relations, 1941), pp. 39–40.

9. William Appleman Williams, *The Tragedy of American Diplomacy,* 2d ed., rev. and enl. (New York: Dell Publishing, Delta Books, 1972), pp. 178–79.

10. Albert O. Hirschman, *National Power and the Structure of Foreign Trade* (Berkeley: University of California Press, 1945).

11. As indeed it did during the "safer" years of the 1920s and early 1930s, when American-British commercial rivalry in Latin America and elsewhere was at its peak. For an instance of this rivalry in the case of one strategic mineral,

petroleum, see Ludwell Denny, *We Fight for Oil* (New York: Alfred A. Knopf, 1928).

12. Undated report of early 1939 on political relations between the United States and South America, Harry Hopkins Papers, container 301, Economic Warfare (I), Franklin D. Roosevelt Library.

13. For a skeptical view of Schacht's financial "genius," see John Kenneth Galbraith, *Money: Whence It Came, Where It Went* (Boston: Houghton Mifflin, 1975), pp. 160–61. Schacht's side of the story is given in *My First Seventy-Six Years: The Autobiography of Hjalmar Schacht,* trans. Diana Pike (London: Allan Wingate, 1955). A balanced account is Amos E. Simpson, *Hjalmar Schacht in Perspective* (The Hague: Mouton, 1969).

14. Percy W. Bidwell, *Economic Defense of Latin America,* America Looks Ahead, no. 3 (Boston: World Peace Foundation, 1941), pp. 36–41; Feuerlein and Hannan, *Dollars in Latin America,* pp. 34–35. For Britain's involvement in bilateral trade arrangements, see J. Hurstfield, "The Control of British Raw Material Supplies, 1919–1939," *Economic History Review* 14 (1944): 14.

15. Arnold A. Offner, *American Appeasement: United States Foreign Policy and Germany, 1933–1938* (Cambridge: Harvard University Press, Belknap Press, 1969), p. 98; Norman P. Macdonald, *Hitler over Latin America* (London: Jarrolds, 1940), pp. 22–26; Schacht, *My First Seventy-Six Years,* pp. 328–29.

16. Cleona Lewis, *Nazi Europe and World Trade* (Washington: Brookings Institution, 1941), pp. 142–43; Herbert Feis, *The Changing Pattern of International Economic Affairs* (New York: Harper & Bros., 1940; reprint, Port Washington, N.Y.: Kennikat Press, 1971), pp. 58–62.

17. Commerce Department memorandum on German economic competition in Brazil, prepared by J. C. Corliss and George Wythe, 8 February 1939, Hopkins Papers, container 301, Economic Warfare (II), FDRL.

18. In 1935, the askimark had been valued 23 percent below the free mark; four years later, the differential was 16 percent.

19. Mordecai Ezekiel, "Economic Relations between the Americas," *International Conciliation,* no. 367 (February 1941), pp. 123–24.

20. Quoted in John D. Wirth, *The Politics of Brazilian Development, 1930–1954* (Stanford: Stanford University Press, 1970), p. 55.

21. E. Bradford Burns, *A History of Brazil* (New York: Columbia University Press, 1970), p. 292. Between 1931 and 1943, Brazilians burned more than 75 million sacks of coffee. Fiona Gordon-Ashworth, "Agricultural Commodity Control under Vargas in Brazil, 1930–1945," *Journal of Latin American Studies* 12 (May 1980): 91–92.

22. Herbert M. Bratter, "Foreign Exchange Control in Latin America," *Foreign Policy Reports* 14 (15 February 1939): 283.

23. José Bernal de León, *La Quinta Columna en el Continente Americano* (México, D.F.: Ediciones Culturales Mexicanas, 1939), p. 32.

24. Pedro Motta Lima and José Barboza Mello, *El Nazismo en el Brasil: Proceso del Estado Corporativo* (Buenos Aires: Editorial Claridad, 1938), p. 86.

25. Although the askimark system was a disguised devaluation, it was still a devaluation, which meant that German consumers ultimately paid a higher than

normal price for raw materials acquired through bilateral trading: for example, in 1935 each ton of raw cotton from Brazil commanded an average price of 1,115 reichmarks, compared with 805 and 1,000 reichmarks, respectively, for American and Egyptian cotton, both of which were of finer quality than the Brazilian fiber. Eugene Staley, *World Economy in Transition: Technology vs. Politics, Laissez Faire vs. Planning, Power vs. Welfare* (New York: Council on Foreign Relations, 1939), p. 112.

26. Howard J. Trueblood, "Trade Rivalries in Latin America," *Foreign Policy Reports* 13 (15 September 1937): 157; John Gunther, *Inside Latin America* (New York: Harper & Bros., 1941), p. 13.

27. Haas memorandum on Latin American trade, drafted for Secretary of the Treasury Morgenthau, 31 January 1938, Morgenthau Diary, 107:267–79, FDRL.

28. Trueblood, "Trade Rivalries in Latin America," p. 154.

29. James MacGregor Burns, *Roosevelt: The Soldier of Freedom* (New York: Harcourt Brace Jovanovich, 1970), p. 52, has written that "Bernard Baruch had long enjoyed a friendly relation with the President, who paid the Old Wilsonian every compliment except following his advice." Joseph Lash, *Roosevelt and Churchill: The Partnership that Saved the West* (New York: W. W. Norton, 1976), p. 241, has stated that Roosevelt was "not a Baruch enthusiast."

30. Baruch to Roosevelt, 29 April 1938, PSF C.F. War Department, box 14, FDRL. (My emphasis.)

31. *Press Conferences*, 23 June 1939, 13:463–64.

32. Military Intelligence Division memorandum, 17 June 1939, report on 16 June meeting of Standing Liaison Committee, Standing Liaison Committee Minutes, 1938–40 vol., box 912, National Archives, Record Group 165.

33. For the strategic role of the Canal in the first half of the twentieth century, see Sheldon B. Liss, *The Canal: Aspects of United States-Panamanian Relations* (Notre Dame, Ind.: University of Notre Dame Press, 1967), chap. 2.

34. Roosevelt to Woodring, 11 July 1939, OF 25–i, FDRL.

35. O'Connor to Roosevelt, 1 June 1939, OF 338, FDRL.

36. Quoted in Lourival Coutinho, *O General Góes Depõe*, 2d ed. (Rio de Janeiro: Livraria Editôra Coelho Branco, 1956), pp. 363–64.

37. Naval Attaché in Mexico to Office of Naval Intelligence, 21 July 1939, copy of report in 812.00N/59, SDDF.

38. H. Rutledge Southworth, "The Spanish Phalanx and Latin America," *Foreign Affairs* 18 (October 1939): 152.

39. *Public Papers*, 8:462–64.

40. Philip E. Jacob, "Influences of World Events on U.S. 'Neutrality' Opinion," *Public Opinion Quarterly* 4 (March 1940): 49–50.

41. Daniels to Roosevelt, 12 September 1939, in *Roosevelt and Daniels: A Friendship in Politics*, ed. Carroll Kilpatrick (Chapel Hill: University of North Carolina Press, 1952), p. 189.

42. Charles A. Beard, *Giddy Minds and Foreign Quarrels: An Estimate of American Foreign Policy* (New York: Macmillan, 1939), p. 69.

43. Not until June 1940 would each service be expanded to the maximum allowed by the National Defense Act of 1920. As late as the autumn of 1939,

the United States Army was only the world's seventeenth largest. See Forrest C. Pogue, *George C. Marshall*, vol. 1: *Education of a General, 1880–1939;* vol. 2: *Ordeal and Hope, 1939–1942;* vol. 3: *Organizer of Victory, 1943–1945;* 3 vols. (New York: Viking Press, 1963–73), 2:2–6.

44. *Public Papers*, 8:484–85.

45. Thomas Russell Ybarra, *America Faces South* (New York: Dodd, Mead, 1939), p. 66.

46. Berle Diary, 4 September 1939, box 211, FDRL.

47. Ibid., 13 September 1939.

48. Ibid., 22 September 1939.

49. Ibid.

50. Ibid., 21 September 1939.

51. U.S. Congress, *Congressional Record*, Proceedings and Debates of the 76th Congress, 2d sess., vol. 85, pt. 1 (Washington: United States Government Printing Office, 1939): 12.

Chapter 8

1. Berle Diary, 6 September 1939, box 211, FDRL; *FRUS: 1939,* 5:22. Making up the remainder of the American delegation were Edwin C. Wilson, minister-designate to Uruguay; Herbert Feis, State Department adviser for international economic affairs; Warren Kelchner, State Department officer in charge of international conferences; Marjorie M. Whiteman, State Department legal adviser; and Paul C. Daniels, Foreign Service officer.

2. Harold F. Peterson, *Argentina and the United States, 1810–1960* ([Albany]: State University of New York, 1964), pp. 400–401.

3. Charles Wertenbaker, *A New Doctrine for the Americas* (New York: Viking Press, 1941), p. 114.

4. Meynen to Foreign Ministry, 28 September 1939, *DGFP–D,* 8:157–58.

5. M/A Argentina, 12 September 1939, 2657–L–133/1, MID.

6. Memorandum from Political Division IX, 17 September 1939, *DGFP–D,* 8:86–88.

7. Sumner Welles, *The Time for Decision* (Cleveland: World Publishing, 1945), p. 211. For German attempts to generate anti-Americanism within the Latin delegations, see Alton Frye, *Nazi Germany and the American Hemisphere, 1933–1941* (New Haven: Yale University Press, 1967), pp. 118–19; Saul Friedländer, *Prelude to Downfall: Hitler and the United States, 1939–1941,* trans. Aline B. Werth and Alexander Werth (London: Chatto & Windus, 1967), pp. 45–47; and Irwin F. Gellman, *Good Neighbor Diplomacy: United States Policies in Latin America, 1933–1945* (Baltimore: Johns Hopkins University Press, 1979), p. 85.

8. Berle Diary, 26 August 1939, box 210, FDRL.

9. Resolution 14, Panama conference, cited by William L. Langer and S. Everett Gleason, *The Challenge to Isolation, 1937–1940* (New York: Harper & Bros., 1952), p. 212.

10. Gordon Connell-Smith, *The Inter-American System* (London: Oxford University Press, 1966), p. 112.

11. Cordell Hull, *The Memoirs of Cordell Hull,* 2 vols. (New York: Macmillan, 1948), 1:690.

12. On the morning the war began, 1 September 1939, Roosevelt summoned Welles and told him that he wanted him to have the State Department convene a meeting of the hemisphere's foreign ministers, so that the United States could propose the creation of an inter-American neutrality zone. Troubled by the lack of a juridical precedent, the president "jumped at the idea" suggested by Welles, namely that the administration cite a proposal Brazil and Colombia had made in 1915, calling for a Western Hemisphere zone within which belligerent activity would be prohibited. Joseph Alsop and Robert Kintner, *American White Paper: The Story of American Diplomacy and the Second World War,* 6th ed. (New York: Simon & Schuster, 1940), pp. 60–61. Hull would later remark of his rival, "every department has its thun of a bitch, but I've got the all-American." Quoted in James MacGregor Burns, *Roosevelt: The Soldier of Freedom* (New York: Harcourt Brace Jovanovich, 1970), p. 350. For details of the Hull-Welles antipathy and its sordid denouement, see Randall Bennett Woods, *The Roosevelt Foreign-Policy Establishment and the "Good Neighbor": The United States and Argentina, 1941–1945* (Lawrence: Regents Press of Kansas, 1979), pp. 103–5.

13. Berle Diary, 10 October 1939, box 211, FDRL.

14. John T. Flynn, *Country Squire in the White House* (Garden City, N.Y.: Doubleday, Doran, 1941), pp. 18–19.

15. Franklin D. Roosevelt, "The Problem of Our Navy: I," *Scientific American* 110 (28 February 1914): 177–78.

16. The actual limits of the zone in the Atlantic were as follows: from Quoddy Head east to longitude 60 degrees west; then south to latitude 20 degrees north; then along a line to latitude 5 degrees north, longitude 24 degrees west; then south to latitude 20 degrees south; then along a line to latitude 58 degrees south, longitude 57 degrees west. The Panama conference officially adopted the zone on 23 September, nearly three weeks after Roosevelt had ordered the Navy to begin its patrols. Samuel Eliot Morison, *The Battle of the Atlantic: September 1939–May 1943* (Boston: Little, Brown, 1947), pp. 14–15.

17. Ernst Woermann, Foreign Ministry Political Division chief, to ambassador to Italy, 27 October 1939, *DGFP–D,* 8:347–48. This decision notwithstanding, Hitler ordered his navy to make no provocative moves in the Pan-American zone, in hopes of avoiding a repetition of the kind of maritime incidents that had brought the United States into the last war. At times, Hitler was deliberately blind to American acquiescence in British violations of the security zone, as, for example, on the several occasions early in the war when the United States permitted the Royal Navy to round up German commercial ships breaking for home from Western Hemisphere ports. See Friedländer, *Prelude to Downfall,* pp. 61–62. For an account of American tolerance of British violations of the security zone, see Thomas A. Bailey and Paul B. Ryan, *Hitler vs. Roosevelt: The Undeclared Naval War* (New York: Free Press/Macmillan, 1979), pp. 38–47.

18. Churchill to Roosevelt, 5 October 1939, *Roosevelt and Churchill: Their Secret Wartime Correspondence,* ed. Francis L. Loewenheim, Harold D. Langley,

and Manfred Jonas (New York: Saturday Review Press, E. P. Dutton, 1975), p. 90 (hereafter cited as *Roosevelt and Churchill*).

19. See below, pp. 156–57.

20. Welles, *Time for Decision*, p. 212.

21. *Peace and War: United States Foreign Policy, 1931–1941* (Washington: Department of State, 1943), p. 493.

22. William Everett Kane, *Civil Strife in Latin America: A Legal History of U.S. Involvement* (Baltimore: Johns Hopkins University Press, 1972), p. 135. Another scholar dismissed the "prophyl-Axis" Declaration of Panama as a gross departure from international law: "That such an attack on belligerent rights and freedom of the seas should be made by twenty-one neutrals, led by the most powerful neutral, all of whom had always insisted on full respect for freedom of the seas and for their own neutral rights, verged on the preposterous." Frederick L. Schuman, *Design for Power: The Struggle for the World* (New York: Alfred A. Knopf, 1942), pp. 250–51.

23. For the foreign economic policy of the Roosevelt administration, see Dick Steward, *Trade and Hemisphere: The Good Neighbor Policy and Reciprocal Trade* (Columbia: University of Missouri Press, 1975).

24. *Peace and War*, pp. 491–92.

25. Nicholas John Spykman, *America's Strategy in World Politics: The United States and the Balance of Power* (New York: Harcourt, Brace, 1942), p. 326.

26. The committee's activities are discussed in J. Lloyd Mecham, *The United States and Inter-American Security, 1889–1960* (Austin: University of Texas Press, 1961), pp. 184, 202–5, 235–36.

27. Duncan Aikman, *The All-American Front* (Garden City, N.Y.: Doubleday, Doran, 1942), p. 10.

28. U.S. Congress, *Congressional Record*, Proceedings and Debates of the 76th Congress, 2d sess., vol. 85, pt. 1 (Washington: United States Government Printing Office, 1939): 250.

29. Ibid., p. 896.

30. For the relative absence of security worries in respect of Canada, see David G. Haglund, " 'Plain Grand Imperialism on a Miniature Scale': Canadian-American Rivalry over Greenland in 1940," *American Review of Canadian Studies* 11 (Spring 1981): 15.

31. J. Edgar Hoover to Col. E. R. Warner McCabe, Asst. Chief of Staff for Military Intelligence, 29 September 1939, 2801–304/8, MID.

32. *Public Opinion Quarterly* 3 (October 1939): 597–99.

33. Quoted in J. Benoist-Méchin, *Sixty Days that Shook the West: The Fall of France, 1940*, ed. Cyril Falls, trans. Peter Wiles (London: Jonathan Cape, 1963), p. 31.

34. Philip E. Jacob, "Influences of World Events on U.S. 'Neutrality' Opinion," *Public Opinion Quarterly* 4 (March 1940): 60–61.

35. Ibid., pp. 94–102, 109.

36. Quoted in Langer and Gleason, *Challenge to Isolation*, p. 282.

37. Boetticher to Wehrmacht High Command, 1 December 1939, *DGFP–D*, 8:470–71.

38. The Standing Liaison Committee was also studying how to oust Axis advisers attached to the armies of Ecuador and Bolivia. In addition, the committee debated whether to send armaments to Chile and Haiti, and pondered a rumor that two Russian submarines had been spotted prowling in Caribbean waters. Standing Liaison Committee Minutes, 7 December 1939, 1938–40 vol., box 912, National Archives, Record Group 165.

39. Stetson Conn and Byron Fairchild, *The Framework of Hemisphere Defense,* United States Army in World War II: The Western Hemisphere, gen. ed. Kent Roberts Greenfield (Washington: Office of the Chief of Military History, Department of the Army, 1960), p. 28.

40. For accounts of the *Graf Spee* and its destruction, see Geoffrey Bennett, *Battle of the River Plate* (London: Ian Allan, 1972); S. W. Roskill, *The War at Sea, 1939–1945* (vol. 1: *The Defensive;* vol. 2: *The Period of Balance;* vol. 3: *The Offensive;* 3 vols.; History of the Second World War: United Kingdom Military Series, ed. J.R.M. Butler [London: Her Majesty's Stationery Office, 1954–61]), 1:111–21; and idem, *The Navy at War, 1939–1945* (London: Collins, 1960), pp. 52–57.

41. Churchill to Roosevelt, 25 December 1939, *Roosevelt and Churchill,* pp. 91–92.

42. *New York Times,* 3 January 1940.

43. Berle Diary, 20 December 1939, box 211, FDRL. Berle's initial reaction to the scuttling of the *Graf Spee* was that it involved no violation of the security zone; after all, the Declaration of Panama did not forbid a captain to sink his own ship. "From our point of view a good job, because it saves us the embarrassment of having to argue out a violation of our neutrality zone, or perhaps send a fleet to stop somebody else's fight (poor sport, at best)." Ibid., 19 December 1939.

44. *New York Times,* 1 January 1940.

45. Roosevelt to White, 14 December 1939, *Personal Letters,* 2:967–68. Also see John DeWitt McKee, *William Allen White: Maverick on Main Street* (Westport, Conn.: Greenwood Press, 1975), pp. 184–85.

46. Roosevelt to Knox, 29 December 1939, *Personal Letters,* 2:975.

47. Welles, *Time for Decision,* p. 75.

48. *Public Opinion Quarterly* 4 (June 1940): 356–61.

49. Ibid., 4 (March 1940): 176–77.

50. Adolf A. Berle, Jr., *New Directions in the New World,* 2d ed. (New York: Harper & Bros., 1940), pp. 5–6.

51. Cited by Joseph P. Lash, *Roosevelt and Churchill: The Partnership that Saved the West* (New York: W. W. Norton, 1976), p. 87.

52. Welles, *Time for Decision,* pp. 92–98, 116.

53. Foreign Ministry memorandum, 12 March 1940, *DGFP–D,* 8:913.

54. Diary entry, 3 March 1940, Adolf A. Berle, Jr., *Navigating the Rapids, 1918–1971: From the Papers of Adolf A. Berle,* ed. Beatrice Bishop Berle and Travis Beal Jacobs (New York: Harcourt Brace Jovanovich, 1973), p. 292; and Berle Diary, 4 March 1940, box 211, FDRL.

55. Berle was not the only person in the West to equate Nazi Germany with Soviet Russia after August 1939. See Thomas G. Paterson and Les K. Adler,

"Red-Fascism: The Merger of Nazi Germany and Soviet Russia in the American Image of Totalitarianism, 1930s–1950s," *American Historical Review* 75 (April 1970): 1946–64.

56. Especially in Brazil, as Stanley E. Hilton has demonstrated in *Hitler's Secret War in South America, 1939–1945: German Military Espionage and Allied Counterespionage in Brazil* (Baton Rouge: Louisiana State University Press, 1981).

57. Berle to Hull, 23 March 1940, Berle Papers, box 211, FDRL.

58. Berle, *Navigating the Rapids*, p. 298.

59. Berle Diary, 29 March 1940, box 211, FDRL.

60. Harold L. Ickes, *The Secret Diary of Harold L. Ickes*, vol. 1: *The First Thousand Days, 1933–1936*; vol. 2: *The Inside Struggle, 1936–1939*; vol. 3: *The Lowering Clouds, 1939–1941*; 3 vols. (New York: Simon & Schuster, 1953–54), 3: 149–50.

Chapter 9

1. *Public Papers*, 9:158–62.

2. *Press Conferences*, 18 April 1940, 15:274–85.

3. Chargé d'affaires Hans Thomsen and M/A Friedrich Boetticher to Foreign Ministry, 11 May 1940, *DGFP–D*, 9:328–30. It is noteworthy that Boetticher was at last beginning to form a more realistic understanding of the mechanics of policymaking in Washington. He was becoming as fully aware as the more cautious Thomsen of at least the possibility of American intervention in Europe. Nevertheless, he continued to blame "Jewish wirepullers" for spreading tales that Germany was out to conquer Latin America. See James V. Compton, *The Swastika and the Eagle: Hitler, the United States, and the Origins of World War II* (Boston: Houghton Mifflin, 1967), pp. 107–8, 118.

4. See above, pp. 95–96.

5. Lothian to Lady Astor, 20 May 1940, cited by Philip Goodhart, *Fifty Ships that Saved the World: The Foundation of the Anglo-American Alliance* (Garden City, N.Y.: Doubleday, 1965), p. 27.

6. Ibid.

7. Kennedy to Roosevelt, 15 May 1940, *FRUS: 1940*, 3:29–30.

8. John Morton Blum, *From the Morgenthau Diaries*, vol. 1: *Years of Crisis, 1928–1938*; vol. 2: *Years of Urgency, 1938–1941*; vol. 3: *Years of War, 1941–1945*; 3 vols. (Boston: Houghton Mifflin, 1959–67), 2:150.

9. William Frye, *Marshall: Citizen Soldier* (Indianapolis: Bobbs-Merrill, 1947), p. 276.

10. Cited by Mark Lincoln Chadwin, *The Hawks of World War II* (Chapel Hill: University of North Carolina Press, 1968), p. 84.

11. Richard M. Leighton and Robert W. Coakley, *Global Logistics and Strategy, 1940–1943*, United States Army in World War II: The War Department, gen. ed. Kent Roberts Greenfield (Washington: Office of the Chief of Military History, Department of the Army, 1955), p. 33.

12. Forrest C. Pogue, *George C. Marshall*, vol. 1: *Education of a General, 1880–1939*; vol. 2: *Ordeal and Hope, 1939–1942*; vol. 3: *Organizer of Victory, 1943–1945*; 3 vols. (New York: Viking Press, 1963–73), 2:46. For a different

interpretation, see David G. Haglund, "George C. Marshall and the Question of Military Aid to England, May–June 1940," *Journal of Contemporary History* 15 (October 1980): 745–60. Marshall, it seems, advocated the United States taking measures in diametric opposition to British interests not only during May and June 1940, but also during the middle of American participation in World War II, as is shown in Mark A. Stoler, "The 'Pacific-First' Alternative in American World War II Strategy," *International History Review* 2 (July 1980): 432–52.

13. Roosevelt to Churchill, 16 May 1940, *Roosevelt and Churchill*, pp. 95–96.

14. *Public Papers*, 9:198–205. Although a billion dollars may not seem like a vast sum in light of current military budgets, it is useful to recall that for all of 1938 the United Staes spent only 1.2 billion dollars for defense. Klaus Knorr, *Military Power and Potential* (Lexington, Mass.: D. C. Heath, 1970), p. 48.

15. Hadley Cantril, "America Faces the War: A Study in Public Opinion," *Public Opinion Quarterly* 4 (September 1940): 393.

16. Survey of recent public opinion polls, ibid., pp. 549–53.

17. Thomsen to Foreign Ministry, 16 May 1940, *DGFP*–D, 9:350–51.

18. Cordell Hull, *The Memoirs of Cordell Hull*, 2 vols. (New York: Macmillan, 1948), 1:822.

19. *Public Papers*, 9:238.

20. Adolf A. Berle, Jr., *Navigating the Rapids, 1918–1971: From the Papers of Adolf A. Berle*, ed. Beatrice Bishop Berle and Travis Beal Jacobs (New York: Harcourt Brace Jovanovich, 1973), p. 326. For a study of the fear that gripped Berle and countless others, see Louis de Jong, *The German Fifth Column in the Second World War*, trans. C. M. Geyl (Chicago: University of Chicago Press, 1956; reprint, New York: Howard Fertig, 1973).

21. M/A Argentina, 16 May 1940, 2657–L–133/3, MID; idem, 21 May 1940, 2657–L–133/6, MID. The pro-Allied Buenos Aires press beat the drum for an eradication of the fifth column, *Crítica* assuming the leadership by issuing the warning that Germany was out to steal Patagonia from Argentina. Military Attaché M. A. Devine reported that "the Fifth Column activity is directed by prominent Nazi chiefs, apparently independent although reportedly supplied with almost unlimited funds by the Embassy." Idem, 21 May 1940, 2657–L–133/7, MID; idem, 22 May 1940, 2657–L–133/8, MID.

22. Quoted in João Frederico Normano, *The Struggle for South America: Economy and Ideology* (London: George Allen & Unwin, 1931), p. 78.

23. "We were all in favor of France. Every fiber of our being thrilled unanimously with the cult of a tradition and thought which have such a powerful influence in the development of Latin American life." Manuel Ugarte, *The Destiny of a Continent*, ed. J. Fred Rippy, trans. Catherine A. Phillips (New York: Alfred A. Knopf, 1925; reprint, New York: AMS Press, 1970), p. 260.

24. Normano, *Struggle for South America*, p. 78.

25. Ludwig Bemelmans, *The Donkey Inside* (New York: Viking Press, 1941), p. 30.

26. Vera Micheles Dean, *Latin America and the War* (New York: Oxford University Press, 1942), p. 46.

27. Juan E. Carulla, *Al filo del medio siglo* (Paraná, Argentina: Editorial Llanura, 1951), p. 241.

28. Matt. 26:40–41.

29. M/A Argentina, 28 May 1940, 2657–L–133/9, MID.

30. Armour to Hull, 24 May 1940, *FRUS:* 1940, 5:21–22.

31. Robert A. Potash, *The Army and Politics in Argentina: Yrigoyen to Perón* (Stanford: Stanford University Press, 1969), p. 121; Frank D. McCann, Jr., *The Brazilian-American Alliance, 1937–1945* (Princeton: Princeton University Press, 1973), p. 183.

32. Memorandum of conversation between Armour and Zar, 5 June 1940, PSF Diplomatic, box 32, FDRL.

33. FBI report on Uruguay, July 1942, Harry Hopkins Papers, Group 24, container 143, FDRL.

34. Hugo Fernández Artucio, *The Nazi Underground in South America* (New York: Farrar & Rinehart, 1942), pp. 5–7.

35. Idem, *Nazis en el Uruguay* (Montevideo: Talleres Gráficos Sur, 1940), pp. 26–30, 98–104.

36. Wilson to Hull, 30 May 1940, *FRUS:* 1940, 5:1151–52. Also see Wilson to Hull, 15 May 1940; and Roosevelt to Welles, 20 May 1940; both ibid., p. 1147.

37. *New York Times*, 29 May 1940; Fernández Artucio, *Nazi Underground*, pp. 7–8.

38. De Jong, *German Fifth Column*, pp. 111–14.

39. *New York Times*, 30 May 1940.

40. Memorandum from Political Division IX, October 1940, *DGFP–D*, 11:442.

41. T. G. Brena and J. V. Iturbide, *Alta traición en el Uruguay* (Montevideo: Editorial A.B.C., 1940), pp. 190–93, 263–68. American scholars who have accepted the argument that Germany intended to colonize Uruguay, or at least overthrow the Baldomir government, are Russell H. Fitzgibbon, *Uruguay: Portrait of a Democracy* (New Brunswick, N.J.: Rutgers University Press, 1954), pp. 256–57; and Marvin Alisky, *Uruguay: A Contemporary Survey* (New York: Frederick A. Praeger, 1969), p. 144.

42. Charles Wertenbaker, *A New Doctrine for the Americas* (New York: Viking Press, 1941), pp. 47–48.

43. Berle Diary, 2 June 1940, box 212, FDRL.

44. Stark to Roosevelt, 2 June 1940, *FRUS:* 1940, 5:1155–56.

45. Duggan to Welles, 31 May 1940, ibid., 5:1153.

46. Vargas's announcement that Brazil would maintain an impartial neutrality came on 10 May at Blumenau, in the heart of the heavily German state, Santa Catarina. The Brazilian leader proclaimed that Brazil was "neither English nor German," and would brook no interference from either power. He reiterated this position at Belo Horizonte two days later. See Paulo de Queiroz Duarte, *O Nordeste na II Guerra Mundial: Antecedentes e Ocupação* (Rio de Janeiro: Record, 1971), pp. 39, 65–66.

47. M/A Brazil, 22 May 1940, 2657–K–123/4, MID. For an account of German undercover activity in Brazil, see Stanley E. Hilton, *Hitler's Secret War in South America, 1939–1945: German Military Espionage and Allied Counterespionage in Brazil* (Baton Rouge: Louisiana State University Press, 1981).

48. Caffery to Welles, 24 May 1940, *FRUS:* 1940, 5:42–43. Even before the

resident had instructed Stark to explore
nha from being used by any European bel-
spreads." Roosevelt to Stark, 30 April 1940,

26... , 30 May 1940, 2657–K–110/3, MID.
Duarte, *Nordeste na II Guerra Mundial*, p. 36.

51. Details of the POT OF GOLD plan can be found in Mark Skinner Watson, *Chief of Staff: Prewar Plans and Preparations*, United States Army in World War II: The War Department, gen. ed. Kent Roberts Greenfield (Washington: Office of the Chief of Military History, Department of the Army, 1950), pp. 96, 106; Stetson Conn and Byron Fairchild, *The Framework of Hemisphere Defense*, United States Army in World War II: The Western Hemisphere, gen. ed. Kent Roberts Greenfield (Washington: Office of the Chief of Military History, Department of the Army, 1960), pp. 33–34; Pogue, *Marshall*, 2:54–55; and John Child, "From 'Color' to 'Rainbow': U.S. Strategic Planning for Latin America, 1919–1945," *Journal of InterAmerican Studies and World Affairs* 21 (May 1979): 250–2.

52. Edward Mead Earle, *Against This Torrent* (Princeton: Princeton University Press, 1941), pp. 18–21. On 26 July 1940, Secretary of War Henry Stimson and Chief of Staff Marshall approved a memorandum from military intelligence recognizing that, while the United States certainly sought "better mutual understanding" with Latin militaries," our objective does *not* comprise expectations on our part of being able to use Latin American forces as effective allies in war." Cited by Conn and Fairchild, *Framework of Hemisphere Defense*, p. 179. (Emphasis is in the source.)

53. Roosevelt to Bowers, 22 May 1940, in Claude G. Bowers, *Chile through Embassy Windows, 1939–1953* (New York: Simon & Schuster, 1958), pp. 60–61.

54. Bowers to Roosevelt, 25 May 1940, PSF Diplomatic, box 36, FDRL.

55. Bowers to Welles, 25 May 1940, ibid.

56. Karl Loewenstein, *Brazil under Vargas* (New York: Macmillan, 1942), p. 281· Walter R. Sharp, "Methods of Opinion Control in Present-Day Brazil," *Public Opinion Quarterly* 5 (March 1941): 9; Harold N. Graves, Jr., "Propaganda by Short Wave: Berlin Calling America," ibid., 4 (December 1940): 604; Felipe Barreda Laos, *¿Hispano América en guerra?* (Buenos Aires: Linari, 1941), pp. 122–23; Kathleen Romoli, *Colombia: Gateway to South America* (Garden City, N.Y.: Doubleday, Doran, 1941), p. 325.

57. Taylor to War Department, 29 July 1940, WPD 4115–29.

58. MID report, "Forms of Fifth Column Activity," September 1940, copy in Morgenthau Diary, 24 September 1940, 308:98–106, FDRL.

Chapter 10

1. Churchill to Roosevelt, 20 May 1940, *Roosevelt and Churchill*, p. 97.

2. Joseph Lash, *Roosevelt and Churchill: The Partnership that Saved the West* (New York: W. W. Norton, 1976), pp. 134–35.

3. For an account of the White House meeting, see Stetson Conn and Byron Fairchild, *The Framework of Hemisphere Defense*, United States Army in World

War II: The Western Hemisphere, gen. ed. Kent Roberts Greenfield (Washington: Office of the Chief of Military History, Department of the Army, 1960), p. 32. For the War Plans Division memorandum of 22 May, see William L. Langer and S. Everett Gleason, *The Challenge to Isolation, 1937–1940* (New York: Harper & Bros., 1952), p. 475.

4. Thomas to Roosevelt, 22 May 1940; Roosevelt to Thomas, 3 June 1940; both PPF 6148, FDRL.

5. *Press Conferences*, 23 May 1940, 15:360–61.

6. A lively account of the German advance is J. Benoist-Méchin, *Sixty Days that Shook the West: The Fall of France, 1940*, ed. Cyril Falls, trans. Peter Wiles (London: Jonathan Cape, 1963).

7. Berle Diary, 26 May 1940, box 211, FDRL.

8. Quoted in Robert E. Sherwood, *Roosevelt and Hopkins: An Intimate History* (New York: Harper & Bros., 1948), p. 160.

9. See Herbert Agar, *Britain Alone, June 1940–June 1941* (London: Bodley Head, 1972), pp. 70–73; and Robert Wright, *Dowding and the Battle of Britain* (London: Macdonald, 1969), pp. 101–12.

10. Bullitt to Roosevelt, 28 May 1940, *FRUS: 1940*, 1:236–37.

11. Hull to Bullitt, 30 May 1940, cited by William L. Langer, *Our Vichy Gamble* (New York: Alfred A. Knopf, 1947; reprint, Hamden, Conn.: Archon Books, 1965), pp. 14–15.

12. Whitney to Roosevelt, 27 May 1940, OF 249, box 5, FDRL.

13. *Press Conferences*, 30 May 1940, 15:412–13.

14. Berle Diary, 31 May 1940, box 212, FDRL.

15. Harold L. Ickes, *The Secret Diary of Harold L. Ickes*, vol. 1: *The First Thousand Days, 1933–1936*; vol. 2: *The Inside Struggle, 1936–1939*; vol. 3: *The Lowering Clouds, 1939–1941*; 3 vols. (New York: Simon & Schuster, 1953–54), 3:178.

16. Joseph Alsop and Robert Kintner, *American White Paper: The Story of American Diplomacy and the Second World War*, 6th ed. (New York: Simon & Schuster, 1940), pp. 82d–82e.

17. Joint Army & Navy Basic War Plan—RAINBOW 4, 13 June 1940, WPD, JB 325, ser. 642–4. The "quartersphere" concept is treated in John Child, "From 'Color' to 'Rainbow': U.S. Strategic Planning for Latin America, 1919–1945," *Journal of Interamerican Studies and World Affairs* 21 (May 1979): 234–36.

18. Braden to Welles, 11 June 1940; Welles to Braden, 12 June 1940; both *FRUS: 1940*, 5:60–63.

19. Braden to Welles, 13 June 1940, ibid., 5:64–65.

20. Graeme K. Howard, *America and a New World Order* (New York: Charles Scribner's Sons, 1940), pp. 80, 87–90.

21. Commerce Department memorandum on hemisphere defense, 11 June 1940, Harry Hopkins Papers, container 311, Latin American Affairs folder, FDRL.

22. Berle Diary, 9 June 1940, box 212, FDRL.

23. Quoted in Mark Lincoln Chadwin, *The Hawks of World War II* (Chapel Hill: University of North Carolina Press, 1968), pp. 279–80.

24. Barry Bingham, "Shall We Go to War?" in *Defense for America*, ed. William Allen White (New York: Macmillan, 1940), p. 40.

25. Raymond Leslie Buell, *Isolated America,* 2d ed. (New York: Alfred A. Knopf, 1940), pp. 254, 265–66. For the perceived significance of Latin resources during these years, see David G. Haglund, " 'Gray Areas' and Raw Materials: Latin American Resources and International Politics in the Pre-World War II Years," *Inter-American Economic Affairs* 36 (Winter 1982): 23–51.

26. Cited by Walter Johnson, *The Battle against Isolation* (Chicago: University of Chicago Press, 1944), pp. 86–87.

27. Ibid.

28. As Warren S. Cohen has demonstrated in *The American Revisionists: The Lessons of Intervention in World War I* (Chicago: University of Chicago Press, 1967).

29. Quoted in John DeWitt McKee, *William Allen White: Maverick on Main Street* (Westport, Conn.: Greenwood Press, 1975), p. 188.

30. Geoffrey S. Smith, *To Save a Nation: American Countersubversives, the New Deal, and the Coming of World War II* (New York· Basic Books, 1973), p. 164.

31. *Press Conferences,* 11 June 1940, 15:557.

32. *Public Opinion Quarterly* 4 (December 1940): 711–12.

33. Hadley Cantril, "America Faces the War: A Study in Public Opinion," *Public Opinion Quarterly* 4 (September 1940):390–93.

34. Philip Goodhart, *Fifty Ships that Saved the World: The Foundation of the Anglo-American Alliance* (Garden City, N.Y.: Doubleday, 1965), p. 72.

35. Hadley Cantril, *The Human Dimension: Experience in Policy Research* (New Brunswick, N.J.: Rutgers University Press, 1967), pp. 41–42.

36. For the contrary view that Roosevelt, as early as the end of May, was convinced that "the best means of defending American security was through expanded aid to Britain and France," cf. Robert Dallek, *Franklin D. Roosevelt and American Foreign Policy, 1932–1945* (New York: Oxford University Press, 1979), p. 227.

37. *Public Papers,* 9:259–64.

38. Langer and Gleason, *Challenge to Isolation,* p. 516, contend that "for the moment pure isolationism was all but dead." Robert E. Osgood, *Ideals and Self-Interest in America's Foreign Relations: The Great Transformation of the Twentieth Century* (Chicago: University of Chicago Press, Phoenix Books, 1964), p. 416, sees the Charlottesville address as the definitive rejection of the "fortress" concept of defense, although Roosevelt, for domestic political reasons, had to mask his true intentions

39. Vargas's remarks quoted in Paulo de Queiroz Duarte, *O Nordeste na II Guerra Mundial: Antecedentes e Ocupação* (Rio de Janeiro: Record, 1971), pp. 67–68.

40. Lourival Coutinho, *O General Góes Depõe,* 2d ed. (Rio de Janeiro: Livraria Editôra Coelho Branco, 1956), pp. 365–68.

41. Cited by Hubert Herring, *Good Neighbors: Argentina, Brazil, Chile and Seventeen Other Countries* (New Haven: Yale University Press, 1941), p. 136.

42. Karl Loewenstein, *Brazil under Vargas* (New York: Macmillan, 1942), pp. 274–75; Alton Frye, *Nazi Germany and the American Hemisphere,*

1933–1941 (New Haven: Yale University Press, 1967), pp. 126–27; Albert E. Carter, *The Battle of South America* (Indianapolis: Bobbs-Merrill, 1941), pp. 65–67; Frank D. McCann, Jr., *The Brazilian-American Alliance. 1937–1945* (Princeton: Princeton University Press, 1973), pp. 185–87; John Gunther, *Inside Latin America* (New York: Harper & Bros., 1941), p. 380; and Stanley E. Hilton, "Brazilian Diplomacy and the Washington-Rio de Janeiro 'Axis' during the World War II Era, "*Hispanic American Historical Review* 59 (May 1979): 208. In fairness to Vargas, he was not the only person in the hemisphere to recommend that people get used to Hitler's new order; for a contemporary American view, cf. Anne Morrow Lindbergh, *The Wave of the Future: A Confession of Faith* (New York: Harcourt, Brace, 1940).

43. Churchill to Roosevelt, 11 June 1940, *Roosevelt and Churchill*, pp. 98–99.

44. *Press Conferences,* 14 June 1940, 15:571–72.

45. Swarts to Eleanor Roosevelt, 13 June 1940, Harry Hopkins Papers, container 301, Economic Warfare (II), FDRL.

46. Churchill to Roosevelt, 15 June 1940, *Roosevelt and Churchill*, pp. 104–6.

47. Strong to Marshall, 17 June 1940, WPD 4250–3.

48. Marshall statement to Standing Liaison Committee, 17 June 1940, ibid. (Marshall's emphasis.)

49. For a different interpretation, cf. George Fielding Eliot, *Hour of Triumph* (New York: Reynal & Hitchcock, 1944), p. vi: "When Franch went down, the involvement of this nation in the struggle against totalitarianism became instantly inevitable."

Chapter 11

1. For the argument that it did, cf. Warren F. Kimball, ed., *Franklin D. Roosevelt and the World Crisis, 1937–1945* (Lexington, Mass.: D.C. Heath, 1973), p. xv: "From that point on American entry into the war against Hitler proceeded in a seemingly mechanical step-by-step progression."

2. Cited by Mark Skinner Watson, *Chief of Staff: Prewar Plans and Preparations,* United States Army in World War II: The War Department, gen. ed. Kent Roberts Greenfield (Washington: Office of the Chief of Military History, Department of the Army, 1950), p. 312.

3. Pp. 201–2.

4. Keith D. McFarland, *Harry H. Woodring: A Political Biography of F.D.R.'s Controversial Secretary of War* (Lawrence: University of Kansas Press, 1975), pp. 224–32.

5. Kirk to Hull, 17 June 1940, cited by Hans L. Trefousse, *Germany and American Neutrality, 1939–1941* (New York: Bookman Associates, 1951), pp. 55–56.

6. Quoted in *Roosevelt and Churchill*, pp. 104–6.

7. Marshall and Stark to Roosevelt, 24 June 1940, WPD 4250–3. This memorandum had been drawn up on 22 June, the day France surrendered.

8. Marshall to Strong, 24 June 1940, ibid.

9. Marshall and Stark to Roosevelt, 27 June 1940, ibid.

10. For the story of the destroyers-bases exchange, see James R. Leutze, *Bargaining for Supremacy: Anglo-American Naval Collaboration, 1937–1941* (Chapel Hill: University of North Carolina Press, 1977), pp. 72–93, 114–27; and Philip Goodhart, *Fifty Ships that Saved the World: The Foundation of the Anglo-American Alliance* (Garden City, N.Y.: Doubleday, 1965). Although Roosevelt approved the transfer on 2 August, two weeks before the beginning of the Battle of Britain (not to be confused with the London Blitz, which commenced in the middle of September), it was not until 2 September that the final details of the swap were worked out and the announcement of the transaction was made public. In return for the destroyers and other military aid, the United States received leases on naval and air bases in Newfoundland, Bermuda, the Bahamas, Jamaica, St. Lucia, Trinidad, and British Guiana.

11. Stetson Conn and Byron Fairchild, *The Framework of Hemisphere Defense*, United States Army in World War II: The Western Hemisphere, gen. ed. Kent Roberts Greenfield (Washington: Office of the Chief of Military History, Department of the Army, 1960), p. 62. Also see Thomas A. Bailey and Paul B. Ryan, *Hitler vs. Roosevelt: The Undeclared Naval War* (New York: Free Press/Macmillan, 1979), p. 88, where it is argued that the destroyers-bases deal constituted a prima facie violation of neutrality: "From the point of view of Hitler, the United States by this time had so far overstepped the bounds of neutrality as to be waging an undeclared war. . . ."

12. For an account of Hitler's poorly conceived invasion planning, see Peter Fleming, *Invasion 1940: An Account of the German Preparations and the British Counter-Measures* (London: Rupert Hart-Davis, 1957); and especially Ronald Wheatley, *Operation Sea Lion: German Plans for the Invasion of England, 1939–1942* (Oxford: Clarendon Press, 1958).

13. Corey Ford, *Donovan of OSS* (Boston: Little, Brown, 1970), pp. 88–94.

14. Quoted in Joseph Lash, *Roosevelt and Churchill: The Partnership that Saved the West* (New York: W.W. Norton, 1976), pp. 212–13.

15. The inconstancy of memory, especially when the matter being recalled is a fear that was shown later to have been exaggerated, is a major problem confronting scholars who work with memoirs. A good example of the pitfall of memoirs is Matthew B. Ridgway, *Soldier: The Memoirs of Matthew B. Ridgway* (New York: Harper & Bros., 1956), pp. 47–48, where the author gives a highly misleading impression of his service with the War Plans Division prior to United States entry into the war. Ridgway was one of the keen young officers sent to Latin America in the summer of 1940 to arrange the bilateral staff talks. At that time, as War Department documents reveal, he was quite concerned about the coming Nazi invasion of the hemisphere. Nearly twenty years later, however, after having been in the thick of battle in both Europe and Korea, Ridgway recalled his time at WPD in a bemused, condescending manner, remarking that "there was nothing of great significance about my service [there]."

16. Steinbeck to Roosevelt, 24 June 1940, OF 3858, FDRL; Roosevelt to Appointments Secretary Edwin Watson, 25 June 1940, ibid.

17. Capt. Daniel Callaghan, presidential naval aide, to Missy LeHand, 13 December 1939, OF 18–x, FDRL.

18. Vanderbilt to LeHand, 27 August 1940, PPF 104, FDRL.

19. Roosevelt to Hopkins, 15 June 1940, Hopkins Papers, container 311, Latin American Affairs folder, FDRL.

20. Carleton Beals, *The Coming Struggle for Latin America* (Philadelphia: J.B. Lippincott, 1938), pp. 260–68.

21. Sumner Welles, *Seven Decisions that Shaped History* (New York: Harper & Bros., 1950), p. 12.

22. Max Lerner, *It Is Later than You Think: The Need for a Militant Democracy* (New York: Viking Press, 1938), p. 149. E.H. Carr's thinking on laissez-faire is found in his classic work, *The Twenty Years' Crisis, 1919–1939: An Introduction to the Study of International Relations* (London: Macmillan, 1939). In defense of Hull, liberal economists pointed out that the seeming success of German bilateral trading could only be matched if the United States was willing to abandon democracy. Percy W. Bidwell, "Latin America, Germany, and the Hull Program," *Foreign Affairs* 17 (January 1939): 382–85; Francis Bowes Sayre, *The Way Forward: The American Trade Agreements Program* (New York: Macmillan, 1939), p. 112. For a recent study of the Hull trade program, see Dick Steward, *Trade and Hemisphere: The Good Neighbor Policy and Reciprocal Trade* (Columbia: University of Missouri Press, 1975).

23. Roosevelt to Hopkins, 15 June 1940, Hopkins Papers, container 311, Latin American Affairs folder, FDRL.

24. Berle Diary, 17 June 1940, box 212, FDRL.

25. *Press Conferences*, 21 June 1940, 15:587. For an analysis of the cartel plan, see Forrest Davis and Ernest K. Lindley, *How War Came: An American White Paper, from the Fall of France to Pearl Harbor* (New York: Simon & Schuster, 1942), pp. 127–30.

26. Morgenthau Diary, 27 June 1940, 276:177–78, FDRL.

27. Berle Diary, 30 June 1940, box 212, FDRL.

28. *New York Times*, 6 January 1940. In June, the *United States News* calculated that if the cartel had been in effect in 1938, America would have imported—in addition to her regular purchases from abroad—some 65 million bushels of wheat, 10 million bags of coffee, 1.5 million bales of cotton, and more than 20 million tons of oil. Cited by Howell M. Henry, "The Nazi Threat to the Western Hemisphere," *South Atlantic Quarterly 39* (October 1940): 379.

29. Willy Feuerlein and Elizabeth Hannan, *Dollars in Latin America: An Old Problem in a New Setting*, Studies in American Foreign Relations, no. 1, ed. Percy W. Bidwell (New York: Council on Foreign Relations, 1941), pp. 89–91.

30. Quoted in William Diebold, Jr., *New Directions in Our Trade Policy*, Studies in American Foreign Relations, no. 2, ed. Percy W. Bidwell (New York: Council on Foreign Relations, 1941), pp. 126–28.

31. Economic Policy Department memorandum, 16 July 1940, *DGFP–D*, 10:229.

32. Berle Diary, 2 July 1940, box 212, FDRL.

33. William L. Langer and S. Everett Gleason, *The Challenge to Isolation, 1937–1940* (New York: Harper & Bros., 1952), pp. 634–36.

34. For Roosevelt's lack of confidence in Hull's stewardship of the State Department, see Robert Dallek, *Franklin D. Roosevelt and American Foreign Policy, 1932–1945* (New York: Oxford University Press, 1979), p. 532.

35. Assistant Chief of Staff for MID, Sherman Miles, to Marshall, 2 July 1940, "Possible Activities of the Axis Powers in the Western Hemisphere," 2657–244, MID.

36. Ibid.

37. War Plans Division memorandum for Stark, 10 July 1940, WPD 4115.

38. Ibid.

39. War Plans Division memorandum for Assistant Chief of Staff George V. Strong, 6 September 1940, WPD 4115–38.

40. Langer and Gleason, *Challenge to Isolation*, pp. 626–27.

41. Munro's remarks quoted in "A Brief Abstract of the Proceedings of the Conference on 'Changes in the Economic and Political Situation in the Western Hemisphere and Problems Arising therefrom, as a Result of the War in Europe,' "*Hispanic American Historical Review* 20 (November 1940): 655–56. (This conference was held 2 and 3 July at the University of Texas, Austin.)

42. *Public Opinion Quarterly* 4 (December 1940): 715.

43. Stephen Duggan, "The Western Hemisphere as a Haven of Peace?" *Foreign Affairs* 18 (July 1940): 614.

44. William L. Langer, *Our Vichy Gamble* (New York: Alfred A. Knopf, 1947; reprint, Hamden, Conn.: Archon Books, 1965), p. 6.

45. Sumner Welles, *The Time for Decision* (Cleveland: World Publishing, 1945), p. 215.

46. Cordell Hull, *The Memoirs of Cordell Hull*, 2 vols. (New York: Macmillan, 1948), 1:822–23.

47. Weizsäcker memorandum to Latin missions, 8 August 1940, *DGFP–D*, 10:488.

48. Hull, *Memoirs*, 1:824.

49. Alberto Conil Paz and Gustavo Ferrari, *Argentina's Foreign Policy, 1930–1962*, trans. John J. Kennedy (Notre Dame, Ind.: University of Notre Dame Press, 1966), p. 57.

50. Berle to Roosevelt, 18 July 1940, Berle Papers, box 212, FDRL.

51. *Public Papers*, 9:303–5.

52. Memorandum of 2 August 1940, Berle Papers, box 212, FDRL. On 26 September Congress voted the funds requested by the president, increasing the lending authority of the Export-Import Bank from 200 million dollars to 700 million dollars. The first Eximbank had been set up in February 1934 to handle trade with the Soviet Union; it was joined in the following month by a second bank, created to facilitate trade with Cuba. Both banks were merged in 1936. As the drift toward war began to grow apparent in the late 1930s, the Export-Import Bank assumed a greater role in the conduct of American diplomacy. Before 1938 it had been mainly concerned with furthering the commercial interests of the United States, but in the year of Munich it started to show signs that it "would become more aggressive in expanding United States interests in the hemisphere." Following the invasion of Poland, its lending power was increased to 100 million dollars. Frederick C. Adams, *Economic Diplomacy: The Export-Import Bank and American Foreign Policy, 1934–1939* (Columbia: University of Missouri Press, 1976), p. 209. Also see the unpublished report by George D. Holliday, "History of the Export-Import Bank of the United States," Library of Congress,

Congressional Research Service, 29 August 1974.

53. Memorandum of 2 August 1940, Berle Papers, box 212, FDRL. It was indeed fortunate for the United States that the Act of Havana, which required no ratification, was approved along with the Convention, because a full year after the foreign ministers conference the Convention had only been ratified by six states. *Documents on American Foreign Relations*, 13 vols. (Boston: World Peace Foundation, 1939–53), 3:85–89.

54. *Press Conferences*, 6 August 1940, 16:97.

55. Harold L. Ickes, *The Secret Diary of Harold L. Ickes*, vol. 1: *The First Thousand Days, 1933–1936*; vol. 2: *The Inside Struggle, 1936–1939*; vol. 3: *The Lowering Clouds, 1939–1941*; 3 vols. (New York: Simon & Schuster, 1953–54), 3:289.

56. The Hague Convention of 1907 prohibited transactions such as the destroyers-for-bases exchange. See Arnold A. Offner, *The Origins of the Second World War: American Foreign Policy and World Politics, 1917–1941* (New York: Praeger, 1975), p. 182.

57. For a statement of the view that American supplies alone would suffice to defeat Hitler, see Fritz Sternberg, *Fivefold Aid to Britain: To Save Her and Keep Us Out of War* (New York: John Day, 1941).

58. For an account of that undeclared war, see Bailey and Ryan, *Hitler vs. Roosevelt.*

59. Orville H. Bullitt, ed., *For the President, Personal and Secret: Correspondence between Franklin D. Roosevelt and William C. Bullitt* (Boston: Houghton Mifflin, 1972), p. 498. The president had read Bullitt's speech in advance; recognizing it as a valuable trial balloon for the deal he was working out with Britain, he gave it his approval.

60. Charles Eade, comp., *The War Speeches of the Rt. Hon. Winston S. Churchill*, 3 vols. (London: Cassell's, 1951–52), 1:244.

61. Berle Diary, 6 and 15 October 1940, box 212, FDRL.

Index

271

172–3; training pilots in U.S., 112;
U.S. aid to, 96, 130–1, 148, 194;
U.S. public opinion, 114, 116;
viability questioned, 187
Franco, Francisco, 55, 59, 60,
100–101
Franklin, Benjamin, 172, 206
*Franklin D. Roosevelt and American
Foreign Policy*, 26
Frye, Alton, 108
Frye, William, 168
Fuentes, Carlos, 10
Fuhrmann, Gero Arnulf, 176

Gardner, Lloyd C., 19
Gaspar Dutra, Eurico, 179
Geopolitik, 72
Germany: activities in Latin
America, 16, 36, 78, 82, 95; and
Anti-Comintern agreement, 66;
and Argentina, 116–7, 173; and
Brazil, 52, 66, 83, 111–2, 179; and
Chile, 88; and Declaration of Lima,
110; and Declaration of Panama,
150; and economic leverage in
Latin America, 52, 56, 64, 134–9,
152, 165; German populations in
Latin America, 16, 51, 53–4, 76,
79, 84, 172, 174, 179; ideology in
Latin America, 43; and Integralistas,
83; intentions in New World,
13–14, 85, 109, 199; and
Inter-American Trading Corporation,
212; and Latin American raw
materials, 71, 73, 91; and Mexico,
71, 74–75, 81, 93–94, 140; and
origins of World War I, 24; and
Paraguay, 139; and Peru, 101–4;
propaganda, 69, 113; and Soviet
Union Pact, 158; threat to Latin
America, 34, 55, 120, 163, 170–1,
215; and Uruguay, 156, 174
Gil, Enrique, 60
Giudici, Ernesto, 38, 80
Gleason, S. Everett, 212
Glenn, John B., 72
Goering, Hermann, 160
Góes Monteiro, Pedro Aurelio de,
139–40, 179–80, 199
González, Antonio, 102

González von Marées, Jorge, 87,
89
Goodhart, Philip, 196–7
Good Neighbor Policy: and Brazil,
66; and cultural rapprochement, 4;
and dictatorships of Latin America,
78; and economics, 47, 133; and
Mexico, 24, 93–94; and protection
of Latin America, 109; and Spanish
fascism, 101
Gran, Miguel, 60
Grassi, Alberto J., 116
Great Britain: activities in Latin
America, 119, 137; and aid to
France, 188; alliance with U.S., 5,
9, 18–19, 22, 28, 34, 59, 91; and
Argentina, 38, 117–8; and Brazil,
67; and Declaration of Panama,
150–1; and German assault, 90,
131–2, 141, 156, 207; intelligence,
52; navy, 58–59, 167, 185–6. 193,
207, 221; possibility of German
alliance, 162–3; and Roosevelt, 65,
95; U.S. aid to, 148, 166, 168–9,
193–203, 206, 214, 220–1; U.S.
public opinion, 114, 116; viability
of, 131, 184, 187, 198, 202–7
Guatemala, 75–76, 78

Haas, George, 137
Hague Convention of 1907, 25,
156–7
Haiti, 46, 215–6
Hanfstaengl, Ernst "Putzi", 76
Hartley, Livingston, 21, 58–59, 67,
90–91
Havana conference, 45–46, 217–9
Hearst, William Randolph, 27
Hemingway, Ernest, 23
Herring, Hubert, 4, 24, 38, 72–73
Hirschman, Albert O., 134
Hitler, Adolf: and Argentina, 37–38;
and Chamberlain, 91–92; and
cooperation with U.S., 160–1; and
Czechoslovakia occupation, 115;
and economic power, 5, 52; and
German self-sufficiency, 71; and
Great Britain, 206–7; intentions in
Latin America, 14, 196, 199; and
Latin American Germans, 76; and
Mexico, 72; and Panama Canal, 76;